FOUNDATIONS OF
ENGLISH OPERA

FOUNDATIONS OF ENGLISH OPERA

A STUDY OF MUSICAL DRAMA IN ENGLAND DURING THE SEVENTEENTH CENTURY

by

EDWARD J. DENT

With an Introduction to the Da Capo edition by
MICHAEL M. WINESANKER
Texas Christian University

Da Capo Press
New York
1965

A Da Capo Reprint Edition

First Da Capo Printing — April 1965
Second Da Capo Printing — March 1967
Third Da Capo Printing — May 1968

This unabridged republication of the
original edition, first published in 1928,
is reprinted by permission of the
Cambridge University Press, England

Library of Congress Catalog Card No. 65-18501

© 1965 Da Capo Press
A Division of Consultants Bureau Enterprises, Inc.
227 West 17th Street • New York, N.Y. 10011

Printed in the United States of America

INTRODUCTION

In recent years there has been a profusion of books about opera, even a plethora of writing in the field. Some studies dwell solely on musical matters; others are concerned with literary values. Some are general in nature; others focus attention on a specific, limited area. Few are a blend of detailed scholarship, depth of perception, and felicitous expression.

The question may then arise in this modern musicological age of expanded scope and facility: why reprint yet another book on this subject which appeared as recently as 1928? The reasons, though manifold, may be summarized succinctly in the nature of the work and the skill of the man who wrote it.

In *Foundations of English Opera*, Edward J. Dent embraces a broad point of view. The importance of librettist and composer, the place of designer and producer — all facets of the hydra-headed art form are considered in appraising the successive attempts to establish a native operatic genre in England. Thus the author, "a vigorous digger and careful sifter," examines scores and stories, discusses designs and staging, consults contemporary critiques, methodically explores every avenue of information, in reconstructing the picture of English musico-dramatic productions from the masques of Ben Jonson to Purcell's semi-operas.

Dent's book, however, is no mere account of events. There are synopses of operatic plots, including at times lengthy extracts from librettos (D'Avenant's *The Siege of Rhodes*). There are extensive musical quotations (Shirley's *Triumph of Peace* and *Cupid and Death*). There are keen aesthetic judgments and evaluations. Always there is the hallmark of the well-trained musical scholar, the analytic touch of the critic as composer. With meticulous care, Dent charts modulations, marks triumphs of tonal balance, stresses, where evident, a sense of symphonic principle expressed in one or another of these early, trail-blazing masterpieces. Although the gifts of dramatist and producer are fully appreciated, the author clearly regards the ordered intelligence of the music in an opera — its clarity of form — as being of prime importance. That "the music is itself the drama: that is the fundamental principle of opera."[1]

It is not surprising, therefore, to find substantial space devoted to a work like *Dido and Aeneas:* it embodies much that Dent deems essential in opera. The methods by which Henry Purcell secured intensity of dramatic expression are carefully explored. The swift bold strokes, the utter concentration of energy in the work elicit well-deserved encomiums. Not that Professor Dent heaps unqualified praise on this superb little opera. In lauding its greatness, he notes its limitations; in hailing its originality, he admits its indebtedness. But a full appreciation is expressed for the great composer's undeniable genius for the theatre, whether in this lone specimen of through-composed opera or in the numerous plays in which Purcell's incidental music graced the Restoration stage. Particular attention is drawn, for example, to his extensive semi-operas, *Dioclesian, King Arthur,* and *The Fairy Queen.* Of Purcell's undisputed skill in this field, Dent writes

> When we consider his marvellous power of setting English words to music, the massive nobility or the racy humour of his declamation, his unerring perception of a stage picture, his unrivalled fertility of invention and his unsurpassed handling of all technical resources, it is difficult not to believe that he only wanted an equally skilful librettist and the reasonable support of an intelligent public to have become the greatest operatic composer of his time in Europe.[2]

Strong praise indeed considering the presence of a Lully in France or a Scarlatti in Italy. And Dent does not discount

[1] Edward J. Dent, *Foundations of English Opera* (Cambridge: The University Press, 1928) , 233.
[2] *Ibid.,* 230.

their presence. On the contrary, wherever pertinent, he delves into the diverse aspects of the theatrical scene on the Continent. There is information on the *ballet de cour* and the *canti carnascialeschi*. The early history of opera in France is traced in some detail. French literary influence, Italian vocal style, the peculiar problems of word setting — these and other deserving topics are freely discussed in an effort to determine the relative merits of opera in France, Italy, and England, their similarities and their differences. Little wonder that the French musicologist, Henry Prunières, writing soon after the appearance of Dent's book and cognizant of its non-insular cast, labeled the *Foundations of English Opera* "la plus utile contribution à l'histoire de l'opéra en Europe au XVIIe siècle."[3] For all its universal approach, the chief emphasis in the book is nonetheless focused on the British Isles and proper consideration is given every aspect of operatic activity in seventeenth-century England.

To Edward J. Dent, English opera (Blow's *Venus and Adonis,* the *Dido* of Purcell) was clearly the offspring, the heir apparent of the Masque. That a whole chapter is devoted to the English Masque is therefore fitting and appropriate. What may seem surprising is the special attention given to D'Avenant's *Siege of Rhodes.* This "first English attempt at an opera," presented at Rutland House in 1656, survives only as a play, the music by a miscellaneous group of composers having been lost. It is the modern subject of the work that intrigues Mr. Dent, for, as he points out, a piece of this nature, with the siege of the city of Rhodes by the Turks as background, "is utterly unthinkable in Italian opera of that period."[4] He, therefore, discusses at some length the nature and effectiveness of the scenery as designed by John Webb, a pupil of Inigo Jones. The libretto, whose merit Dent feels is considerable, is then studied as a play and as a poem for musical setting. An effort also is made to reconstruct the place and

[3] See review of *Foundations* by Henry Prunières, *La Revue musicale* X/1 (November 1928) , 74.

[4] Dent, *op. cit.,* 65.

order of recitative, song, and chorus. Altogether there are two chapters of material on this and other "operas" of D'Avenant, the Poet Laureate who was able to catch "the public taste with foreign fashions." Professor Dent deplores the total loss of the music, especially "since this was the only period at which serious opera in English, set to music all through and almost all in recitative . . . has ever enjoyed a real and supreme popularity with English audiences."[5]

Dent is the first to admit "that the mind of the English public was not really attuned to the true operatic idea,"[6] to what the author calls "the operatic principle." The early opera, a court entertainment maintained by the monarchy in other countries, depended in England for its tenuous being on the support of the general public, a public which approached the genre with "complete ignorance and bewilderment."[7] To the majority of spectators the favorite attraction was the drama, in which music appeared — to be sure — but only as an incidental appendage.

Throughout the years there would seem to have been in England a disinclination toward the through-composed species of native musical drama. The eighteenth century is a case in point. A man like Lord Chesterfield appeared willing enough, even while criticizing it, to tolerate the unrealities of Italian opera,

> Whenever I go to an opera, I leave my sense and reason at the door with my half guinea, and deliver myself up to my eyes and my ears.[8]

The fact is that Lord Chesterfield and many others of the

[5] *Ibid.*, 77.

[6] See review of *Foundations* by N. C. Gatty, *Music and Letters* IX/4 (October 1928) , 392.

[7] Edward J. Dent, *A Theatre for Everybody: The Story of the Old Vic and Sadler's Wells* (London: T. V. Boardman & Co., 1945) , 55. Writing in 1940, Dent called attention to the fact that "many of our most eminent leaders of music, both living and dead, have taken the view that opera is a form of music which ought not to be encouraged." See Dent's *Opera* (Harmondsworth: Penguin Books, Ltd., 1945) , 12 [this statement appears in each of the several editions of this work, from 1940 through at least 1949].

[8] [Philip Dormer Stanhope, 4th] Earl of Chesterfield, *Letters to His Son* . . . , 2 vols. (London: M. W. Dunne, 1901) , II, 57.

cognoscenti did attend the King's Theatre in the Haymarket in great numbers. It was another matter, however, with "the people" at Drury Lane and Covent Garden, where the average playgoer came to hear the main business of the piece unfold in English spoken dialogue. Musical appurtenances, even there, gradually came into favor and, as the century wore on, musical settings, accompaniments, and interludes began to outweigh the dramatic interest in the presentation. Thus "operatic" productions came increasingly into vogue. Aside from the ballad and comic operas which abounded, more and more plays from the legitimate stage, much like our modern-day practice, were converted into "musicals." Yet, throughout, there still remained the thread of ordinary, everyday speech. This, for the English audience, was the touchstone to ensure some semblance of reasonableness.[9] In one of his books, Dent suggests that the English are still haunted by Dr. Johnson's definition of an opera as being an exotic and irrational entertainment. "So it was," says he, "and why not? Since the days of ancient Rome people have always enjoyed the exotic, something foreign and strange, and it might quite well be argued that it was the business of music, and indeed of all art, to be irrational."[10]

Dent had implicit faith in the peculiar power of the musical drama, despite the fact that the history of English opera had been, in his own words, a record largely of failure. He acknowledged the enormous problems that beset both creator and audience — the difficulty of clothing words, especially English words, in meaningful music; the importance of enlisting the talents of the adventurous in the artistic firmament; the need for a public to accept certain conventions however ridiculous and absurd they may at times appear, the idea of "singing a play instead of talking it" being itself a convention sometimes hard to accept. It was his conviction that the use

[9] Not that the English comic opera escaped the sharp thrust of the critic's pen; see Michael Winesanker, "Musico-Dramatic Criticism of English Comic Opera, 1750-1800," *Journal of the American Musicological Society* II/2 (Summer 1949), 87-96.

[10] Dent, *Opera, op. cit.,* 92.

of music in the theatre helped create a world of make-believe, that with its magic spell it could intensify the drama to the point of lifting the spectator "on to a higher emotional plane." And so Dent labored constantly in behalf of opera, devoting much of his long and fruitful life (1876-1957) to its cause, longing for the day when the trail nobly blazed by the early promising works of a Blow or a Purcell would inevitably lead to "a noble school of English opera."

Who was this man whose great and abiding love was opera? The eulogies expressed by fellow musicologists at the time of his death leave no doubt about the man and his place in the musical world. "A towering figure in Western music," judged one writer;[11] a person with tremendous "width of . . . learning and comprehensiveness of . . . taste, . . . urbanity, . . . style, . . . wit," ventured another.[12] That "he thought and wrote and spoke cleanly and clearly and precisely and unsentimentally"[13] was the view of all who came within his orbit. For he "possessed in a rare degree the power to form keen critical estimates on the results of close and accurate research."[14]

A Professor at Cambridge for some fifteen years (1926-1941), Dent also served as the Messenger lecturer at Cornell University during the 1937 session.[15] A composer of commendable merit, he was largely responsible for the birth in 1922 of the International Society for Contemporary Music, serving as its president for many years.[16] A scholar of repute,

[11] Geoffrey Sharp, "Edward J. Dent," *The Music Review* XVIII/4 (November 1957), 319.

[12] [Eric Blom,] "Editorial: Edward Joseph Dent (1876-1957)," *Music and Letters* XXXVIII/4 (October 1957), 368.

[13] [Anonymous editorial,] "Notes of the Day," *The Monthly Musical Record* LXXXVII [No. 984] (November-December 1957), 202.

[14] Henry C. Colles, "Edward Joseph Dent," *Grove's Dictionary of Music and Musicians*, 5th edition, Eric Blom, editor, 10 vols. (New York: St. Martin's Press, 1954-61), II, 669.

[15] Edward J. Dent, "Otto Kinkeldey," *The Musical Quarterly* XXIV/4 (October 1938), 409-10.

[16] Egon Wellesz states: "It was clear from the first that only one person had all the necessary qualities for this position: Edward Dent." See Egon Wellesz, "E. J. Dent and the International Society for Contemporary Music," *The Music Review* VII/3 (August 1946), 205-8.

he headed the Société Internationale de Musicologie for a prolonged period beginning in 1931.

A man is measured by his works and here Edward J. Dent achieved a remarkable record. Judging from the wide scope of his interests, his writing as theorist, historian, commentator, critic, translator, editor, lecturer, stage director, he must surely have been indefatigable. He also practiced what he preached. His firmly held theories and vast knowledge of the institution of opera received practical application in the revivals of old English musical stage pieces which he undertook with zest and enthusiasm. Throughout he seemed particularly partial to the works of Henry Purcell. It is noteworthy that his efforts to revive interest in Purcell's music coincided with the genesis of his book on *Foundations of English Opera*. The author tells us in his Preface that the book "was begun in 1914 in view of a projected performance of *The Fairy Queen* at Cambridge."[17] As it turned out, the actual presentation waited until 1920 and the appearance of the book until 1928.

An invaluable facet of Dent's operatic activity manifested itself in the preparation of English texts for operas originally written in other languages. As a translator of more than two dozen librettos of operas by Mozart, Beethoven, Berlioz, Verdi, Wagner, and Tchaikovsky, among others (some of which remain unpublished) , Dent set a high standard in the field, believing firmly in the need for giving opera in English in his native land. J. A. Westrup has called attention to his verbal facility and affirms "that for hundreds of people he has made opera a new experience."[18] All would agree with Arthur Jacobs that "Dent is no narrow translator; some of his happiest touches seem less to translate the original than to reinterpret it in a style suited to English-speaking audiences."[19] Above all, he believed in creating texts that were "suitable for singing" and easy to comprehend. As he stated in a paper

[17] See Preface, ix.

[18] Jack Allan Westrup, "Dent as Translator," *The Music Review* VII/3 (August 1946) , 204.

[19] Arthur Jacobs, "Edward J. Dent: The noted English scholar celebrates his 75th birthday," *Musical America* LXXI/9 (July 1951) , 5.

read before The Musical Association of London, "the first business of a translator is to make the play intelligible to the audience."[20] In other words, "the plot must be made clear, and also its development," and this "demands the very simplest possible language." Nevertheless, Dent continues, "the translator must try to give the impression that his words were those to which the music was originally composed." Dent develops his theories and principles of opera translation by discussing the treatment of rhymes, of recitative and aria, ensembles and choruses, the difficulties peculiar to various foreign languages, the problems arising out of musical structure. Altogether it is a thoroughgoing study of a challenging subject. There is no question that the author, in his many ventures in this field, followed his own prescription,

> A translator must necessarily know something of the language from which he is translating, but it is more important that he should have a good command of his own, and perhaps even more important still that he should have a sensitive understanding of music, an understanding based not merely on inborn musical feeling, but on scientific analytical knowledge.[21]

Certain it is that here was an opera lover who did not merely advocate the desirability, the necessity of presenting a piece in the language of the audience; he did something about it.

As editor, Dent was responsible for issuing a number of older opera scores. There were editions of *The Indian Queen, The Tempest, The Fairy Queen, Dido and Aeneas,*[22] and other pieces by Purcell. The *Beggar's Opera,* that well-known progenitor of ballad and comic operas, was arranged and published in vocal score at the request of Tyrone Guthrie for the Sadler's Wells Company. A full-score version of *Cupid and Death* by Matthew Locke and Christopher Gibbons was issued in the *Musica Britannica* series. The respectable number of titles in the printed and manuscript lists confirms the wide

---

[20] Edward J. Dent, "The Translation of Operas," *Proceedings of the [Royal] Musical Association,* 61st Session (1934-5), 81.

[21] *Ibid.,* 82.

[22] The *Dido* is in reality a performing edition, with detailed instructions on how an amateur group might approach the presentation of this opera.

range of Dent's interest in the field of operatic music, including works by Vecchi, Monteverdi, and Scarlatti.

In addition to service as editor and translator, Dent acted as helpful consultant during the staging of many operas in England throughout his career. He worked in this capacity not only at the Old Vic and Sadler's Wells Theatres in London, but at Cambridge University, where his scholarly supervision of pieces like *The Fairy Queen* and *King Arthur* added immeasurably to the authoritative productions directed by Cyril Rootham.

It is amply clear, then, that Dent's love of opera was not confined to that of a student writing on the subject, far removed from the vital scene of production and performance. He successfully translated into concrete reality his interest in the theatre "as a live creation of flesh and blood and sound." And where he could not directly participate or where he met with the frustrations of resistance to innovations, his seemingly endless flow of writing fulfilled the role of good-humored gadfly to the artistic world.

It is clear, too, that while opera became for Dent "the devotion of a lifetime," his musical interests were many and varied. He studied and wrote on a wide spectrum of subjects, ever displaying a depth of humanistic understanding. The list of books and articles, pamphlets and program notes, translations and reviews is both impressive and inspiring. Lawrence Haward's *Bibliography,* published in 1956 as a tribute to Dent in his eightieth year, fills thirty-seven closely printed pages.[23] While it includes some musical scores, the record of Dent's creativity is largely along literary lines marked by amazing diversity. There are the biographies of Alessandro

[23] Lawrence Haward, *Edward J. Dent: A Bibliography* (Cambridge: Privately Printed at the University Press for King's College, 1956). This is a revision and extension of his earlier bibliography of Dent's output which appeared in the 70th birthday commemorative issue of *The Music Review* VII/4 (November 1946), 242-62.

Scarlatti,[24] Ferruccio Busoni,[25] and Handel,[26] the extensive, critical study of Mozart's operas,[27] articles and papers on such unrelated topics as "The Historical Approach to Music,"[28] "Ensembles and Finales in 18th-Century Italian Opera,"[29] "Music of the Renaissance in Italy,"[30] "Social Aspects of Music in the Middle Ages,"[31] "The Pianoforte and Its Influence on Modern Music,"[32] and "The Teaching of Strict Counterpoint."[33] The list is long and imposing, all the more so because of the large number of contributions in French, German, and Italian, underscoring the author's linguistic flair and fluency.

The name of Edward J. Dent commands respect in the musicological world. It is also a name to be conjured with in theatrical circles. He had a thorough knowledge of opera and possessed the scholarly background to write about it with authority. To this add insight, charm, and an unerring knack for appropriate expression and there emerges the inimitable author of a book like the *Foundations of English Opera.*

[24] *Alessandro Scarlatti: His Life and Works* (London: Edward Arnold, 1905); a new impression [i.e., a reprint], with preface and additional notes by Frank Walker (London: Edward Arnold, 1960).

[25] *Ferruccio Busoni: A Biography* (London: Oxford University Press, 1933).

[26] *Handel* (London: Duckworth, 1934); revised edition (New York: A. A. Wyn, Inc., 1948).

[27] *Mozart's Operas: A Critical Study* (London: Chatto & Windus, 1913); radically revised 2nd edition (London: Oxford University Press, 1947); paperback edition (New York: Oxford University Press, 1963).

[28] A paper delivered at the Harvard Tercentenary Conference of Arts and Sciences in September 1936 when Dent received the first honorary degree of Doctor of Music conferred by Harvard University; this paper first appeared in *Authority and the Individual* (Cambridge: Harvard University Press, 1937), 350-71; it was reissued separately by Harvard University Press; republished in *The Musical Quarterly* XXIII/1 (January 1937), 1-17. Mr. Dent also held doctorates of music from Oxford and Cambridge.

[29] *Sammelbände der Internationalen Musikgesellschaft* XI/4 (July-September 1910), 543-69; XII/1 (October-December 1910), 112-38.

[30] *Proceedings of the British Academy* XIX (1934), 294-317; reissued separately (London: H. Milford, 1934).

[31] Chapter VIII, *Introductory Volume* (ed., Percy C. Buck), *The Oxford History of Music* (London: Oxford University Press, 1929), 184-218.

[32] *The Musical Quarterly* II/2 (April 1916), 271-94.

[33] *The Music Review* I/3 (August 1940), 201-13.

Writing on the occasion of the noted scholar's seventy-fifth birthday, Arthur Jacobs said

> No London operatic first night is complete unless the tall, lean figure of Edward J. Dent is seen in the auditorium. It is an unpretentious figure. . . . He moves about unassumingly, with none of the airs of the consciously prominent man. Yet he is one of the world's leading musical scholars, and is certainly without a peer in Britain.[34]

The spirit of such a man has been immortalized in his many significant publications. These have continued to exert an enormous influence within the world community of scholars, nowhere more so than in his commentary about the various aspects of English opera. Quite apart from any present and future work on the subject, this volume is and will remain the "foundation" of all other efforts in the field. It is a pity that he did not adopt a suggestion to convert his book into the first of a series on the history of English opera to the present. Perhaps it was that other fields of musical knowledge and activity beckoned and distracted him. Perhaps it was that he felt the subsequent years — the eighteenth century, the nineteenth century, even the twentieth — burned dimly by the light of the earlier seventeenth century promise. Other scholars in other years will have to sift, study, compare, and judge.

The Da Capo Press is to be congratulated on reissuing Edward J. Dent's excellent, out-of-print classic.

MICHAEL M. WINESANKER
Texas Christian University
Fort Worth, Texas
October 12, 1964

---

[34] Jacobs, *op. cit.*

FOUNDATIONS OF
ENGLISH OPERA

Cambridge University Press
Fetter Lane, London

▼

New York
Bombay, Calcutta, Madras
Toronto
Macmillan

▼

Tokyo
Maruzen-Kabushiki-Kaisha

FOUNDATIONS OF ENGLISH OPERA

A STUDY OF MUSICAL DRAMA
IN ENGLAND DURING THE
SEVENTEENTH CENTURY

by

EDWARD J. DENT

Professor of Music in the
University of Cambridge

CAMBRIDGE
AT THE UNIVERSITY PRESS
1928

Doch erfrischet neue Lieder,
Steht nicht länger tief gebeugt;
Denn der Boden zeugt sie wieder,
Wie von je er sie gezeugt.

To

CLIVE CAREY

AND

A. F. SCHOLFIELD

P R E F A C E

The purpose of the following pages is to trace the early development in England of what may be called the operatic principle. As is well known, the first attempts at opera in Italy were the result of accident; they were indeed not attempts at opera, but attempts at something quite different. Neither poets nor composers saw very clearly at first whither their ventures were going to lead them; and when the spirit of commercialism began to make itself felt, they naturally took less and less conscious account of artistic principles. Even after three centuries of experiment there seems to be no very well-defined idea of what an opera ought to be, although there is no lack of tradition and experience to guide those whose only object is financial success. Yet in opera, as in all forms of music, composers seem to be directed not merely by tradition and experience, but by a quasi-subconscious and hardly analysable mental process which is really the fundamental logical basis of the art, though it is the most elusive factor and the most difficult for the historian to trace —the most difficult too to present to the reader, because it is of its nature impossible to express directly in terms of language. The combination of music with drama might be thought to lessen the difficulty; but a little consideration will show that this aggravates rather than eases it. Essential musical principles may sometimes be modified under the influence of the stage, and the normal dramatic values are often entirely altered by the concomitance of music. There arises therefore an operatic principle which is neither the normal musical principle nor the normal dramatic principle. History shows us only too clearly that neither poets nor musicians have grasped it except spasmodically and intuitively. Yet it underlies all their efforts, and the task of the historian only becomes more interesting as it becomes more difficult.

The history of the operatic principle in England during the seventeenth century has been strangely neglected, although perhaps no century of our history has been the subject of so much minute research in the separate domains of literature, music and stage-craft. Writers on the drama seldom concern themselves with music at all; at most they do no more than summarize such information as may be obtained from the ordinary musical works of reference. When a poet of the eminence of Dryden writes a play for music, it is dismissed in a line as hardly worthy of his genius. Shadwell, who evidently had ideas of his own as to the combination of drama and music, is treated still worse; he may be thankful if he gets a contemptuous mention as the author of *Epsom Wells* and *The Libertine*. The operatic arrangements of Shakespeare are considered only in relation to the original texts, and the curious contemporary parodies of them are hardly even alluded to outside *Notes and Queries*. The leading authority on the stage-craft of the century, Mr W. J. Lawrence, has brought to light a very large number of important facts and documents relative to musical details, but he abstains entirely from any kind of musical technicalities or from general musical criticism; M. Paul Reyher, the most learned investigator of the Masques, is equally reticent on the aesthetic side of musical history. The purely musical historians are of little help; they can tell us plenty about scores, but nothing about librettos.

It is fundamentally important that the historian of opera should always study his documents with the eye of a producer. A writer who deals with opera from Gluck onwards may reasonably be expected to have at least seen on the stage most of the works that he mentions, even if he has not become more closely acquainted with them from behind the curtain. The musical drama of earlier days is practically unknown to the modern theatre; Purcell's *Dido and Aeneas* is probably the only opera anterior to Gluck which the ordinary opera-goer is likely to have seen acted. A considerable effort of imagination is therefore needed in reading such records as still remain of early experiments in musical drama. In a few cases there is material enough for us to combine into a fairly complete reproduction; in others much is of necessity left to conjecture. Yet it is not so absurd as it might seem at first sight to discuss an opera the music of which is entirely lost, as is the case with *The Siege of Rhodes*; for it is of comparatively little importance to know what the music sounded like—we can make a sufficient guess at that by looking at other compositions of the men who contributed to it—whereas it is of the greatest interest to know what relation the music bore to the dramatic action and how far it intensified the emotional values of the play. This we can find out to some extent by a careful examination of the libretto.

This book was begun in 1914 in view of a projected performance of *The Fairy Queen* at Cambridge. The performance had to be postponed to 1920, and the publication of my book, though ready for press in 1915, for a still longer period. During the intervening years there has been a great revival of interest in the Restoration Theatre and much valuable research has been done. I have therefore revised the book to a large extent, and in view of other works on the stage and its appurtenances I have thought it superfluous to give any illustrations beyond musical extracts. I hope I need not apologize for the absence of a bibliography. The works on musical history to which I refer are well known, and copious bibliographies of the Theatre are easily accessible elsewhere.

From the time when I first took up musical research, nearly thirty years ago, I was constantly helped and encouraged by the late Mr William Barclay Squire until his death in January

1927. It is my first duty to record here my deep sense of gratitude for his unfailing generosity and his wise counsel. I am also indebted to Mr G. E. P. Arkwright and Mr Dennis Arundell for valuable material, as well as to the late Dr W. H. Cummings and his son, Mr Arthur Cummings, for the loan of MSS. I must also thank the compositors and proof-readers of the University Press for much patience and forbearance. The musical illustrations have been written out by Mr Archibald Jacob of King's College.

Cambridge, March 1928

CONTENTS

⬦————————————⬦————————————⬦

Chapter One

The MATERIALS *of* ENGLISH OPERA

The history of English Opera has been for the most part the record of three centuries of failure. From the first attempt to introduce opera to English audiences down to the present day *1965* there has never been any period at which serious musical drama in the language of the country has been as firmly established among ourselves as it has been in Italy and France since the middle of the seventeenth century, or in Germany during the last hundred years. At the same time England has not been without opera, quite apart from the imported Italian opera which dominated London musical life from the reign of Anne onwards, and which still continues its existence, though France, Germany and Russia have latterly disputed its exclusive rights. There have even been three moments at which English opera of a certain kind has been strong enough to make its influence felt on the Continent. At the beginning of the seventeenth century, when Germany was over-run with English actors, our musical comedies or 'drolls' were at once translated into Dutch, German, and Danish; *The Beggar's Opera* started a similar wave of enthusiasm a hundred years later, and within recent years *The Geisha* and its successors have been applauded all over Europe. Such works as these, it might be thought, are England's most characteristic con-tribution to the musical drama. The musician prefers to turn to the less conspicuous pages of musical history on which are recorded the continual efforts of our more serious composers to realize a national opera. One after another they have failed: some could never find the right form in which to express themselves; some found the form, but not the audience to understand it; others have had the technique, even the audience as well, but not enough fundamental poetic power to make their work live. Yet in spite of public apathy, in spite of inadequate means of presentation, in spite of uncertainty of method, the effort has been continuous, determined and persistent.

At the moment when Italian poets and composers brought opera to birth in Florence, music in England was at its highest level. It was an age when the English mind was peculiarly susceptible to the influence of all Italian ideas, literary as well as musical. How was it that we did not at that wonderful moment develop an English form of opera in which Jonson and Shakespeare might have collaborated with Douland and Wilbye?

The answer lies simply in our national attitude towards music. To the Italian music is a means of self-expression, or rather of self-intensification; to the Englishman music is a thing apart, a message from another world. The Italian singer creates the music that he utters, or at least appears to create it; the English singer is a sensitive medium through which music is made audible. Music for the Italian is the exaggeration of personality—for the Englishman its annihilation.

If this were a scientific statement of fact, instead of being the roughest of momentary generalizations, English opera would be an absolute impossibility; for opera in its completest form depends essentially on the principle that music —that is, the music of the voice—should be the ideal language in which the persons of the drama express themselves. And it is curious to note that some years before Peri and his friends had evolved their system of musical declamation English composers had arrived by a very different road within sight of the same idea. In the odd naïve tragicomedies acted by the children of the royal chapels during Elizabeth's reign music of a comparatively elaborate nature was introduced in the form of songs sung by the principal characters at moments of emotional crisis. But the movement was short-lived, and the Shakespearean drama, though it made copious use of music, employed both voices and instruments in a totally different way. Shakespeare and his contemporaries never show us speech intensified into song under stress of emotion, but only the emotional effect produced by music on the characters represented. The germ of English opera is to be found not in the drama proper but in the masques of the early seventeenth century. In these the poet and the composer could collaborate on more nearly equal terms, although both were held in subjection by that far more important personage the scenic architect. The masque offered the composer the chance of combining various musical forms into a consistent whole; but it gave him little opportunity of producing anything that could really be considered as musical drama. The fact was that in England the spoken drama was already far too highly developed and far too deeply rooted in the heart of the people for its musical counterpart to be accepted as an equivalent, much less as a transfiguration of its most powerful emotional workings. It was only when the Puritans succeeded in suppressing the drama that masques were able to assume a more definitely dramatic form, and that a real systematic attempt at English opera could be made.

The operas organized by Sir William D'Avenant in 1656 were a curious and original experiment in a form which had little in common with the Italian operas which at that time were the only models in existence. Their ultimate influence was in the main literary rather than musical; Dryden acknowledged *The Siege of Rhodes* as the starting point of the heroic drama of the Restoration. It very soon became clear that English audiences, passionately devoted though they still were to music, could never be brought to regard music as a normal language of dramatic expression. From the Restoration to

3

the end of the century a quantity of plays were produced in which music was a very important feature; but in almost all cases the music was confined to those episodes in which supernatural or quasi-supernatural characters appeared.

Interesting experiments were made by Locke and Blow, which will be considered in detail later on. Locke, in spite of strong Italian tendencies in musical technique, never adopted the Italian view of musical drama; his *Psyche* follows the model of Lulli and Molière in carrying on the main business of the play in spoken dialogue. Blow's *Venus and Adonis* is of greater importance. It is set to music all through, and is certainly operatic in its fundamental principle; but its dramatic construction is extremely slight and its technique primitive and crude. With the appearance of Purcell stage music underwent considerable development, and the heroic drama with incidental music began regularly to bear the name of opera. Yet although it was frankly admitted that the music was the main attraction of the evening's entertainment, the so-called operas were hardly more than a series of masques. There can be little doubt that Purcell himself had a more artistic ideal in view; *Dido and Aeneas*, inspired no doubt to some extent by Blow's *Venus and Adonis*, shows that he fully understood the possibilities of real opera in English. But *Dido and Aeneas* was an isolated experiment, and though it may have been instrumental in converting Dryden to a better appreciation of its composer, it did not apparently convert him to its principles of dramatic construction. *King Arthur* was a compromise, and apparently a compromise which satisfied the public, for it was revived frequently in the eighteenth century, and occasionally even in the nineteenth. With the untimely death of Purcell English 'dramatic opera' of this type came to an end, and later operatic developments are beyond the scope of this book.

In considering the history of these early attempts at opera in England we must bear in mind that English composers and dramatists were subject to the influence not only of their own native traditions, but also to that of their French and Italian contemporaries. These influences made themselves felt at different times and in different directions. Generally speaking, the poets seem to have been influenced more by French writers than by those of Italy, whereas with the composers it is the Italian influence which predominates. This is very noticeable in the case of Dryden and Purcell. Further, it is important to realize the way in which Italian and French influences acted on each other during the earlier part of the century.

Let us now consider in more detail the earlier attempts at combining music and drama in England. The drolls, interesting as they are from the point of view of popular drama and popular song, had no influence on serious opera. They consisted generally of primitive plays on coarse and obvious subjects, written in the metre of some popular tune such as *Walsingham*, *Brave Lord Willoughby* or *Fortune my foe*, to which they were sung, the tune and metre being sometimes varied in the course of the play.[1] Acted by the lowest types of actors for the amusement of uneducated audiences only, they naturally received no consideration from the poets and composers who were attached to the court. But we may regard them perhaps as the poor relations of that earlier type of musical play which became obsolete before the sixteenth century came to an end—the semi-classical tragicomedies acted for the entertainment of the Queen by the children of the Royal Chapels. The acting of plays by the choir of the Chapel Royal is first mentioned in the reign of Henry VIII, and since the excellence of English singing at that time is attested by the descriptions of the Venetian ambassador and other distinguished foreigners, it was not unnatural that music should be introduced in performances of this kind. After the accession of Mary the gentlemen of the chapel ceased to take part; but the children still continued to act by themselves, and in the

---

[1] Johannes Bolte, *Die Singspiele der englischen Komödianten und ihrer Nachfolger in Deutschland, Holland und Skandinavien*, Hamburg and Leipzig, 1893.

first twenty years of Elizabeth's reign the boy players acquired a considerable importance, the Children of St Paul's and the Children of the Chapel Royal being in fact duly licensed as regular companies of actors.

Not many of these plays have survived. The best known is the play of *Damon and Pythias* (1565), written by Richard Edwards, which was parodied by Shakespeare in 'the most lamentable comedy and most cruel death of Pyramus and Thisby'. Ridiculous as their alliterations and repetitions may appear to the modern reader, it must be remembered that devices of this kind take on a very different value when the words are set to music. About a dozen of these settings were discovered recently by Mr G. E. P. Arkwright[1] in the British Museum and in the library of Christ Church, Oxford. Some are anonymous, some by Richard Farrant, who was Master of the children at Windsor, Robert Parsons, Robert Johnson and others. They are written for a treble voice, accompanied by three or four viols. The favourite metre for the words appears to be that known in hymn-books as 'short metre', and the melody is generally of an equally simple character. We might therefore suppose that both these songs and the songs of the drolls were descended from a common source. But the songs of the choristers' plays are in almost every case remarkable for the elaborate nature of their accompaniments. Thus the lullaby 'Ah sellie poor Joas' by an anonymous composer, printed in *The Musical Antiquary*, IV. 115, has a straightforward melody of popular type which is almost entirely in rhythm of three beats; it is accompanied however by four viols playing entirely independent parts with points of imitation in a rhythm of four beats. The other specimen given, 'Pour downe your eares divine' by Robert Parsons, (*The Musical Antiquary*, I. 35) is more directly expressive, and here the frequent repetitions of the words 'Pandolpho, some

---

[1] They are described by him in two articles on 'Early Elizabethan Stage Music', in *The Musical Antiquary*, I. 30 and IV. 112. Two specimens are printed there, and I am indebted to the kindness of Mr Arkwright for copies of the others.

pity, Pandolpho' between the stanzas, set to notes in different parts of the singer's compass, give the song a decidedly personal and dramatic character. The accompaniment is as contrapuntal as that of the previous song, but the imitations are more skilfully managed, and the instruments at the same time are contrived so as to be less obtrusive. The important fact about these songs is that they were introduced as an integral part of the drama, the favourite moment being on the occasion of a death-scene. Like Pyramus and Thisbe, the characters of these plays love to repeat the words 'I die' over and over again; but so far from the repetitions being ridiculous, the skill with which they are set to music makes them genuinely pathetic.[1]

For some reason or other these plays came to an end before their musical traditions could be handed on for development by later composers. With the rise of the Shakespearean drama there came a reaction against the boy-players, and this might well have led the dramatists to avoid all effects that suggested the children's efforts, and the more learned musicians to refuse their collaboration to those who had poured scorn upon them.[2] Had it been possible to continue the principle of heightening the effect of a dramatic moment by making the actor break from speech into song, the English would have been true pioneers in opera instead of timid and not always intelligent imitators of other nations.

The Shakespearean drama, though it never employed music in the most essentially operatic way, was none the less addressed to an audience highly susceptible to the art. The fact that music was played in English theatres for some time before the play began need not concern us here; it amounts to no more than that the play was habitually preceded by a concert. We may disregard equally a large number of the songs

---

[1] See also O. Kinkeldey, *Orgel und Klavier im XVI Jahrhundert*, Leipzig, 1910 (pp. 176–7).
[2] See also C. W. Wallace, *The Evolution of the English Drama up to Shakespeare*, Berlin, 1912; and W. J. Lawrence, 'New facts about the Blackfriars', in *The Elizabethan Playhouse and other studies*, First Series, Stratford-on-Avon, 1912.

scattered through the plays for no other purpose than to give an excuse for the appearance of a singer. On the other hand such songs as those of the Clown in *Twelfth Night* are part of the singer's personality, though not in the ordinary operatic sense; like Old Merrythought in *The Knight of the Burning Pestle*, the Clown is a man whose peculiarity is that he tends to express himself more in music, one might almost say, than in words. It is a first step towards opera: does not Macheath do much the same thing in the prison scene of *The Beggar's Opera*? The next step brings us to Ariel, whose songs are more intimately indicative of his personality; and here we see the typical English attitude clearly illustrated. Old Merrythought is drunk, the Clown is mad, and Ariel is a supernatural being. English poets could never accept the idea of a normal man expressing himself in song. Incidentally it may be remarked that Wagner held practically the same view, at any rate in theory, whereas the Italians, even in their earliest experiments, approached the problem quite differently. Orpheus and Eurydice are no less mythological than Siegfried and Brünnhilde; but while Wagner is perpetually concerned to make his characters appear supernormal, Peri's only end in view is to bring out their essential humanity. The attitude of Dryden and Purcell on this question must be reserved for a later chapter.

Another point which must be noticed is the frequent employment of music, generally instrumental, sometimes vocal, as a background to some action which requires emphasis of a special kind. I do not wish to include in this category the occasions on which musicians are brought on to the stage as actual characters—not infrequently speaking characters—in the play; I refer rather to such episodes as the casket scene in *The Merchant of Venice*, the prison scene in *Richard II*, besides various scenes in other plays of a supernatural or quasi-supernatural character.[1] One of the most effective of these

[1] See Percy A. Scholes, 'The Purpose behind Shakespeare's use of Music', *Proceedings of the Musical Association*, London, 1917.

is the coming to life of the statue at the end of *The Winter's Tale*.[1] Another interesting stage effect is the scene in *The Duchess of Malfi* where the ceremony is witnessed of the Cardinal putting off his ecclesiastical robes in the church of Loreto; and one of the most remarkable instances of music as a dramatic factor occurs in *The Revenger's Tragedy*, where the Duke is murdered just as his Duchess and her lover cross the stage to the gay strains which accompany their revels.[2]

Another very important employment of music on the stage is connected with the masques which were introduced in many Elizabethan plays. It is desirable however that, before considering these, we should trace the history of the masque proper, as far as it is to be considered a musical entertainment, since the masque is the prototype of almost all the English operas of the seventeenth century.

During the fourteenth and fifteenth centuries 'disguisings' and 'mummings', as they were called in English, were favourite forms of entertainment both in this country and at most of the courts of Europe. The main principle of these diversions was a torchlight procession of men on horseback, wearing masks and dressed in fantastic costumes of various kinds. They were generally accompanied by musicians, and when they arrived at their destination, they seem to have danced and acted some sort of dumb-show, and to have played at dice with their hosts. Gradually the practice grew up of introducing the masquers with some sort of explanatory speech in verse, and a few of these have been preserved. Under the influence of the Renaissance these festivities be-

---

[1] Those who witnessed the production at the Savoy Theatre in 1912 will not fail to remember the beautiful effect of the music in this scene—the song 'If love's a sweet passion' in Act III of Purcell's *Fairy Queen*, played by strings behind the scenes. It should be noted that this business is very carefully stage-managed by Paulina with a view to putting Leontes into a suitable frame of mind. Similarly it is customary, I am told, to sing hymns at spiritualistic séances.

[2] For further illustrations of similar scenes see G. H. Cowling, *Music on the Shakespearian Stage*, Cambridge, 1913.

came more elaborate and more definitely artistic in character. In Italy there were the *trionfi* and *canti carnascialeschi* of Lorenzo de' Medici, the music of which has to some extent been made accessible lately.[1] As in more northern countries, these masques 'lasted till three or four hours into the night, with a multitude of masked men on horseback following, richly dressed, exceeding sometimes three hundred in number, and as many men on foot with lighted torches. Thus they traversed the city, singing to the accompaniment of music arranged for four, eight, twelve or even fifteen voices, supported by various instruments'.[2]

The earlier masques were in the main processions of this nature, and the procession survived as an essential part of the entertainment down to the end of the classical period of English masques. The procession, however, was not capable of developing into anything of the nature of opera; and we must turn our attention rather to that part of the masquerade which took place within doors. One of the most important features of the sixteenth-century pageants was the use of stages on wheels, a device borrowed from the miracle-plays and moralities. These conveyances, known in Italy as *trionfi* or *carri*, began to assume certain traditional shapes, the favourite designs being those of castles, mountains and ships, in which various actors in the masquerade were seated. When the cavalcade arrived at the palace where the dancing was to take place, these actors did not dismount, but were wheeled in on their car, and used it as a scene for some kind of dramatic action.

The year 1513 has been generally accepted as the date of the first introduction of the Masque into England, since Hall in that year records that 'on the daie of the Epiphanie at night the kyng with xi other wer disguised, after the manner of Italie, called a maske, a thing not seen afore in Englande'.

---

[1] *Chants de Carnaval Florentins (Canti Carnascialeschi) de l'époque de Laurent le Magnifique*, edited by Paul-Marie Masson, Paris, 1913.
[2] "Il Lasca", quoted in Symonds' *Renaissance in Italy*, vol. IV, Italian Literature.

This passage has led to much controversy, into which it is not necessary to go further in this place, since the difficulties involved are not concerned with music. One thing however seems clear from this and other sources, that an essential feature of the masque was the custom by which the masquers, after having danced in character by themselves, selected partners from the ladies in the audience and danced with them. This custom was kept up consistently to the end of the masque era. Whatever the precise novelty of the masque of 1513 may have been, it is clear from Marlowe and from Ronsard that both the French and the English acknowledged the entertainment to be of Italian origin.[1]

From Italy, too, came the humanistic movement which devoted so much ingenuity to the problem of reconstructing the ideal drama of antiquity in which poetry, music and dance were all to be combined. South of the Alps the number of small princely courts, each determined to make itself into a modern Athens, greatly facilitated the opportunities for experiments, however costly, in whatever direction the poets, composers and architects might feel themselves inspired to move. In France and England matters proceeded more slowly, in spite of the enthusiasm in both countries for everything Italian. Henry VIII maintained Italian musicians, and the same speech of Piers Gaveston in Marlowe's *Edward II* which speaks of 'Italian masks' goes on to describe such representations of mythological scenes as were the habitual

---

[1] Marlowe, *Edward II*, Act I, sc. i:

> Therefore I'll have Italian masks by night,
> Sweet speeches, comedies, and pleasing shows.

Ronsard in the sonnet beginning

> Mascarade et cartels ont prins leur nourriture
> L'un des Italiens, l'autre des vieux François.

and ending

> L'accord Italien quand il ne veut bastir
> Un Théâtre pompeux, un cousteau repentir,
> La longue Tragédie en Mascarade change.
> Il en est inventeur: nous suyuons ses leçons,
> Comme ses vestemens, ses mœurs et ses façons,
> Tant l'ardeur des François aime la chose estrange.

subject of the Italian *intermezzi*.[1] Francis I imported from
Italy not only the painters and decorators of Fontainebleau,
but also Italian instrumentalists in large numbers. Princes
and ambassadors from Italy brought their musicians with
them to Paris, and the Italian Cardinal Ippolito d'Este, when
Archbishop of Lyons, entertained Henry II and his queen
Catherine de' Medici with a performance of Cardinal Bib-
biena's comedy *La Calandra* accompanied by musical *intermezzi*
between the acts representing Apollo, Aurora and Night
appearing in 'machines' of the characteristic Italian type.
This was in 1548. The carnival festivities at Fontainebleau
in 1565 seem to have been the first occasion on which French
poets applied their ingenuity to representations of this kind.
A comedy on a subject from Ariosto was acted by the ladies
of the court, followed by a masque of Cupid and Charity for
which Ronsard supplied the verses. The Italian custom of
intermezzi became the rule in French comedies of this period,
and although Italian dances were not introduced into this
particular form of diversion, they formed an important part
of the *mascarades* at the court of Charles IX. Brantôme gives
a detailed description of a ballet performed in honour of the
Polish ambassadors in 1573.[2] Sixteen ladies, representing the
sixteen provinces of France were seated on clouds round a
mountain of silver. They were accompanied by music, to
which each of them sang in turn. The mountain was carried
round the hall for everyone to see, and after this the ladies
descended and formed up in military array, while the thirty
fiddlers played a warlike air. The ladies advanced to the
King and Queen, and executed a complicated dance which
lasted a whole hour. During part of the dance they wore
masks. At the end they presented the King and Queen and

[1]   Sometimes a lovely boy in Dian's shape
        *   *   *   *   *   *
      Shall bathe him in a spring; and there hard by,
      One like Actaeon peeping through the grove,
      Shall by the angry goddess be transformed, etc.
  [2] Quoted by H. Prunières in *Le Ballet de cour en France avant Benserade et Lully*,
Paris, 1914.

the other great personages with enamel plaques representing the products of their several provinces.[1]

This description might serve equally for masques of the period in Italy or England, subject to slight variations. There is the germ of dramatic action, but no deliberate dramatic principle. On the other hand, Italy had achieved, and France had copied, the idea of plays with spectacular and musical *intermezzi*. To make further progress towards opera it was necessary to combine the two. It was the moment when that group of writers known as the *Pléiade*, of whom Ronsard was the chief, was engaged in applying new methods and principles to the art of poetry in France. 'The result of their efforts was the creation of something hitherto lacking in French literature—a poetical instrument which, in its strength, its freedom, its variety of metrical resources, and its artistic finish, was really adequate to fulfil the highest demands of genius.'[2] But the work of the *Pléiade* was not confined to literature. Verse for them was inseparable from music, music inseparable from verse. Ronsard held that 'la poésie sans les instruments ou sans la grâce d'une ou plusieurs voix n'est nullement agréable, non plus que les instruments sans estre animez de la mélodie d'une plaisant voix' (*Abrégé de l'Art Poétique*, 1565). As in Italy and in England, this point of view was not shared with much friendliness by the musicians of an older generation. They doubtless felt that they knew more about their art than the men of letters who wished to subvert all their most cherished principles. What they refused to attempt was carried out by a generation that was less skilled, but more enterprising. Among the poets of the *Pléiade* was Jean Antoine de Baïf, who was himself something of a musician as well. With the assistance of Thibaut de Courville, a composer who is now completely forgotten, he founded an academy of music and poetry, which was recognized by

---

[1] Another item in the festivities was a Latin dialogue between France, Peace and Prosperity, set to music by Orlando Lassus.

[2] Lytton Strachey, *Landmarks in French Literature*, London, n.d.

Charles IX with great cordiality in 1570. It started its career under difficulties, and came to an end about 1584. Its most important musical collaborators were Claude Lejeune and Jacques Mauduit. For various reasons the new academy did not achieve in its own name any remarkable result. But it served to disseminate the new ideas, and they bore fruit in 1581 with the *Balet comique de la Royne*.

The designer and producer, as we should now say, of the *Balet comique* was an Italian, Baldassarino da Belgiojoso, better known by the name of Balthasard de Beaujoyeulx, who had come over as one of the band of fiddlers sent to the French court about 1555. How far he was really responsible for the invention of the new scheme it is impossible to say. It is clear that he was at least influenced by the ideas of Baïf, and also by the *Aminta* of Tasso, which had been produced at Ferrara in 1573. Moreover, the company of the *Gelosi* which had acted *Aminta* on this famous occasion visited Paris not long afterwards, and although no record has survived of the pieces performed by them, there can be little doubt that their repertory included the drama which had suddenly given its author European fame.

A short summary of the *Balet comique* will show how far it was in advance of previous ballets; it will also show how it provided a model for the English masques of a later generation. The performance took place not in a theatre, but in the hall known as the Petit-Bourbon. It was about a hundred feet long and nearly fifty wide, with a semicircular apse at one end. The seats for the spectators were arranged in rising tiers round three sides, with two galleries above them; but the greater part of the floor space was left vacant. The royal party occupied seats on the floor level, facing the stage directly. The stage proper represented the palace and garden of Circe, who is the principal character in the ballet. The engraving from which the description is taken[1] shows us a series of three large arches of masonry at the end of the room,

---

[1] Reproduced in H. Prunières, *Le Ballet de Cour en France*.

through which we catch a glimpse of a palace, perhaps painted on a back-cloth in the apse. In front of this is another group of arches, representing a trellis of foliage, and in front of the trellis a low balustrade enclosing the animals into which the enchantress has transformed her admirers. At this point a gentle slope descends to the main floor level, and at the foot of it we see on the right an arbour of trees, representing the grotto of Pan, and on the left, opposite to this, what is called the *voûte dorée*, a sort of cage made of clouds and stars, big enough to hold several people. From this point to the King's seat there still remains a considerable area of floor space.

The performance began at ten in the evening with 'a noise of hautboys, cornets, sackbuts and other sweet instruments of music' placed behind the scenes. A gentleman then comes running down from the garden of Circe, presents himself to the King and explains in spoken verse how Circe has taken him prisoner. He begs the King to attack the enchantress, who appears herself at the moment to look for the fugitive. She is in a great rage, but retires again having done nothing. Then follows an entry of tritons and sirens, singing, followed by a car representing a fountain, on which are Thetis and Glaucus attended by naiads. These nymphs were represented by the Queen and various other illustrious ladies. Last comes a chorus of tritons with lutes, harps, flutes, and other instruments. The procession advances to the middle of the room; there is a dialogue set to music between Thetis and Peleus, and the nymphs descend from their car and dance. Circe reappears and reduces them to immobility; a cloud descends from above bearing Mercury, who sings a long solo and releases the dancers. Circe however fixes them to the ground again, and even does the same by Mercury; after a long monologue she takes them as prisoners into her garden. Satyrs and dryads come to the rescue; Pan and the four Virtues—a curious alliance—join them. Minerva enters on a car drawn by a monstrous serpent and summons Jupiter, who descends from heaven on his eagle, accompanied by a chorus of voices in the *voûte dorée*. An attack is made on the palace of Circe, who is taken prisoner by Jupiter and led by him to the King, to whom he also presents Minerva and Mercury. The dryads perform a dance and then fetch the naiads from Circe's garden, upon which there follows the *grand ballet, i.e.* the main dance, which is of considerable length, and takes place on the floor level. They then present gifts to the King and his party, after which they take partners from the audience and a general dance begins. The entertainment lasted until half-past three in the morning.

The novelty of the *Balet comique* lay in its form, in the combination of speech, song, and dance to illustrate a definite plot and form an organic whole,[1] though it seems rather ridiculous to us nowadays to read the commendatory verses in which Beaujoyeulx is hailed as the first man who has succeeded in reconstructing the tragedy of ancient Greece. Beaujoyeulx moreover was not himself the author either of the words or the music; these were written by various other persons under his superintendence. Both from a literary and a musical point of view, *Circe*, it must be frankly admitted, is a very disappointing affair, and it would be a great mistake to suppose that it was all on a level with the charming dance-tune reprinted by Burney and various other writers.[2] The spoken verse is heavy and devoid of interest; the musical monologues are neither recitative nor aria, but a strange awkward mixture in which the rhythm of the verse is completely ignored with no charm of melody to compensate us for the loss. The dance tunes are harmonized continuously in five parts with no attempt at counterpoint or variety of any kind. The dances were evidently very elaborate, and

[1] The epithet *comique* does not imply anything of a grotesque nature, although, as we shall see later, the grotesque element was a favourite feature of the *ballet de cour* and the masque; it means merely that Beaujoyeulx aimed at combining ballet with *comédie, i.e.* with a kind of drama that was not tragic.
[2] Burney, *A General History of Music*, III. 282; *Oxford History of Music*, III. 220.

there are constant changes of rhythm which are most be-wildering to anyone who reads them merely as music. But we must remember that they were intended only as accom-paniments to complicated evolutions, and would become much more intelligible when presented to the eye as well as to the ear. We must allow too for the interpretation of the French players of those days, who were generally admitted to have shown a very notable vivacity of execution.[1]

It is not necessary for us to follow the history of French ballets beyond this point. The dramatic element in them gradually declined, and the musical element increased, so that when Mazarin introduced Italian operas to Parisian audiences the transition from ballet to opera was fairly easy. Except for the rapid development of grotesque episodes, which is common to both the English and the French form, the subsequent history of the masque took a different direc-tion in England, and caused the later problem of opera to be more difficult of solution.

[1] All who have had any experience of the practical revival of old music will know how extraordinarily difficult it is to induce modern performers to execute it with life and energy, even when a certain standard of musical intelligence has been attained.

Chapter Two

The ENGLISH MASQUES

The reigns of James I and Charles I saw the development and the decadence of a kind of spectacle which although derived as we have seen from French and Italian sources was in its characteristic details definitely English. The masques, having numbered such poets as Ben Jonson, Thomas Campion and James Shirley among their collaborators, came to be regarded in later days as belonging to the domain of literature, with the result that they have suffered very unfavourable comparison by the side of the contemporary drama. The music to which they were set has to a large extent disappeared; what remains is so scattered as to make it a matter of considerable difficulty—if indeed it be possible at all—to reconstruct any single one of them completely from this point of view. The scenery which may not unjustly be said to have been their principal feature is preserved for us only by stage directions and by a few collections of plans and drawings.

To the spectators who witnessed these productions we may be sure that the words, however beautiful they may be to us, were the least important part of the entertainment. The purpose of this chapter is to consider the masques not as literature or drama, but solely with regard to their influence on what ultimately developed into English opera. In theory the principal feature of the masque was the appearance and evolutions of the 'masquers', that is, of some twelve or sixteen dancers of either one sex or the other, drawn from the highest aristocracy, and sometimes including royalty itself. James I did not dance; but his queen, Anne of Denmark, was quite ready to follow the French fashion of appearing on the stage, and so naturally enough were Charles I and Henrietta Maria.

18

In considering the masque as an artistic form it is very necessary to keep this carefully in mind, since otherwise the masques, when read through in the printed editions, all appear to collapse in interest towards the end. We have to make due allowance for the spirit of the age, for the fact that the masque was exclusively intended for the entertainment of royalty, and that the person of the king's majesty was under all circumstances the central point of interest to which even the magnificence of the spectacle was subordinate.

The masque, then, starts as an elaborate dance in costume by a select body of illustrious persons. To introduce them and explain their assumed character a poet is called in; later on, by way of contrast, a so-called 'antimasque' is provided, generally of a grotesque nature. This 'antimasque' was acted by professional dancers. That all this should be accompanied by music is a matter of course, and the art of the decorator, called in at first merely to provide a passive background, gradually takes a more active part in preparing for and enhancing the spectacular effect of the main dancers' principal entry. Here is the design, here are the materials of the masque; the proportions of its various details will depend for the most part on the relative talents of the various collaborators. An ideal work of art requires them to contribute each his best to the realization of a common ideal, on terms of perfect and amicable equality. If any one collaborator is anxious to make himself a tyrant over the others, the work will be distorted in that particular direction. Among the makers of masques the musicians seem to have been at some disadvantage. In no case could it be said that the music was the predominating partner, although we may be fairly sure that to those who were present at the performances the music probably remained longest in the memory. The struggle was between the poet and the scene painter; and although the chief poet was no less a man than Ben Jonson, the ultimate victory fell to Inigo Jones. The spirit of the age was on his side; theatrical architecture was a new and exciting form of art, and it can at least be said that England came nearer preserving a due sense of proportion than other countries.

Daniel's *Vision of the Twelve Goddesses*, the first masque of the new century, had still kept the system of decoration employed in the *Balet comique de la Royne*: a mountain at the back of the stage, and lower down a temple on the one side, and the cave of Somnus on the other. It was an inconvenient arrangement, for it took up a great deal of space and was monotonous to the eye, since the scene remained unchanged throughout the entertainment. In 1605, with Ben Jonson's *Masque of Blackness*, a new system was introduced by Inigo Jones, then recently returned from Italy, and almost a complete stranger to English audiences. It was not until many years later that he became known as a designer of permanent buildings. The mediaeval stage had employed a series of what were called mansions or *luoghi deputati*, presenting a number of scenes simultaneously, with no attempt at illusion. In the sixteenth century Sebastiano Serlio adopted a system half-way to that of the later period, ranging these 'houses' in the form of a street, running towards the back of the stage. Such an arrangement is still called *scena parapettata*, in which the 'flats' are set more or less at right angles to the line of the proscenium. It was a modification of this principle which Inigo Jones employed in his earlier masques. The architectural proscenium, generally emblematic in its decorations, does not seem to have been used by him before 1612. For some time changes of scene were effected only by drawing aside pairs of flats at the back of the stage, so as to disclose a new pair of flats behind, while the wings remained stationary; but in the later masques interchangeable flats parallel to the line of the proscenium were substituted for the fixed ones ranged in two converging lines towards the back with return pieces at an obtuse angle to mask the openings.[1]

[1] Most of Inigo Jones' designs for scenery are in the collection of the Duke of Devonshire at Chatsworth. Several plans are in the British Museum (Lansdowne MS. 1171) and clear diagrammatic reproductions of them are given in P. Reyher's *Les Masques Anglais*, Paris, 1909.

The *Masque in honour of Lord Hay* (1607), written by Thomas Campion, is of great interest from a musical point of view. Two songs and three dances are all that remain to us of the actual music,[1] but the directions given in the masque itself show that these must have formed only a very small portion of it. Campion being a composer as well as a poet was careful to record the musical arrangements of his masque, and we can at any rate form some idea of the general principles which guided the producers of those days in the combination of the three arts.

The general disposition of the hall was what we have already seen in previous masques and ballets. The dancing place was on this occasion raised above the floor level, and on each side of it were stationed the musicians in three separate groups. Nearest to the audience on the right was a group of ten, two violins to play the melody, a number of lutes and a harpsichord to fill up, and a trombone to give a firm bass; on the opposite side, but further away, was a group of twelve, in which the bowed instruments predominated; lastly, on the right-hand side again, but still further off, and raised on a higher level, were placed six voices and six cornets.[2]

This first stage was connected by a slope with the main stage, three feet higher and eighteen feet deep, which could be curtained off, and was concealed by clouds at the beginning of the masque. On the main stage was a grove of trees, with the nine golden trees, fifteen feet high, which concealed the masquers. On each side a slope led up to the bower of Flora and the house of Night respectively. The hall appears to have had a screen and presumably a gallery above, such as are found in college halls; these two side scenes were placed close to the screen, and above, probably built up from the gallery, was a mountain with the tree of Diana. Behind

[1] Reprinted by G. E. P. Arkwright in *The Old English Edition*.
[2] A similar custom of setting the trumpets on a raised platform was continued at a much later date: see the well-known plan of the Dresden orchestra given by Rousseau in the *Dictionnaire de Musique*, Paris, 1768.

this there seems to have been a group of hautboys in the gallery, more or less concealed by more trees, with another hill rising behind them. The general idea then of the decorations is to carry the eye from the floor level by a series of ascents up to the very top of the hall: this would naturally lend itself to admirable spectacular effects. The dispersal of the music in several groups was the usual practice in masques. Modern opera has continued this to some extent, sometimes with valuable dramatic effect, but always regarding the dispersed groups as subordinate to the main orchestra, which if not actually invisible is so at any rate by convention. This however was not possible until the orchestra had become standardized, and standardization of the orchestra only took place when Italian opera had become a common form of entertainment and could be run as a commercial speculation. The early masques, like the early Italian operas, were staged regardless of cost, and the employment of scattered bands was as extravagant in its way as the employment of scattered scenery. The organization of regular opera-houses necessitated economy, and the later producer, by concentrating his materials in a smaller space, was able to make many things perform a double duty.

The music began with the entrance of the King to the sound of the hautboys in the gallery; after a short pause the 'consort of ten', *i.e.* the group nearest the audience, played whilst the curtains in front of the stage were partially drawn, to reveal the bower of Flora. After a little stage business, Flora, Zephyrus and attendant Sylvans come down towards the lower stage and sing a song in three parts, accompanied by lutes which they play themselves, the 'orchestra' remaining silent. Flora addresses a speech to the audience on the subject of the marriage for which the masque was given, and then follows a dialogue in music for two voices. The whole stage is then revealed, and Night appears attended by Hours; a long dialogue ensues between Flora, Zephyrus, Night and Hesperus. The trees, we are told, are knights of Phoebus, transformed into this shape by the anger of Cynthia; Hesperus announces that Cynthia has in honour of this occasion agreed to their being restored to human shape. The Sylvans on the stage begin to play their instruments and to sing, on which the trees execute a dance. This is the well-known song 'Move now with measured sound'.[1] The transformation then takes place, and as it was a somewhat cumbrous business, and Inigo Jones' 'engine' could only accommodate three trees at a time, Campion has done his best to cover up the awkwardness by giving Night a separate speech for each group of three, followed by a song, sung and played by the Sylvans. The trees sank below the stage, and the masquers came up as if appearing out of the topmost branches. When the transformation is complete, Campion very effectively brings in his entire musical apparatus. A short chorus is sung in praise of the King, 'in manner of an echo' distributed ingeniously between the different groups of singers and players, there being five voices placed on each side of the stage. The total number of musicians is given as forty-two, but if the hautboys above and the musicians on the stage are included there must have been a good many more. The dances of the masquers follow, accompanied by the three orchestras, and interspersed with speeches from Night and Hesperus, choruses and songs. In this part of the entertainment come the further transformation of the masquers (who wore a second kind of dress underneath their first) and the dances of the masquers with the ladies of the audience.

, Even from the above short summary it will be seen that there is nothing really operatic in the masque, as compared with such a work as Peri's *Euridice*. The principal characters, Flora, Night, Hesperus and Zephyrus do not sing at all; the music is mainly choral, with a few dialogues between Sylvans or Hours which contribute nothing to the drama. They are in fact described sometimes merely as voices. It is simply a series of agreeable songs and dances, which are organized

[1] Quoted in the *Oxford History of Music*, III. 201.

into a sort of drama, because the dramatic episodes are introduced for no other purpose than to effect this. The loss of
the greater part of the music is of small moment; the stage
directions show us that Campion had a considerable idea of
employing his musical resources with a sense of the theatre,
though hardly with a sense of the drama. More than this
we must not look for; the musical technique of the age, even
in Italy, had not yet achieved any sort of symphonic sense of
construction towards a definite climax. Such construction
was in fact only made possible by the later development of
the key-system, of which the gradual extension of 'sonata-
form' was the natural and inevitable result.

With Ben Jonson the literary element, and more especially
the comic element, assumes greater prominence. The *Masque
of Queens* (1609) is the first to employ the 'antimasque', and
of this it has been said, 'the dramatic force of the antimasque
is such that it quite eclipses the main masque, which nothing
but the magnificence of the spectacle and the skill of the
dancers and musicians can have rescued from producing the
effect of an anti-climax'.[1] In this case it seems that it was
a positive advantage to have had scarcely any music during
the antimasque of witches, which is of great length and extremely elaborate. Some 'strange and sudden music' was
provided for their dances; but the nine incantations appear
to have been spoken, not sung. The 'loud music', therefore,
which heralded the transformation scene would have come
in with extraordinary force, and we may well suppose that
the audience were much more impressed by that and by
the appearance of the twelve queens than with the learned
eloquence of the poet, however different the judgment of a
modern reader may be. But in any case the antimasque was
not without musical importance. The witches of the *Masque
of Queens* are exceptional characters, judged by the standard
of later masques, but even they executed characteristic dances,
for which no doubt characteristic music was composed. The

[1] H. A. Evans, *English Masques*, London, 1897.

masque now contained three distinct types of dances, for which distinct types of music were required. The final revels, in which the masquers danced with partners from the audience, were the ordinary social dances of the period, galliards, corantos and the like; the 'grand dance' of the masquers was a much more intricate affair, involving geometrical figures and frequent changes of *tempo* in the music. The dances of the antimasque, like the music of the *ballet à entrées* into which the French ballet soon degenerated, were intended to be expressive of the characters represented, and are the foundation of the modern dramatic ballet.

Ben Jonson's *Masque of Oberon* (1611) is less startling but more attractive, and more organic in its arrangement. The Satyrs who form the antimasque have a considerable length of dialogue, and the main entry is ingeniously led up to by a preliminary transformation-scene showing two Sylvans on guard before the palace of Oberon. A catch, a song and a dance of Satyrs[1] are here introduced. The appearance of the masquers takes place with the usual pomp, and a number of fairies are discovered in attendance on Oberon. Instead of causing the antimasque to vanish at once, as was done in the case of the witches, the satyrs remain and continue to take part in the dialogue; and another effective point is made by the main dance of the masquers being preceded by a song of fairies and a dance for the 'lesser faies', who were young ladies of tender years, encircling the little prince Charles. In *Oberon*, as in Campion's masque, there are dialogues set to music, but these are not really of a dramatic character. A later work of Campion's, *The Lord's Masque* (1613), is of interest as having a speech spoken to the accompaniment of music. Further progress in a musical direction is made in

---

[1] This was possibly the 'Satyrs' Maske' in the British Museum Add. MS. 10444. It appears there without any composer's name; but in Thomas Simpson's *Taffel-Consort Erster Theil*, Hamburg, 1621, it is ascribed to Robert Johnson, who is known to have composed music for the *Masque of Oberon* This piece of music was utilized in the performance of Milton's *Comus* at Cambridge in 1908, and is printed in the *Christ's College Magazine*, vol. XXIII, No. 68.

The Golden Age restored (Jonson, 1616), if M. Reyher is right in suggesting that the whole masque was sung from beginning to end.[1] There is however no evidence for this beyond the metrical structure of the poem, which certainly suggests a very large employment of music. In *The Vision of Delight* (Jonson, 1617) we first meet with the direction *stylo recitativo*, and in *Lovers made Men*, which was given in February of the same year, Jonson tells us that 'the whole masque was sung after the Italian manner, *stylo recitativo*, by Master Nicholas Lanier; who ordered and made both the scene and the music'. *Lovers made Men* is in various respects exceptional. It was not a court masque, but was given by Lord Hay in honour of the French Ambassador and was acted 'by divers of noble quality his friends'; this probably accounts for its being very short, and devoid of elaborate transformation-scenes. Moreover, being entirely acted by amateurs, the antimasque, instead of being a separate entertainment, as was the case when there were professionals there to act it, is here so contrived that the same dancers dance both that and the masque itself. The fact of the whole being set to music was an additional reason for keeping the poem short. The music is unfortunately lost. It is possible that Lord Hay was more than usually interested in music, since Campion's masque to celebrate his marriage was also exceptional in its musical importance.

The court masques continued on the old lines, as far as music was concerned, and the antimasque now begins to develop into an elaborate scene of low comedy. There are sometimes even two antimasques, one before and the second after the appearance of the principal masquers. There had already been friction between Jonson and Inigo Jones before the latter went to Italy in 1613, and the quarrel only became more acute as time went on. Relations were probably not improved by Jonson's satirical allusions to Jones, first under the name of Vangoose, the rare artist and projector of masques in the *Masque of Augurs* (1622), and then in the part of the

---

[1] P. Reyher, *Les Masques Anglais.*

Cook in *Neptune's Triumph* (1624). The final breach was caused by Jones' indignation at finding his name put second to Jonson's on the title page of *Chloridia* (1631). Jones was sufficiently powerful to be able to prevent Jonson from being commissioned to write any more masques; and Jonson retorted upon Jones with the well-known *Expostulation*. From this moment begins the decadence of the masque under Shirley and D'Avenant.

Shirley's *Triumph of Peace* is by far the most ornate and extravagant of all the masques that were produced in this country. It was organized by the Inns of Court at a cost of over £21,000, as an expression of protest against Prynne's *Histriomastix*. The performance of it was preceded by a procession of all the characters on horseback from Ely House in Holborn to Whitehall, which no doubt added considerably to the cost. Whitelocke, who was generally responsible for the music, tells us that the whole of the music cost about £1000, in which is included £100 apiece paid to Simon Ives and William Lawes for its composition. This was liberal recompense compared to what musicians had received previously.[1]

As the form of the Masque differs from that of its predecessors, it must be shortly summarized here. The opening scene represents a large street with sumptuous palaces etc. leading to the Piazza of Peace. A dialogue follows between Opinion, Confidence, Novelty and other personifications, who dance the first antimasque. The characters remaining on the stage and continuing their conversation, the scene is changed to 'a spick and span new tavern'. This leads to a second antimasque of the tavern keeper, his wife and servants, followed by two more dances of beggars and disreputable characters. Opinion being dissatisfied with these, six 'projectors', *i.e.* inventors of strange machines, are introduced one after another, each dancing in turn, being finally joined in a

---

[1] Whitelocke's long account of the Masque is printed in Burney's *History of Music*, III. 369 ff.

pantomimic dance by the tavern keeper and the rest. Opinion asks for another device; the scene changes to a woody landscape, with a pantomimic dance of birds and other characters.

An Owl, a Crow, a Kite, a Jay, a Magpie. The birds dance and wonder at the Owl. When these are gone, enter a Merchant a'Horseback with his portmanteau; two Thieves set upon him and rob him; these by a Constable and Officers are apprehended and carried off. Then four Nymphs enter dancing, with their javelins: three Satyrs spy them and attempt their persons; one of the Nymphs escapeth; a noise of hunters and their horns within, as at the fall of a deer; then enter four Huntsmen and one Nymph; these drive away the Satyrs, and having rescued the Nymphs, dance with them.

The scene again changes to another landscape, with another pantomimic dance of much the same kind. Confidence and the rest return to the stage, 'all drunk', Novelty saying, 'I will have an antimasque of my own, in a new place too'.

At this point the serious part of the masque begins, with the entrance of Irene and Eunomia or Law, who appear in machines, followed soon after by Diche in a third machine, apparently with a train of musicians. There are dialogues in music between the three principal figures and the chorus. Finally they all move towards the King and Queen and address them in a song. The scene changes again, and the sixteen masquers are discovered sitting on the ascent of a hill, with an arbour of trees over them. A 'Genius or angelical person' descends to the stage, and presents them to the audience in a speech, after which they dance their entry and main dance, with a song between the two. No sooner is this over than a great noise is heard of voices and cracking woodwork;[1] then there rush in a carpenter, a painter, the wives of other workpeople, and menials of the royal household, as if forcing an entrance to see the masque. At the tailor's suggestion they dance, after which he says, 'Now let us go off

---

[1] Sabbatini (*Pratica di fabricar Scene e Machine ne' Teatri*, Ravenna, 1638) recommended a false alarm of scaffolding giving way in the audience as a convenient device to distract the spectators' attention while a difficult change of scene was to be effected.

cleanly, and somebody will think this was meant for an anti-masque'. After another song the 'revels' of the masquers and their ladies take place, and the masque is concluded by the appearance of Amphiluche, 'the forerunner of the morning', who appears in an appropriate transformation-scene to call the masquers home to bed.

A few fragments of William Lawes' music to this masque have survived[1], and the following extract will give some idea of the way in which composers approached the problem. It is curious to note that the part of Irene is written for a tenor: it was in fact taken by Nicholas Lanier. The modern reader must also make allowances for certain technical habits of the day; thus in the choruses the alto, tenor and bass parts are always kept low down together, with the treble at some distance.[2] It need hardly be added that the MS. represents only the barest outline of the music, and that we must imagine the chords copiously filled up by lutes, harpsichords and other instruments. The treatment of words proceeds on the lines which by this time were well established in England. William and Henry Lawes were both pupils of the Italianized Englishman Coperario, and their musical declamation, like that of Lanier and Ferrabosco in earlier years, is clearly derived from that of Caccini.[3] That it should follow Caccini rather than the more dramatic style of Peri or Monteverdi is natural enough, since the masques are almost entirely lyrical as compared with the early Italian operas. It is true that the Roman composers Stefano Landi and Domenico Mazzocchi were already departing from the austere ideals of the Florentines, and were preparing the way for the domination of the aria, but the English composers could hardly be expected to be in close touch with this movement. The English vocal

[1] The entrance of Irene as here printed is in the Bodleian Library MS. Mus. Sch. B. 2, and the Song of Amphiluche 'In Envy of the Night' in the British Museum Add. MS. 31432.

[2] The alto parts, as in all English seventeenth-century music, whether secular or sacred, are intended for male altos.

[3] Cf. *Oxford History of Music*, III. 199 ff., where examples from these composers are given.

(The Antimasquers being gone, there appears in the highest and foremost part of the heaven, by little and little to break forth, a whitish cloud, bearing a chariot feigned of Goldsmith's work: and in it sate Irene, or Peace, in a flowery vesture like the spring, a garland of olives on her head, a branch of palm in her hand, buskins of green taffeta, great puffs about her neck and shoulders.)

W. LAWES

light   For such a   glorious night,   Wherein two   skies Are to be

seen,   One   starry,   but an   a - ged sphere,   An - other

here,   Crea - ted   new   and   brighter   from the eyes   Of   king and queen?

Chorus

Hence,   hence, ye   pro - fane,   far hence   away!   Time hath sick

feathers   while you   stay

Symphony

31

Irene

Wherefore do my sisters stay? Appear, appear, Eu - no - mi - a! 'Tis I - re - ne calls to thee, I - re - ne calls; Like dew that

32

falls. Into a stream, I'm lost with them That know not how to or-der ma.

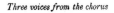
Voice from the chorus

See where she shines, See where she shines, oh see

Three voices from the chorus

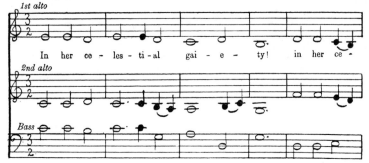

1st alto

In her ce - les - ti - al gai - e - ty! in her ce -

2nd alto

Bass

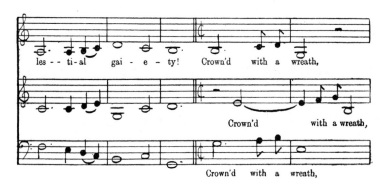

les - - ti - al gai - e - ty! Crown'd with a wreath,

Crown'd with a wreath,

Crown'd with a wreath,

33

crown'd with a wreath of stars to show The eve-ning's

crown'd with a wreath of stars to show The eve - ning's

crown'd with a wreath of stars to show The eve - ning's glo - ry

glo - ry in her brow, the eve - ning's glo - ry in her brow.

glo - ry in her brow, the eve - ning's glo - ry in her brow.

in her brow, the eve - ning's glo - ry in her brow.

*(Here, out of the highest part of the opposite side, came softly descending another
cloud, of an orient colour, bearing a silver chariot curiously wrought, and differing
in all things from the first : in which sate Eunomia or Law, in a purple satin robe,
adorned with golden stars, a mantle of carnation laced, and fringed with gold, a
coronet of light upon her head, buskins of purple, drawn out with yellow. This
chariot attended as the former.)*

Symphony

Eunomia (treble)

Think not I could absent myself this night; But Peace is gentle and doth still invite Eu - no-mi-a; yet should'st thou si - lent be, The rose and lil-y which thou strow-est All the cheerful way thou goest, Would direct to follow thee.

Irene

Thou dost beaut-i — fy increase,

Eunomia

And chain se-cur-i-ty with peace I - rene fair and first di-

35

vine,   All   my bless-ings spring from thine. * Although I etc.

thou abhorr'st What is rude,   or apt to

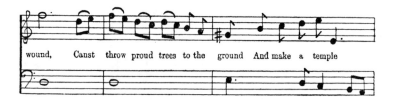

wound,   Canst throw proud trees to the   ground And make a temple

of a fo - rest.   No more,   no more, no more but join Thy

* The text set by Lawes evidently differs here from the printed version.
The MS. gives only the initial words of each song as a rule, and I have filled
in the rest from the printed text, which at this point reads

     Irene. I am but wild without thee, thou abhorrest
           What is rude or apt to wound, etc.

The words *thou abhorst* are written in to the music; but the succeeding lines
do not fit very well, and should perhaps be different. I print the music as
given in the MS. with Lawes' own bar-lines; it will be noted that the second
phrase is a minim short.

voice and lute with mine. The world shall give pre-ro-ga-tive to neither

We cannot flour-ish but togeth-er, we

cannot flourish but to—gether. I-re-ne en-ters like a per-fum'd

spring, Eu-no-mia ripens ever-y-thing, And in the gold-en

harvest leaves To every sic-kle his own sheaves.

37

style represented most typically by the brothers Lawes is indeed a very characteristic product, and it is curiously paralleled by the tendencies of English composers a generation ago. Aiming at a just balance of words and music, the musician sacrificed his own personality to that of the poet, but had either not enough literary sense, or perhaps more probably not enough musical technique, to make his declamation consistently accurate. The musician is in fact expressing not the emotions which led the poet to conceive his poetry, but his admiration for the poet's accomplishment. When William Lawes sets Shirley, still more when Henry Lawes sets Milton,[1] the beauty of the words gives a factitious beauty to the music; when D'Avenant's superficial rhetoric is all that the composer has to inspire him, the baldness of the music is only accentuated. A single song, such as that of the Lady in *Comus*, may produce a touchingly beautiful effect, but a long series of musical movements such as we see in the extract given becomes tedious, owing to the slow monotony of the declamation, and the colourless and self-effacing harmonies which are intended to support it.

On the other hand, considered in connection with the stage effects, William Lawes' music is not without merits. His instrumental movements have dignity and a certain melodic invention, which is well set off by the free and independent movement of his basses.[2] As with Coleman and other writers of the time, the themes are of so declamatory a type that they seem almost to have been intended for words, until we look at the vocal numbers and see how comparatively feeble these are in melodic line. We see a similar kind of thing happening in the Italian and Italianizing music of the next century: the break-up of the melodic line in the arias of Pergolesi and

---

[1] Although the most celebrated of the masques, *Comus* need not be discussed here. It entirely disregards the conventional masque form, and has no bearing on the development of English opera.

[2] William Lawes was a voluminous composer of instrumental music. The Bodleian Library contains a quantity of his works, which are elaborately polyphonic in character.

others for the sake of verbal effect leads to a conception of short rhythmical phrases as material for thematic development in the vocal and instrumental work of Mozart and Haydn.

We must not expect at this period any strong sense of steady musical development to a climax such as we find in Purcell; the technique of the period did not admit of it. Musicians were only just emancipating themselves from the modal system, and it is indeed remarkable that Lawes should show so strong a sense of balanced tonality as he does in our extract. It begins and ends in C major; this key is steadily maintained to the end of the second 'symphony', the incidental modulations being almost always to the dominant, with only the most momentary allusions to the relative minor. But with Irene's second song, complaining of the absence of her sisters, the key of A minor is at once strongly emphasized; the trio which follows begins and ends in A minor, and so does the symphony to which Eunomia appears. Eunomia starts singing in the same key, but in the course of the duet the music modulates to various keys, even as far as D major. The key of C is ingeniously avoided, except for the one very effective entry at 'yet should'st thou silent be': but the transitions which follow lead fairly logically back to it when Eunomia invites Irene to 'join thy lute with mine', and the concluding chorus settles the movement firmly in the key in which it began.

The historians of English music have hitherto failed to recognize the importance of this broad sense of tonality, although they have carefully considered details of declamation or harmony. But it cannot be too strongly insisted that opera as an artistic form depends largely on symphonic principles, that is, on the composer's realization of the drama as one continuous and organized piece of music from beginning to end, even if interrupted here and there by spoken dialogue. That is the system of Mozart and Wagner, and it is in the tentative anticipation of it that we can see the masques to be real forerunners of opera.

Carew's *Caelum Britannicum* (1634)[1] shows how completely the art of Inigo Jones now dominated the masque. There must have been a good deal of music,[2] for the songs in the serious part are elaborate and much divided among the voices; there are also seven antimasques, introduced by Mercury and Momus in very lengthy though often amusing speeches. The influence of Inigo Jones is apparent even in the literary portion of the masque, since the subject is very Italian in character, with an unending succession of figures from classical mythology, which are, however, treated at times with a very English sense of humour. With the next year we come to *The Temple of Love*, the first masque written by William D'Avenant. The principal masquers in this were ladies, the Queen herself being one of them. The antimasques were comparatively few, which may account for the masque having been less successful than its predecessors, in spite of the magnificence of its scenery. It included a great deal of music, but this is never of a dramatic character. The music to D'Avenant's next masque, *The Triumphs of the Prince d'Amour* (1636), was by the brothers Lawes. This masque was entirely set to music, except for a short prologue spoken before the curtain rose. It consists merely of dances and songs alternated, if we may class as dances the business performed in dumb show by the characters of the antimasque. In this it resembles a French *ballet de cour* much more than the typical English masque of Ben Jonson. Its exceptional character may have been due to the fact that it was 'hastily prepared' and 'devised and written in three days' for presentation by the Middle Temple to 'the Prince Elector', *i.e.* the Elector Palatine Karl Ludwig, whose mother was sister of James I. Some of the music by William Lawes has survived,[3] but it is less interesting than *The Triumph of Peace*, at any rate from a dramatic point of view. The first antimasque represents

---

[1] It is printed among D'Avenant's works in the collected edition of 1673.
[2] By Henry Lawes.
[3] Bodleian Library MS. Mus. Sch. B. 2.

soldiers and others drinking at a village tavern. Next appears a temple of Mars with a camp. Priests of Mars come out of the temple and sing a chorus describing a battle. The principal masquers then appear as Knights Templars. Cupid descends with a song and shoots at them; the scene changes to 'a square Piazza resembling that of Venice, with Courtizans looking out of Windows and Balconees'. The second antimasque represents lovers of different nationalities paying their addresses to these ladies. The scene then changes to the Temple of Venus; priests sing a chorus, and the masquers make their second entry. The scene changes again, to the Temple of Apollo; more priests sing another chorus and a party of dancers bring in a banquet. This is set in front of the 'state', and, while the princes partake of it, more music is sung by the three groups of priests. The music which is extant begins with the second chorus of the priests of Apollo, in which they invite the 'industrious slaves of plenty' to bring in the banquet, and goes down to the end of the masque. The movements are all in the keys of C major or minor and are mostly very short, but with a fair amount of characterization. The minor mode is well brought in at the moment when the 'twelve men wildly habited' enter with the banquet.

D'Avenant's last masque, and the last that was presented before the Civil War, was *Salmacida Spolia*, which is constructed on much the same plan as *The Triumphs of the Prince d'Amour*. In addition to a first antimasque of furies, there is later on a series of no less than twenty consecutive antimasques, none of which has any connection either with the whole or with any other. There were two sets of principal masquers, led by the King and Queen respectively. The music was by one Louis Richard, a Frenchman in the service of Henrietta Maria. We are told that all the antimasques were 'well set out and excellently danced', and the tunes 'fitted to the persons'. No compositions of Louis Richard appear to be in existence, and we have no means of judging how he differentiated the characters of his dancers.

It has been necessary to consider the music to the masques in some detail, although not one can properly be regarded as an opera, because, as we shall see in the next chapter, it was out of the masque that English opera developed. The court masques were not accessible to the general public, and even for those who gained admission they were not of frequent occurrence. But the public were evidently interested in them, even if they did not witness them, as is shown by the popularity of masques introduced into plays. On the Elizabethan stage these cannot have been of a very elaborate nature; the theatres did not possess the necessary machinery, and the expense put them out of the question for any company that expected to make a profit out of its performances. But the ingenuity of Inigo Jones may be said to have made for economy as well as for extravagance, and it was due to him and his pupil John Webb that D'Avenant was in later years enabled to present the public with plays and masques, elaborated into what were given the name of operas, on a scale which though hardly magnificent was at any rate compatible with financial success.

Chapter Three

'*The* SIEGE *of* RHODES'

D'Avenant's treatment of the masque is from some points of view retrograde; but there can be no doubt that he gave his audiences what they wanted. Besides, he gave them what was in fashion at the French court, and that was naturally above criticism. But he was already cherishing ideas of a more ambitious order, and in 1639 he obtained a patent from Charles I for the erection of a theatre of his own. The document authorized him 'from time to time to act plays in such house to be by him erected, and exercise musick, musical presentments, scenes, dancing, or any other the like, at the same or other houses at times, or after plays are ended'. The importance of this document was first pointed out by Mr W. J. Lawrence,[1] who draws from it the conclusion that D'Avenant intended his theatre for performances of opera and for evening concerts as well. It is probable that concerts would have been quite successful, as a concert before the play was a regular feature of some of the ordinary theatres.

As regards operas, D'Avenant, if this interpretation is correct —and there seems every reason to suppose that it is—was remarkably early in the field. There was nothing to be seen at Paris which could be called an opera, though it is of course possible that under 'musical presentments' D'Avenant contemplated nothing more dramatic than the *ballet de cour*. And although it was almost half a century since the first experiments of Peri and Rinuccini in musical drama, the opera was still something of a novelty even in Italy. For a long time Rome was the only city where steady progress was being made, and that was due almost entirely to the extravagance

---

[1] 'The Origin of the English Picture-Stage', in *The Elizabethan Playhouse and other Studies*, Second Series, Stratford-on-Avon, 1913.

of the Barberini family. It was not until 1637 that the first public opera-house was opened, the Teatro S. Cassiano at Venice. However, England was always closely in touch with Venice, and it is noticeable throughout the seventeenth century that, in spite of strong French influences on dramatic literature, the musical tendencies of this country remained very constantly Italian. For some reason or other D'Avenant did not build his opera-house, and within the same year he gave up his right to the particular site which had been assigned to it. But he still retained his licence, to make use of it when a more favourable occasion arose.

By the time the Civil War was over and the influence of Puritan repression had begun to wane many new events had taken place elsewhere in the world of music. The old-fashioned *ballet de cour* came practically to an end with the death of Louis XIII in 1643, and it was during the early years of Louis XIV's minority that Cardinal Mazarin endeavoured by dint of persistent effort to establish Italian opera as a permanent institution at the French court.[1] Mazarin's motives in doing so were very largely political, but he was none the less a passionate lover of music. In his early days he had been in the service of Cardinal Antonio Barberini, the leading organizer of operatic performances at Rome, and it was alleged that he was the lover of Leonora Baroni, the singer whom Milton heard at Rome and celebrated in a Latin poem.[2] When he transferred himself definitely to Paris he soon found that his musical interests were of service to him in cultivating the favour of Richelieu and Louis XIII, who were both devoted to the art. Music seems to have been Louis XIII's principal occupation during the later years of his life: even after he had received extreme unction he had motets of his own composition performed and sang in them

[1] For the full details of this movement see H. Prunières, *L'opéra Italien en France avant Lulli*, Paris, 1913.

[2] It has been suggested that it was to the same Leonora that he addressed his Italian sonnets, but this has been disputed. See J. S. Smart, 'The Italian singer in Milton's sonnets', in *The Musical Antiquary*, IV. 91.

himself. In 1643 Mazarin determined to have an Italian opera performed at Paris before the King and Queen, and wrote to engage the Roman composer Marco Marazzoli and a troupe of Italian singers. The death of Richelieu during the course of his negotiations made him all the more anxious to secure his position at court by gratifying the passion of Anne of Austria for Italian music. Before anything was definitely arranged the King died, and Mazarin was obliged to postpone his entertainment. But he brought Leonora Baroni to Paris in 1644, and the charm of her singing, coupled with her intellectual abilities, soon gave her an extraordinary influence over the Queen. The following year he ventured to organize the performance of an Italian opera before the Queen and a small but select audience. This opera cannot be definitely identified, but was probably a little pastoral entitled *Nicandro e Fileno*, set to music no doubt by Marazzoli. In December of the same year another Italian opera, *La Finta Pazza*, was given, probably with the music of Sacrati, whose setting had been performed at Venice. The music however seems to have counted for very little in this work, which was represented not by regular singers but by a company of actors. The chief attractions were the ballets of monkeys, bears, eunuchs and ostriches planned for the special amusement of the *Roi soleil*, then aged seven, and the magnificent scenery designed by Giacomo Torelli, the greatest theatrical architect of the day. In February 1646 Cavalli's *Egisto* was performed with singers specially sent over from Italy, and it was this entertainment of which Mme de Motteville spoke so slightingly in the passage often quoted from her memoirs.[1] But Mme de Motteville, like most typical French spectators of the period, did not understand the essential principle of Italian opera; and this particular work was in fact not very representative of Cavalli's dramatic genius.

---

[1] 'Nous n'étions que vingt ou trente personnes dans ce lieu et nous pensâmes mourir d'ennui et de froid. Les divertissemens de cette nature demandent du monde et la solitude n'a pas de rapport avec les théâtres.'

There is also reason to suppose that it was not mounted with any great elaboration of scenery.

Among the scanty audience on that chilly February evening was Cardinal Antonio Barberini, who had come to Paris with his two brothers to seek the protection of France from the persecutions of the new pope Innocent X. Cardinal Antonio brought with him a secretary, the abbé Francesco Buti, who had written the libretto of *Il Palazzo d' Atlante*, an opera recently produced in Rome, and either because he himself could not bear to be separated from his musicians, or more probably at the instigation of Mazarin, sent a letter to Rome in March 1646 summoning the composer, Luigi Rossi. Rossi, who was a courtier as well as a musician of exceptional genius—perhaps after Monteverdi the most remarkable Italian composer of the first half of the seventeenth century—very soon established himself in the affections of the French court, and even won the esteem of the French musicians by his cordial appreciation of their singing, their instruments, and their delicate style of performance. He and Buti were at once set to work upon an opera, for which Torelli was to furnish the scenery. This opera was *Orfeo*, produced after many difficulties and delays on March 2, 1647. The opera was received with the greatest enthusiasm by those who were privileged to witness it, though outside the court circle it engendered a violent outburst of feeling against Mazarin and his Italian protégés. But the defeat of the Fronde restored Mazarin to power in 1653, and in 1654 he followed up *Orfeo* with *Le Nozze di Peleo e di Theti*, composed for the occasion by Carlo Caproli, another Roman musician, to a libretto by Buti. The score of the opera has not survived. Its main interest lies in the fact that it combined the Italian opera form with that of the *ballet de cour* which was still dear to the hearts of the French. The actors included several French musicians, and among the dancers was Lulli, who had just entered the service of the French King. He was then twenty-four, and had not yet been heard of as a composer.

During the whole of this period Henrietta Maria had been living in Paris with her son, the future Charles II, and their names are constantly mentioned in the records of the time as having been present at the performances of these operas. It is highly probable that D'Avenant also had seen some of them, since, after having been accused in 1641 of taking part in a conspiracy to subvert the army from its adherence to Parliamentary authority, he fled to France, and was constantly in attendance on the English Queen, who sent him on various missions to England. In 1650 however he was taken prisoner and narrowly escaped being condemned to death. He owed his release, it is said, to the good offices of Milton and Whitelocke, both of whom, it may be noted, were keen amateur musicians.

D'Avenant during his visits to Paris probably saw not only the Italian operas of the court but also another kind of spectacle, the *tragédies à machines* of the Théâtre du Marais. These were plays in alexandrines, with occasional songs or ballets, depending, as their name implies, on scenic effects as their principal attraction, although they could only provide machinery of a very primitive order as compared with the marvels of Torelli's ingenuity. When Luigi Rossi's *Orfeo* was the talk of Paris in 1647, the actors of the Théâtre du Marais catered for those who could not go to the opera, and in 1648 they revived an *Orphée aux Enfers* by Chapoton of the year 1640, with new scenery cleverly imitated from Torelli's, and some additional new music. It may have been the popularity of the French *Orphée* which induced Buti to suggest to Mazarin that Rossi's *Orfeo* should be translated into French. It is possible that a project was entertained of entrusting Corneille with the translation; but in any case it was not carried out, and what did happen was that Corneille was commissioned to write a new play, *Andromède*, for which the scenery of *Orfeo* could be used over again. Its performance was abandoned owing to Louis XIV's attack of smallpox in the autumn of 1647, but Corneille succeeded in getting it finally produced in February 1650.

D'Avenant, if he did not see the performance, was fairly certain to have read the printed play, which appeared in the previous autumn. It is generally passed over as a mere spectacular piece or operatic libretto, of no importance compared with *Medée* or *Le Cid*; but it is interesting as the experiment of an accomplished dramatist in the combination of speech, song and machinery, and though its influence on French opera was only slight, it ought probably to be regarded as the model for D'Avenant's version of *The Tempest* and the later English operas.

When we read the libretti of the Roman and Venetian operas of the early seventeenth century, it is difficult to imagine that the poet designed his drama on any clearly defined principle. One episode succeeds another without any appearance of reason; tragedy and farce are so intermingled that we may find them even in one and the same piece of music; when inspiration comes to an end, a transformation-scene—the more incongruous the better—will fill up the deficiency. The art of a Luigi Rossi will give a magical reality to the whole by the exquisite beauty of its emotional expression.

Corneille, like most Frenchmen, viewed the drama from a different standpoint. Romantic as he was by temperament, he still had a sense of system. He explains his system in the preface to his play.

Vous trouverez cet ordre gardé dans les changements de Théâtre, que chaque Acte aussi-bien que le Prologue a sa décoration particulière, et du moins une machine volante avec un concert de Musique, que je n'ay employée qu'à satisfaire les oreilles des spectateurs, tandis que leurs yeux sont arrestez à voir descendre ou remonter une machine, ou s'attachent à quelque chose qui leur empesche de prester attention à ce que pourroient dire les Acteurs, comme fait le combat de Persée contre le Monstre: mais je me suis bien gardé de faire rien chanter qui fust nécessaire à l'intelligence de la Pièce, parceque communément les paroles qui se chantent estant mal entendues des auditeurs, pour la confusion qu'y apporte la diversité des voix qui les prononcent ensemble, elles auroient fait une grande obscurité dans le corps de l'ouvrage, si elles avoient eu à instruire l'Auditeur de quelque chose d'important. Il n'en va pas de mesme des machines, qui ne sont pas dans cette Tragédie comme des agréements détachez, elles en font le nœud et le desnouement, et y sont si nécessaires que vous n'en sçauriez retrancher aucune, que vous ne faciez tomber tout l'édifice....En attendant recevez celuy-cy comme le plus achevé qui aye encor paru sur nos Théâtres, et souffrez que la beauté de la représentation supplée au manque des beaux vers que vous n'y trouverez pas en si grande quantité que dans *Cinna*, ou dans *Rodogune*, parceque mon principal but icy a esté de satisfaire la veue par l'esclat et la diversité du spectacle, et non pas de toucher l'esprit par la force du raisonnement, ou le cœur par la delicatesse des passions.

The names of the characters are divided into two classes, gods in the machines, and mortals. Of the first class there are eight, besides three Nereids and eight Winds. The play begins with a prologue spoken by Melpomene (descending a mountain) and the Sun (in a celestial chariot drawn by four horses) in praise of Louis XIV. They sing a duet, joined by a chorus which repeats the refrain

Louys est le plus jeune et le plus grand des Rois,

after which Melpomene gets into the Sun's chariot and they go off together 'pour aller publier ensemble la mesme chose au reste de l'Univers'.

The first scene represents the capital of Cepheus' kingdom. Perseus is politely listening to the lengthy explanation of Cassiopea, Andromeda's mother. Enter Cepheus and Phineus, here his nephew, rival candidate for Andromeda's hand. Phineus and Perseus are agreed in trying to persuade Cepheus not to give up his daughter to the monster. Perseus' argument is characteristic of the age:

Differez son Hymen sans l'exposer au choix,
Le Ciel assez souvent doux aux crimes des Rois,
Quand il leur a monstré quelque légère haine,
Répand sur leurs sujets le reste de leur peine.

Venus appears in a machine, and advances slowly to the middle of the stage while the chorus sing a hymn to her. She delivers an ambiguous pronouncement, and returns to the skies to the music of another chorus. Perseus declares his love for Andromeda.

The second act introduces the heroine, serenaded by a page of Phineus, to whom one of her attendants replies, the two singers then joining in a duet. The news is brought that Andromeda's name has been drawn as the next victim of the monster, and in spite of Phineus' protests she is carried off then and there by Aeolus and the eight Winds. Perseus announces his intention of rescuing her. The next act shows us the sea-shore, with the Winds fastening Andromeda to a rock. The chorus and other characters watch the arrival of the monster, which is duly slain by Perseus, while the chorus and a soloist encourage him With a piece of music. The winds bring Andromeda back; Perseus, 'après avoir fait un caracol admirable au milieu de l'air' on the back of Pegasus, disappears to more choral music. Three Nereids rise from the sea and complain of the injustice that has been done to them; Neptune appears and undertakes to avenge them.

In the fourth act Phineus finds himself discarded in favour of Perseus. To console him Juno appears, drawn by peacocks; 'elle se promène au milieu de l'air, dont nos Poètes luy attribuent l'Empire, et y fait plusieurs tours, tantost à droite, et tantost à gauche, cependant qu'elle asseure Phinée de sa protection'. The chorus sing a song in praise of the bride and bridegroom, and the company proceed to the temple.

In the fifth act Phineus and his friends attack Perseus, but Perseus by the aid of Medusa's head turns them to stone statues. This is told to the audience by a messenger. Perseus appears and the whole company are just about to enter the temple when Mercury descends and announces the arrival of Jupiter. The chorus sing a hymn; Jupiter appears, with Juno and Neptune now completely pacified, and carries off the happy pair together with Andromeda's parents to celebrate their marriage in the skies.

Although there is plenty of music[1] in the drama, it is less essential to the action than the machinery, which is laid out so as to form a very effective *crescendo*. Corneille seems to have had no idea whatever of piling up music as Mozart or Verdi do towards the end of an act, but generally concludes each with a few spoken lines, which appear to make a painful anti-climax after the appearance of a divinity and the singing of the chorus. But there was a reason for this which we moderns are apt to forget. No curtain fell at the end of each act; the scenery was transformed in view of the spectators.[2] A big musical climax was only practicable when a curtain fell on its conclusion. This applies not only to finales in which principals and chorus combine to build up an ever-increasing volume of sound, but also to endings where the interest is centred on a few figures, or on one. There is not a single act in the operas of Wagner which does not imperatively require the fall of a curtain, even such acts as end with an empty stage, for in these the final effect depends not on the exit of the last character, but on the empty stage itself and the continuation of the drama, interpreted by the orchestra, in the imagination of the audience. This idea of drama is purely German and modern. It was impossible in France or Italy in the seventeenth century. Moreover it is clear from Corneille's preface that he simply could not conceive of the music expressing in itself the most important part of the drama; what was dramatic could be interpreted only in terms of speech. This idea seems to have held its ground in France even into the days of Rameau, who, though he does not employ spoken dialogue, frequently ends his acts with a recitative after what constitutes the real musical climax.

As M. Prunières says, Corneille's play would have made an excellent opera libretto if it had not been written in alexandrines. It has the merit of being very clearly designed;

[1] The music was composed by Dassoucy, who was a friend and admirer of Rossi. Only a few fragments of his score have survived.

[2] The stage directions leave no doubt on this point.

the characters may be conventional, but their emotions are vigorously and effectively indicated, and there is not a single scene that does not contribute something necessary to the development of the drama. In this respect it is a great contrast to the Italian libretti of the period. As regards the versification, it is evident that the tradition of the alexandrine in France and that of either blank verse or the heroic couplet in England were serious obstacles to the development of opera. None of these metres lends itself easily to recitative. The Italians, on the other hand, had developed a recitative style of their own in poetry, derived from the irregular metres of the madrigals and other lyrical forms. It may be seen in Tasso's *Aminta*, though about half the play is in blank verse, and is admirably exemplified in Rinuccini's *Euridice*, a poem which can be read with delight quite apart from its musical setting. But *Aminta* and Guarini's *Il Pastor Fido* were almost isolated achievements in Italian literature, not casual specimens of a national drama which could count its examples by hundreds. For Italy that national drama was to be the drama of music. In France and England it could never hope to supplant the drama of poetry in the affections of the public.

In May 1656 D'Avenant took his first step towards the establishment of opera in England. The theatres were still closed, but the Puritans had no objection to music, and Cromwell himself was a supporter of the art. To what extent D'Avenant's own motives were musical it is difficult to say. He was a writer of plays, had been made Poet Laureate, and evidently believed in himself as a poet and dramatist; it is probable too that he hoped to make his theatre a source of financial profit. He began very cautiously with what was described as 'The First Dayes Entertainment at Rutland-House by Declamations and Musick: after the manner of the Ancients'. Rutland House was in Charterhouse Yard, Aldersgate Street. Five shillings a head was charged for admission; the audience numbered not more than a hundred and fifty, though there was space for four hundred. The room seems to have been a very inconvenient one. A stage was erected at one end, with curtains of gold and purple; the audience sat in rows facing each other at right angles to the stage. The entertainment began with a 'flourish of musick' after which the curtain was drawn and the Prologue entered. He apologizes for the discomforts of the room, which was low and narrow, and indicates plainly the future intentions of the author:

> Think this your passage, and the narrow way
> To our Elisian field, the Opera:
> Tow'rds which some say we have gone far about,
> Because it seems so long since we set out.
> Think now the way grown short, and that you light
> At this small Inn, to bait, not stay all night:
> Where you shall find, what you will much despise;
> The Host grown old, and worse than old, half wise.

The speaker refers here to the long time that had elapsed since D'Avenant's unsuccessful attempt to build an opera-house in 1639. A 'consort of instrumental musick adapted to the sullen disposition of Diogenes' was then performed, after which the curtain was drawn again, and there appeared Diogenes and Aristophanes, sitting in 'rostras' of purple and gold. Diogenes makes a long speech in condemnation of 'publick entertainment by Moral Representations'; another piece of music is played to illustrate the cheerful disposition of Aristophanes, who thereupon argues the case from the other side. The speeches are lengthy and tedious, but were perhaps appreciated by an audience accustomed to Puritan sermons. The curtains close, and a song with chorus and instruments follows. The second part of the entertainment consisted of similar speeches by a Parisian and a Londoner, each abusing the other's city. Each speech was preceded by appropriate music, and the speeches were followed by a song deriding Paris and the French. The Epilogue, despite its apparent regret for the suppression of the drama, alludes ironically to its old-fashioned principles of construction.

Perhaps, some were so couzen'd as to come,
To see us weave in the Dramatique Loom:
To trace the winding Scenes, like subtle Spies,
Bred in the Muses Camp, safe from surprize:
Where you by Art learn joy, and when to mourn;
To watch the Plots swift change, and counterturn:
When Time moves swifter then by Nature taught;
And by a *Chorus* Miracles are wrought;
Making an Infant instantly a man:
These were your Plays, but get them if you can.

The music was composed by Henry Lawes, Charles Coleman, Captain Cooke and George Hudson. Charles Coleman had composed music for masques in Charles I's day; Captain Cooke was a famous singer and choir trainer; of Hudson little is known. The principal singers were Coleman's son Edward and his wife. Edward Coleman had already composed music for Shirley's *Contention of Ajax and Ulysses* in 1653.

The entertainment, it will be seen, was really little more than what nowadays would be called a 'lecture-recital in costume', and it seems strange that so much caution was necessary when two masques by Shirley, *Ajax and Ulysses* and *Cupid and Death* had both been performed during the Commonwealth. But these had been private entertainments, and it is clear from the speeches at Rutland House that a distinction was drawn in such cases.

The 'Declamations' were apparently repeated for ten days, and other performances of a similar kind were intended to follow them; whether they took place is not known. The next event recorded is the production of *The Siege of Rhodes*, in the autumn of 1656. This also took place at Rutland House, and was on a correspondingly small scale. *The Siege of Rhodes* has always been described as the first English opera, and there seems to be little doubt that it was sung from beginning to end; but as none of the music has come down to us, it is very difficult to form a judgment on it. It was extremely successful, and besides being followed by other operas, it was repeated in various years, with considerable enlargements. Whether the first edition represents the original idea of the poet, subsequently enlarged, or whether the later version is the original and the first an abridgement of it, is uncertain. The latter hypothesis is on the whole the more probable, for reasons which will appear later.

The play was divided into five 'entries', which were set by three composers: the first and last by Henry Lawes, the second and third by Captain Cooke, and the fourth by a younger man, Matthew Locke. Besides this there was instrumental music by Charles Coleman and George Hudson. Cooke and Locke both appeared as singers as well, taking the parts of Solyman and the Admiral; Mustapha was 'Mr. Henry Persill', *i.e.* the father of the great Henry Purcell, while Edward Coleman and his wife appeared as the hero and heroine, Alphonso and Ianthe. The scenery, which in spite of the small space available, was a very important feature of the play, was designed by John Webb, a pupil of Inigo Jones, who had died in 1652.

Of the music not a note appears to have survived. We may form some vague idea of its style from the masque-music of Henry Lawes, and from Locke's music to Shirley's *Cupid and Death*; but in neither case have we the chance of seeing how these composers would have treated such long stretches of recitative as D'Avenant required. As regards the scenery we are better informed, and it will be convenient to give an account of that before proceeding to consider the structure of the play itself.

Inigo Jones' successive designs for masques show the gradual process by which he abandoned the old-fashioned system, based on the idea of scattered 'mansions', for the principles which have remained fundamentally in use up to the present day. The general idea of the early masques was to build up the scenery solid. Designed for employment not in theatres but in halls generally used for other purposes, it was obliged to fill up all the available space; the further end of the hall was turned into a sort of mountain range rising almost to the roof, with temples, caves, arbours, etc. erected on different portions of it, smaller no doubt than they would be in nature, but still making little or no use of perspective to deceive the eye as to size or distance. When the Italian fashion of flying-machines and transformation-scenes came in, the old system could not be utilized any longer. Machinery required a certain space in which to place the contrivances that were not intended to be seen, and this was no doubt one of the reasons why the proscenium in the form of a picture-frame was introduced. It limited the area visible to the spectators, and allowed of concealed lights at the sides and above; it also permitted the employment of clouds from which machines could be let down. A careful system of artificial lighting could greatly enhance the illusive effect of perspective-painting, and this combination brought with it a double advantage: the temple, cave and arbour instead of being seen side by side all the evening could be seen separately and successively, and could therefore each be made large enough to occupy the whole stage.

Modern spectacular pieces depend largely on the solid building up of architectural masses, the actual erection and removal of which very seldom take place in view of the audience. Inigo Jones and the Italians from whom he learned his art laid less emphasis on the solidity of their scenes, and paid more attention to their transformation as a part of the spectacle, as well as to the machines which could carry as many as forty people at once suspended in mid air. It is probable that if we could witness an actual performance of a masque or an old Italian opera we should think all the stage machinery ludicrously crude and clumsy; but it must be remembered that scene-painting is as much a convention as any other kind of painting, and that the most realistic modern scenery still depends for its effect on the spectator's ingrained habit of seeing things from a traditional point of view.

Primitive as some of Inigo Jones' designs may seem to

Wagnerian audiences, they were nevertheless far too costly of execution for use on the regular public stage of his time. A few plays were mounted by him for performance in private, but there can be little doubt that old-fashioned actors would not take kindly to the new system.

It was to D'Avenant's interest, at the outset of his new enterprise, to avoid anything that suggested the ordinary theatre of the preceding reigns. It was not called a play or even an opera,[1] but 'A Representation by the art of Prospective in Scenes and the Story sung in Recitative Musick'. We are reminded of the ingenious way in which the 'German Reed Entertainments' of forty years ago secured a certain constant clientèle by means of a nomenclature which carefully evaded any suggestion of comic opera in a theatre. Masques had been tolerated, and D'Avenant was no doubt glad to connect his new venture with them rather than with the playhouse. The curious disposition of the room for the preliminary declamations may also have been derived from the masques, at which the spectators who had no claim to a place on the royal platform sat facing each other on either side of the dancing-place. Whether this arrangement was maintained at *The Siege of Rhodes* it is impossible to say.

The great architect of the masques being dead, D'Avenant naturally had recourse to Webb, who had been his pupil for a long time and had made the working drawings for masques from his sketches since 1635.[2] The difficulties with which he had to contend may be gathered from the apology in D'Avenant's preface:

It has been often wisht that our scenes (we having obliged ourselves to the variety of five changes, according to the ancient drammatick distinctions made for time) had not been confined to eleven foot in height, and about fifteen in depth, including

---

[1] D'Avenant alludes to it elsewhere as an 'opera', but the word was probably not very familiar to English audiences even as late as 1656.

[2] For a complete account of the scenery of *The Siege of Rhodes* with several reproductions see W. G. Keith's articles, 'The Designs for the first moveable scenery on the English public stage', in *The Burlington Magazine*, April and May, 1914.

the places of passage reserv'd for the musick. This is so narrow an allowance for the fleet of *Solyman* the Magnificent, his army, the Island of *Rhodes*, and the varieties attending the siege of the city, that I fear you will think we invite you to such a contracted trifle as that of the *Caesars* carved upon a nut.

With so small a stage, it was impossible to attempt such elaborate changes as Inigo Jones had employed in the court masques, and there was, no doubt, the further question of expense to be considered. Changes of some sort were however considered to be of prime necessity, and it is interesting to see how Webb attacked his problem.

The complete designs for the scenery have recently been identified in the collection of the Duke of Devonshire at Chatsworth, and a plan and section are in the British Museum. The proscenium corresponds exactly with D'Avenant's own description in the play—a pair of rusticated columns supporting a frieze decorated with military trophies and shields. The opening was 18 ft. 4 in. wide and 9 ft. high; D'Avenant's 11 ft. includes the height of the frieze. Three pairs of wings were set at the sides, each successive pair being wider and nearer to the middle of the stage, so that the space between the furthest pair was only 7 ft. These wings represented conventional rocks with vegetation growing on them. Inigo Jones in *Salmacida Spolia* employed several sets of wings, sliding in grooves close behind each other, so that when those of the first set were all pushed out of sight, the second set was revealed: but Webb had not sufficient space for this device, and the rock wings remained fixed throughout the opera. The changes were effected solely by means of the back flats, of which there were four pairs, each 9 ft. wide altogether. The first represented a view of Rhodes, with the harbour and hills behind in bird's-eye view, and the Turkish fleet approaching; it was based on pictures given in geographical books of the period. This view divided vertically into two parts—the audiences of those days apparently were not troubled by the inevitable line of junction—which were slid off to right and left, revealing the second scene set as close as possible behind it. The second scene, 'The town besieged', shows the fortified walls of the town on the left and the tents and artillery, smoke and all, of the enemy on the right. The bay and the ships are just visible in the distance. Scenes iii and iv were of a different character and shall be described later. Scene v—the general assault—represents the town walls stretching almost right across the picture, with the sea in the distance behind them. The foreground is occupied by the Turkish army, which Webb has represented with much spirit, engaged in the attack on the city.

The third and fourth scenes are in what was called 'releive', and as far as can be deduced from the plans, they were made up in two or perhaps three planes. Scene iii represents the pavilion of Solyman. The three pairs of back flats already described were drawn apart; behind was probably the further pair separated, representing part of a colonnade with a space between, and through this was seen, further behind, the pavilion and throne; behind this, either painted on the same scene, or on a back-cloth seen through the side arches, were 'the quarters of the bassas and inferior officers'. Scene iv represents Mount Philermus, with its castle, and the Turkish army manœuvring in the plain below. Here again the scene was probably divided, the corner of city wall shown at one side in the immediate foreground being on a separate frame.

It will be noted first, that the rocky wings remain as a foreground to all these scenes, in spite of their incongruity; and secondly, that the artist in some cases has no scruple about painting on the back scenes a crowd of human beings in violent action. It was of course the only possible way of representing them, since there obviously was no room for them on the stage; the cast of characters includes no more than seven names. Another result of the restricted space is that the stage has no 'apron', as is evident from the section. The masques had always had a subsidiary stage for dancing in front of the proscenium, and in the later English theatres the apron was for a long time a characteristic feature. Mr Lawrence suggests that its adoption was due to the fact that some early theatres were fitted up in disused tennis-courts, and that the audience in a long narrow room were so far away that the stage had to be brought out nearer to them. But it seems much more likely that the apron was derived from the Elizabethan theatre; an apron is of no use, in fact it cannot be said to exist, unless there are spectators at the sides of it. There was evidently no room at Rutland House for a projecting platform of this kind, and to bring the stage still further forward would have sacrificed more space. It was as a matter of fact some 18 ft. deep, though D'Avenant describes it as having a depth of about 15 ft.[1] There being no apron, there were no proscenium doors, for the same reason, that the proscenium opening had to be made as wide as the room would permit. It is interesting to note that whereas the *Siege of Rhodes* as acted at Rutland House contains no allusions to doors, the second part, first acted in 1663 at the Duke of York's Theatre in Lincoln's Inn Fields, has the stage direction (Act I, sc. i) 'Enter Ianthe and her two women at the other door' in a scene representing 'a Prospect of Rhodes beleaguer'd at Sea and Land'. This clearly points to the presence of proscenium doors at this theatre.[2]

Lastly, we must note the disposition of the orchestra. Webb's plan and section give no indication of its position; but D'Avenant's preface, already quoted, alludes to 'the places of passage reserv'd for the musick'. If the band was not very numerous, it might have been possible to squeeze it in behind the scenes, as was done in French theatres. The account of the 'First Days' Entertainment' in the state

---

[1] Mr Keith holds that there was no dancing-place in front when *Salmacida Spolia* was performed; but the stage directions show that it was possible to pass from the stage to the 'state', and the fact that Jones' plan only shows the stage itself does not necessarily imply that there was nothing else.

[2] For the whole question of proscenium doors see W. J. Lawrence, *The Elizabethan Playhouse* etc., First Series. Mr Lawrence quotes a similar direction from Orrery's *Mustapha*, acted at the same theatre in 1665.

papers[1] says, however, 'The Musick was aboue in a loouer hole railed about and couered with sarcenetts to conceale them'.

If this means that the band was placed in a room or gallery above the stage it is in accordance with Elizabethan custom, and with that modification of it which was for some time carried on in the theatres of the Restoration.[2] The word *louver* (spelt in various ways) signifies a lantern such as was placed on the roof of a hall in mediaeval times for purposes of ventilation. It is also found in the combination *louver-hole* in writers of this period, and is sometimes used in the sense of a chimney. Obviously neither of these places can have been put to a use for which both were so very inadequately fitted. But as the word was also used for a dovecote, there is little difficulty in supposing that D'Avenant had a sort of turret constructed for the musicians above the stage, and if this was the case the draperies would be convenient to conceal the rough nature of the woodwork.

[1] Quoted in full by P. Reyher, *Les Masques Anglais*.
[2] Lawrence, *op. cit.*, First Series, pp. 90–92 and 160 ff.

Chapter Four

'*The* SIEGE *of* RHODES' (*continued*)

The subject of D'Avenant's opera is the siege of the city of Rhodes by the Turks under Solyman the Magnificent in 1522, when the Grand Master Philippe Villiers de l'Isle-Adam and the six hundred knights of the order of St John with a few soldiers held out for nearly six months against an enemy numbering nearly a quarter of a million.[1] It has been shown that D'Avenant derived his plot from Knolles' *Historie of the Turkes* published in London in 1603, and that various details are taken from this work. In the main, however, the siege is merely a background for a series of purely imaginary incidents.[2]

The play is divided into five acts, called 'entries' in order to avoid any word which suggested the theatre. It begins with the Admiral announcing to Villerius, as the Grand Master is called, that the Turkish fleet is approaching. Alphonso, a Sicilian duke, has been visiting Rhodes as the guest of the knights. Villerius advises him to return at once to his wife in Sicily, but he refuses, preferring to share in the fighting. All the characters leave the stage, and Ianthe, wife of Alphonso, enters with her two women. No change of scene is indicated, but it is clear from Ianthe's speech that the scene is supposed to be Sicily, as she announces her intention of taking ship for Rhodes. A chorus 'by soldiers of several nations' concludes the 'entry'.

The second entry shows the city beleaguered, the action taking place apparently three months later. Alphonso sings a song; Villerius and the Admiral inform us that food is scarce and no help expected from outside. They leave the stage, and without any change of scene Solyman and Pirrhus

[1] Baron de Belabre, *Rhodes of the Knights*, Oxford, 1908.
[2] James W. Tupper, *Love and Honour and The Siege of Rhodes*, Boston, 1909.

his 'Vizier Bassa' enter. Solyman orders an assault. Mustapha, another Bassa, introduces Ianthe, veiled, who has been captured by the Turks on the voyage from Sicily. Ianthe refuses to unveil, and the Sultan directs that she and her ships are to be conducted safely to Rhodes. A chorus of women concludes the entry.

The third entry shows Solyman's pavilion and throne. The Sultan orders the erection of a castle on Mount Philermus: the siege is to be continued, but no assault is to be made until Ianthe and Alphonso are safe on the way to Sicily. The scene then changes back to the town besieged. Villerius and the Admiral compliment Ianthe on her courage; Alphonso, after the others have retired, reproves her for her foolhardiness. She tells how she was brought before Solyman, and stayed two days with Mustapha. Alphonso immediately becomes jealous and suspects her of infidelity. The entry as usual concludes with a chorus, in this case of men and women.

The fourth entry shows Mount Philermus, with the castle in process of erection. Mustapha tells Solyman that Alphonso and Ianthe refuse to leave Rhodes: Solyman orders that their lives are to be spared in the assault. The scene changes back to the town besieged. Alphonso and Ianthe have a long argument, she wishing to take advantage of the Sultan's generosity and save her husband's life. They leave the stage separately with mutual indignation. Villerius and the Admiral, finding that the state of Alphonso's feelings causes him to be of less value as a soldier, decide to make a last sally. This is followed by a chorus of the Sultan's wives.

The fifth and last entry shows us the general assault, 'the greatest fury of the army being discern'd at the English station', although none of the English have any principal part in the play. The scene begins with Pirrhus, Mustapha and Solyman indicating the assault by speeches of an excited nature; Mustapha says that at the English station he has seen a warrior

Fairer than woman and than man more fierce,

whom Solyman has also seen and identified as Ianthe. The Turks leave the stage, and the others enter, though there is no change of scene. Alphonso hears that Ianthe is wounded and Villerius in sore straits; after some hesitation as to which he will rescue he decides for his wife, whom he still suspects. Pirrhus and Mustapha return to the stage and explain that the Turks are now being suddenly beaten. The scene changes for a moment to Mount Philermus, to allow the Sultan to observe the state of operations in a monologue of sixteen lines; then it returns to the 'town besieged'. Ianthe 'in a night-gown' is brought in by Villerius and the Admiral, wounded, but not dangerously so. Alphonso, who had been led to believe that she was certain to die, now enters wounded. Ianthe forgives him, but he does not receive her forgiveness with any great cordiality, and the scene concludes with the lines

> Draw all the curtains, and then lead her in;
> Let me in darkness mourn away my sin.

A chorus of soldiers brings the opera to an end.

This summary of the plot gives little idea of the curious style of the poem. Its sudden changes of scene, its short episodes in which nothing happens, and its irregularity of metre are all explained by the author himself in his preface.

As these limits have hinder'd the splendour of our scene, so we are like to give no great satisfaction in the quality of our argument, which is a story very copious; but shrinks to a small narration here, because we could not convey it by more than seven persons; being constrain'd to prevent the length of *recitative* musick,[1] as well as to conserve, without incumbrance, the narrowness of the place. Therefore you cannot expect the chief ornaments belonging to a history drammatically digested into turns and counterturns, to double walls, and interweavings of design....

The story represented (which will not require much apology because it expects but little praise) is heroical, and notwithstanding the continual hurry and busie agitations of a hot siege, is (I hope) intelligibly convey'd to advance the characters of vertue in the shapes of valour and conjugal love. And though the main argument hath but a single walk, yet perhaps the

---

[1] *I.e.* to make allowances for the slower rate of delivery.

movings of it will not seem unpleasant. You may inquire, being a reader, why in an heroick argument my numbers are so often diversify'd and fall into short fractions; considering that a continuation of the usual length of *English* verse would appear more heroical in reading. But when you are an auditor you will finde that in this, I rather deserve approbation than need excuse; for frequent alterations of measure (which cannot be so unpleasant to him that reads as troublesome to him that writes) are necessary to *recitative* musick for variation of *ayres*.

But the most curious thing about *The Siege of Rhodes* is that although it was the first English attempt at an opera it does not bear the least resemblance to the librettos of any operas given in Italy at the time; nor has it any resemblance to the ballets produced in Paris. Italian opera, particularly Venetian opera, had indeed for some time abandoned the purely mythological libretto treated in a classical or would-be classical manner; but the poets still chose their themes from antiquity and gave their characters classical names, even if they made them behave like seventeenth-century Italians. A modern subject, such as *The Siege of Rhodes*, with an almost continuous presentation of the siege itself as a background, is utterly unthinkable in Italian opera of that period. Nor is D'Avenant's libretto at all Italian in the way it is laid out, in the ordering of the songs and choruses.

The plain fact was that D'Avenant was not really attempting to start English opera as a primary object of his efforts. His first desire was to get the theatres re-opened and plays (naturally, his own) performed. It is fairly clear, if we compare the different versions of *The Siege of Rhodes*, that it was originally written not as an opera but as a play. The scenes for the Sultan's wife Roxolana and other persons, which are found in the later versions, were cut out of the first, partly to save time, and mainly for want of people to act the parts. But the chorus of the Sultan's wives at the end of the fourth entry—

1 *woman*. This cursed jealousie, what is't?
2 *woman*. 'Tis love that has lost it self in a mist, etc.—

sung in the version of 1656 has no reason for its existence unless preceded by the scene in which Roxolana explains to the women her jealousy of Ianthe, a scene not restored to the opera until 1661.[1] Although no positive proof can be adduced, it seems highly probable that D'Avenant originally wrote the work as a drama in rhymed heroic couplets, and that it was only when he found it impossible to produce it as a play, that he decided to turn it into an opera by cutting it down, altering the lengths of the lines here and there, inserting songs and choruses, and finally getting the whole set to music.

Thus in Entry 1, ll. 1–28 are irregular, probably added on when the play was altered; ll. 29–86 are heroic couplets. Eight lines given in the edition of 1663 to the High Marshal of Rhodes are here incorporated in the part of Villerius, as the Marshal does not appear in the first version at all. The second scene (ll. 87–136) is also in heroic couplets, with five pairs of shorter lines introduced here and there. The pairs of shorter lines are invariably introduced between two rhyming lines. In two cases the two lines of the heroic couplet make perfectly good sense without the shorter ones:

Ianthe. Go seek out cradles, and with childhood dwell;
    Where you may still be free
    From Love's self-flattery,
  And never hear mistaken lovers tell
  Of blessings, and of joys in such extreams
  As never are possest but in our dreams.
  They woo apace, and hasten to be sped;
  And praise the quiet of the marriage-bed;
  But mention not the storms of grief and care
    When Love does them surprize
    With sudden jealousies,
  Or they are severed by ambitious war.

The speech reads much more naturally without the four short lines. They seem to have been inserted merely to break the monotony of the heroic couplets, a monotony only notice-

---

[1] First printed in 1663.

able if they were set to music. In the other cases a little ingenuity might restore something like the conjectured original reading.

> *Ianthe.* To Rhodes this fatal fleet her course does bear.
> Can I have love, and not discover fear?
> When he, in whom my plighted heart doth live
> (Whom Hymen gave me in reward
> Of vows, which he with favour heard,
> And is the greatest gift he e're can give)
> Shall in a cruel siege imprison'd be,
> And I, whom love has bound, have liberty?

I venture to suggest

> When he, in whom my plighted heart doth live
> (The greatest gift which Hymen e'er could give)

or possibly

> Whom Hymen in reward of vows did give.

In the next case

> *Madina.* Beauty laments! and this exchange abhors!
> Shall all these gems in arms be spent
> Which were by bounteous princes sent
> To pay the valour of your ancestors?

restoration is more easy:

> Shall all these (epithet) gems in arms be spent?
> Gems which were once by bounteous princes sent
> To pay the valour of your ancestors?
> Beauty laments! and this exchange abhors!

The last group of irregular lines

> *Madina.* Love may perhaps the foolish please:
> But he shall quickly leave my heart
> When he perswades me to depart
> From such a hoord of precious things as these,

was probably inserted whole when D'Avenant made his play into an opera, as Ianthe's concluding lines take no notice of what her woman has said, and her speech would be much more effective without this lyric interruption. The chorus of soldiers is simply a song having no connection with the dramatic action at all. Entry II begins with 26 lines of heroic couplets: then Alphonso enters with a song of six 4-line stanzas, followed by ten irregular lines for Villerius, Admiral and Chorus. The next scene (Solyman and Pirrhus) begins in heroic couplets (ll. 61–94); ll. 95–106 are a song for Solyman: after three short lines which are superfluous to the sense, couplets go on to l. 145, and the remainder of the scene (146–198) is irregular. The chorus of women, as in Entry I, is merely a sort of 'act-tune', a piece of music to end the act, as the curtain did not fall. In Entry III, ll. 13–20, 55–66 are heroic couplets; so are in the second scene, ll. 77–90, 159–174, 185–188; in Entry IV, ll. 1–40, except for three alternate-rhyming quatrains and two short lines, also ll. 57–95, except for a few short lines. Lines 96–169 are irregular, but include 24 lines of heroic couplets. In Entry V the lines are almost entirely irregular: heroic couplets only appear here and there for six or eight lines at a time. In the second part of the opera, first performed in 1661, the distribution of metres is much more even, and we meet with no long stretches of heroic couplets; D'Avenant was evidently then more at his ease in writing for music.

Further proof of D'Avenant's underlying ideas may be derived from the preface to his heroic poem *Gondibert*. This poem was begun during his residence in Paris, and though never finished, was sent to press at the time when the author was imprisoned in Cowes Castle and was expecting to be executed very shortly. The preface, dated from Paris, is a long essay on heroic poetry, in which D'Avenant criticizes in turn Homer, Virgil, Lucan, Statius, Tasso and Spenser; it is curious to see that he refuses to consider Ariosto as a heroic poet of the first rank lest he should be therefore obliged to admit Dante and Marino. Lucan, he thinks, chose a subject too near his own time, and was therefore compelled to be a historian rather than a poet, to tell the truth plainly instead of improving on it; Statius and Tasso are both to be censured for their frequent incursions into supernatural regions. 'A Christian Poet', he says, 'whose Religion little need the aids of Invention, hath less occasion to imitate such fables, as merely illustrate a probable Heaven, by the fashion and dignity of Courts; and make a resemblance of Hell, out of the Dreams of frighted Women; by which they continue and increase the melancholy mistakes of the People'. Spenser, the last of the heroic poets, he blames for the archaism of his language, and the unnatural character of his allegory.

In planning his own heroic poem it is interesting to see that he takes as his model not the epics of the past, but the typical English drama, dividing it into five books as the equivalent of five acts, and each book into cantos to correspond with scenes. Bearing in mind then D'Avenant's extraordinary veneration for the very idea of heroic poetry, his firm belief in it as a title to fame for himself and as an unlimited moral influence on his countrymen (all of which is very apparent from the preface to *Gondibert*), and remembering the close connection which he makes between heroic poetry and the drama, it is easy to see how at this particular moment, when the opportunity offered for re-establishing the drama in the disguise of opera to audiences still to a large extent preoccupied with moral considerations, he should have preferred the plain human subject of the siege of Rhodes to the mythological machinery of the French and Italian stage, the more so as he was not in a position to run heavy financial risks in the carrying out of his ideals.

D'Avenant's attitude towards music, and more particularly to the new style of music, is difficult to determine. We find a curious allusion to it in *The Wits*, a comedy of his, acted in 1634, in which a street musician joins with Snore the constable and others to sing 'the Constable's Catch'—a spirited description of London traffic, each verse of which ends with the refrain, 'stay till the constable wakes'. The stage direction is,[1] 'The second catch is sung, and acted by them in Recitative Burlesque'. The preface to *Gondibert* has a further

---

[1] The first catch had been sung earlier in the same scene.

allusion to it in a paragraph explaining why the poem is written not in heroic couplets but in quatrains with alternating rhymes. 'Nor doth alternate Rime by any lowliness of Cadence make the sound less Heroick, but rather adapt it to a plain and stately composing of Musick; and the brevity of the *Stanza* renders it less subtle to the Composer, and more easie to the singer, which in *stilo recitativo*, when the story is long, is chiefly requisite.' He goes on to explain that he hoped the poem might be sung to the people at village feasts. As *Gondibert* was to consist of five books, each in some five or six cantos, and each canto of some eighty quatrains, we may well credit D'Avenant with a serious appreciation of the style of Lawes, though we may be thankful that we are not obliged to listen to a setting of it by him.

Still more interesting is the criticism of opera in D'Avenant's curious entertainment *The Playhouse to be Let*, acted in 1662. After *The Siege of Rhodes* we have no further information of D'Avenant's doings until late in 1658, when he produced another 'opera', *The Cruelty of the Spaniards in Peru*, at the Cockpit in Drury Lane. This was followed by *The History of Sir Francis Drake*, a third opera, in 1659. *The Siege of Rhodes* was revived in the same year, and it is possible that the Second Part of *The Siege of Rhodes* was also produced at this time.[1] With the establishment of D'Avenant and his company at the Duke's Theatre after the Restoration, the two parts of *The Siege of Rhodes*, somewhat expanded, were revived again (1661), and in 1663 the other two operas, *The Cruelty of the Spaniards in Peru* and *The History of Sir Francis Drake*, re-appeared as parts of *The Playhouse to be Let*, a medley in which several short plays are acted by various prospective tenants with the caretaker of the empty theatre and his friends as audience. The first candidate is a Frenchman, who produces a French play in broken English; the next arrival is a Musician, who brings all his instruments with him as he

---

[1] For full details of the evidence see W. J. Lawrence, 'The Origin of the English Picture-Stage', in *The Elizabethan Playhouse*, Second Series.

considers himself certain to be able to make the largest
profits of anybody. The dialogue between him and the
Player, who has been chatting with the 'Housekeeper' and
the Tirewoman, is sufficiently interesting to be quoted here
in full:

Player: Why came you with such confidence to take
             The House, as made you bring your Furniture
             Before we treated for the Rent?
Musician: Because I thought you had been more in love
             With your profit, than with your wit.
Player: I, that's the point? whence should our profit rise?
Musician: I meant to entertain the People with
             A Novelty; which I suppose is no
             Ill bait for those small fishes, which I thought
             Mine own, and purpos'd you a share i' th' Net.
Player: But what's the composition of your Bait?
Musician: I wou'd have introduc'd Heroique story
             In *Stilo Recitativo*.
Player: In *Stilo Recitativo*? 'tis well;
             I understand you, Sir. But do you think
             That natural?
Musician: Because 'tis not in custom
             You therefore think, Sir, it is out of Nature?
Player: It seems so, Sir, to me, unless you would
             Metamorphise men into Birds. Suppose
             I should not ask, but sing, you now a question,
             And you should instantly sing me an answer;
             Would you not think it strange?
Musician: Well, Sir, as how?   (*Plays and Sings*)
Player: Take out your Watch, and tell me, Sir, the hour?
             Then you reply
             My Watch, Sir, is at Pawn, but 'tis past Four.
Musician: Your heart is good, Sir, but y'are an ill Mimick
             In Musick, and your voice does breed some doubt
             Of your Virginity.
Player: You'd make me blush
             If there were strangers here; but if you please
             Cease your rebukes and proceed to instruction.
Musician: Recitative Musick is not compos'd
             Of matter so familiar, as may serve
             For every low occasion of discourse.

71

> In Tragedy, the language of the Stage
> Is rais'd above the common dialect;
> Our passions rising with the height of Verse;
> And Vocal Musick adds new wings to all
> The flights of Poetry.

If the Musician's last words represent D'Avenant's own genuine opinion, it shows him to have understood the essential principles of opera. Whether his audiences understood them or not is another matter: but they were apparently quite ready to come to his operas, although their appreciation was not very intelligent. In the same play, just before *Sir Francis Drake* is acted, there is the following characteristic dialogue:

> *Housekeeper:* Now we shall be in *Stilo Recitativo.*
> I'm in a Trance, when I hear Vocal Musick;
> And in that Trance, inclin'd to prophecie
> That 'twill bring us inundations of shillings.
> *Player:* Thou understand'st Recitative Musick
> As much as a *Dray-horse* does Greek.

We must now return to *The Siege of Rhodes* and consider it from the point of view of an opera libretto.

It is difficult to make a comparison with Italian operas as regards the actual laying out of recitative and aria. The general Italian principle of the later seventeenth century is that each 'scene' (in the French and Italian sense of the word) should end with an aria, that is, that the aria should be the climax of the conversation, and that the singer of the aria should invariably leave the stage directly after it. But even in 1656 Italian opera had not become so firmly standardized, and the principle is not strictly observed. It must be remembered also that the English attitude to recitative and the setting of words was not quite the same as the Italian. The extract already quoted from William Lawes' music to *The Triumph of Peace* shows that composers in England were inclined at this moment to treat the squarest rhythmical stanza as if it were entirely unrhythmical. There are several passages in *The Siege of Rhodes* which I have called songs in the preceding summary, because an Italian composer would have set them in the aria style; but it is quite possible that the English composers preferred to have them declaimed. But I think there can be no doubt about Alphonso's song in Entry II:

> How bravely fought the fiery French,
> Their bulwark being storm'd.
> The colder Almans kept their trench,
> By more than valour warm'd.

This song, which has six stanzas, can hardly have been sung to anything but a ballad tune. Its place in the opera is most curious; Alphonso simply walks on and sings it without any sort of introduction. Villerius and the Admiral follow it up with six lines of prosaic comment, and the chorus sings what is clearly intended as a final stanza to Alphonso's tune. This 'chorus', by the way, is a somewhat mysterious factor in the opera. There are no indications of its entrance and exit in the various entries, and it may possibly be that the lines marked 'chorus' were sung by the principals, as in the final '*coro*' of the later Italian operas. It seems like a survival of the masque chorus, which did not as a rule take part in the action, but was rather an adjunct to the orchestra. Quite separate from these short choruses are the choruses at the end of each entry. Here again the masque is suggested, and probably by D'Avenant's deliberate intention, the 'entry' being the entry of the chorus (who may well have been dancers too) which is led up to by the dialogue of the principal characters. From a literary point of view these choruses are perhaps the best part of the opera, for they have none of the affectations of the heroic manner and are written in a swinging popular style that is characteristically English.

Awkward and irregular as it is, *The Siege of Rhodes* has some considerable merit as a libretto. Its characters are mere puppets, but that is a fault common to many operas of all periods, and a fault less objectionable in an opera than in a play, since the musician, if he be a Mozart or a Verdi, can inspire them with a reality which makes us feel that it is we in the audience who are lifeless and conventional. The atmosphere of the siege is very cleverly suggested and kept up throughout, in spite of the fact that it was impossible to attempt any realistic effects on so small a stage. Another very important merit is that the poem, all due allowance being made for the literary style of the day, maintains a consistent emotional level, and is very careful not to descend to those commonplace matters which always make a musical setting hopelessly ridiculous.

D'Avenant's next venture, *The Cruelty of the Spaniards in Peru*, was a reversion to the 'lecture-recital' type of entertainment. A series of six scenes were shown, each preceded by appropriate instrumental music. Each was explained by a speech in verse from the Chief Priest of Peru, and was followed by a song; there is no indication of whether this was sung by the priest, by other singers or a chorus. In all the entries except the first the song is followed by a dumb show and dance, accompanied by suitable music. The audience were thus presented with the history of Peru from the epoch of primitive happiness, through the reigns of the Incas, to the invasion of the Spaniards and their expulsion by the Peruvians in alliance with the English. This last scene, the author admits, had no historical authority, but 'may pass as a Vision discern'd by the Priest of the Sun'. All the scenes had a considerable number of figures painted on them. The scenery was in fact evidently intended not to serve a dramatic purpose, much less to be decorative; such a conception of scenery was foreign to all English ideas. It was intended as a series of pictures to give information as complete and detailed as circumstances permitted, and as an illustration of actualities such as later generations would have represented by a panorama, a lantern-lecture, or a cinematograph performance. It suggests more than anything the old-fashioned lecture on foreign missions, at which the speaker appeared in 'native' costume, other dresses being disposed on the persons of obliging friends, and the whole liberally interspersed with hymns and other music of edifying character.

The other 'opera', *The History of Sir Francis Drake*, is more in the manner of *The Siege of Rhodes*. Like the other two plays, it is divided not into 'acts' but 'entries' introduced, as before, by instrumental music. In the first entry Drake lands, in the second he is received by the King of the Symerons 'who were a Moorish people, brought formerly to Peru by the Spaniards as their slaves to dig in Mines'; in the third the Peruvians join the alliance, in the fourth Drake is taken to Panama to climb a tree from which the ocean can be seen. In the fourth act Captain Rouse shows Drake a beautiful bride who has been captured by the Symerons and tied to a tree; this is represented by a painted scene, which vanishes as Pedro, a runaway Spaniard in league with the Symerons, announces that she has been set free. The entry ends with the appearance of her father and her bridegroom, who dance with 'castanietos' to express the feelings appropriate to the occasion. In the sixth and last entry a battle takes place 'off' in which the Spaniards are defeated, and their mules, laden with ingots of gold, captured. Drake decides to return to England, and the opera ends with a dance of the 'land-soldiers', two seamen, two Symerons and one Peruvian, 'intimating by their several interchange of salutations, their mutual desires of amity'.

Although the libretto bears some resemblance in style to that of *The Siege of Rhodes*, and seems more obviously written for music, it is dramatically inferior to it. There had been some protests made against the opera in 1658, and when Richard Cromwell appointed a commission to inquire into the matter, D'Avenant no doubt thought it prudent to make quite sure that nobody could accuse him of presenting plays. There having been apparently no objection to *The Cruelty of the Spaniards*, he ventured a little further in a dramatic direction with *Sir Francis Drake*, but preserved the illustrative character of the scenery, the division into 'entries' and the descriptive music between the acts. Most important is it to note that *Sir Francis Drake* has no female characters. The captured bride is a mere piece of painting, and although her father and bridegroom enter and dance on the stage, she herself does not make her appearance at all. As in *The Cruelty of the Spaniards* the interest of the piece is historical and geographical rather than dramatic. But it is effectively put together, and one can well imagine that these tableaux from the life of a national hero plentifully interspersed with spirited sea-songs would obtain considerable popularity and be a source of financial profit to both author and composer.[1]

Of the ultimate success of *The Siege of Rhodes* there can be no doubt. It was revived again by D'Avenant after the Restoration had re-opened the theatres, and provided with a sequel. Another female character, Roxolana, was added to the first part, and is very prominent in the second. The importance of the female element in the theatre, as soon as restrictions on its appearance were removed, is shown by the fact that the prologue to the second part is spoken by a woman. This is clear from these lines:

> Hope little from our poet's wither'd witt,
> From infant-players, scarce grown Puppets yet.
> Hope from our women less, whose bashfull fear,
> Wondred to see me dare to enter here:
> Each took her leave, and wisht my danger past;
> And though I come back safe, and undisgrac'd,
> Yet when they spie the WITS here, then I doubt
> No Amazon can make 'em venture out.

The parts of the women are much more important in the Second Part than in the First, and this becomes the more noticeable since the Second Part is almost twice as long as its predecessor. It is much more of a play and less of an

---

[1] It is not known definitely who were the composers of *The Cruelty of the Spaniards* or *Sir Francis Drake*, but there is a 'Symeron's dance' by Locke in *Musick's Handmaid*, 1678 (reprinted in Stafford Smith's *Musica Antiqua*), which no doubt comes from the latter play.

opera in its style, though the changes of metres are managed more fluently, and the actual diction is often very awkward. Nothing is known of the music to it, and the loss of all the music to D'Avenant's operas is the more deplorable since this was the only period at which serious opera in English, set to music all through and almost all in recitative—a form of music which, as we shall see later on, has been considered to be utterly impracticable in the English language—has ever enjoyed a real and supreme popularity with English audiences.[1]

[1] This is vouched for by Pepys: '4th. (July, 1661). I went to the Theatre and there I saw "Claracilla" well acted. But strange to see this house that used to be so thronged, now empty since the Opera began; and so will continue for a while, I believe.' There is however reason to suppose that after the Restoration much of the recitative in *The Siege of Rhodes* was suppressed, and the dialogue spoken (see Dryden's *Essay of Heroick Plays* prefixed to *The Conquest of Granada*).

Chapter Five

The AMATEURS

The productions of D'Avenant, although they are undoubtedly the first regular operas performed in England, are of significance mainly as the foundation of new and important developments with regard to the drama and to the stage on which the drama was acted. We must now take into consideration certain earlier and contemporary experiments which will tell us more about the musical side of the operatic movement in England.

English music has at all times been peculiarly indebted to the energy of amateurs. It is comparatively seldom that they have been patrons of the art after the manner of the petty princes of the Continent; our sovereigns indeed, in spite of maintaining a certain musical establishment as a matter of course, have done little for the furtherance of distinct and important artistic movements. The few exceptions, such as Henry VI, Henry VIII, Mary and Elizabeth, have been remembered less as patrons than as themselves practical musicians of rare accomplishment. We have never produced amateur composers of world-wide reputation like the Prince of Venosa, Astorga or Benedetto Marcello, but such men as Campion, Pepys, and Aldrich in the seventeenth century, Morell, Gray and Mason in the eighteenth, Oliphant, Pearsall and Pierson in the nineteenth have performed a very valuable service to their country not so much by attaining eminence themselves, as by radiating an influence which raises the general standard of musicianship among those with whom they come in contact.

The average amateur standard at the beginning of the seventeenth century was, as is well known, a very high one, perhaps the highest that this country has ever been able to reach, and though it inevitably declined, yet its rate of sinking was not so rapid as some writers, led astray by changes of musical technique, would have us believe. During the early part of the century the universities, as was natural, were active centres of musical influence, and in the dramatic performances at Oxford and Cambridge, which were often witnessed by the Court, music was frequently a feature of importance. Thus Peter Hausted's comedy *The Rival Friends*, acted before the King and Queen at Cambridge on March 19, 1631, was preceded by an allegorical prologue, all set to music with the exception of two speeches; and there were musical *intermezzi* between the acts, somewhat after the Italian manner, though the resources of Cambridge were not equal to the scenic extravagances of an Italian court. The music is preserved in a MS. attributed to George Jeffreys,[1] an Oxford musician of whom little is known, but it is very possible that he was not the composer but only the copyist of this particular work. Whoever the composer was, his style bears a strong resemblance to that of the brothers Lawes. Like the masque music quoted in an earlier chapter, this prologue shows a definite sense of tonality which is clearly intended to be continuous in spite of the breaks made by the spoken parts. The invitation of Venus to Phoebus to leave the arms of Thetis and the latter's reluctance to let him go, leading up to a salutation of the royal spectators, do not offer any very striking dramatic possibilities, but the composer has done his best to give the dialogue a certain life-like animation. Another example of a play with a large amount of incidental music is *The Royal Slave*, by William Cartwright, acted before the King and Queen at Oxford on August 30, 1636. The composer on this occasion was Henry Lawes.

The court masques, as we have seen, centred on the performance of amateurs as dancers, though the musicians seem generally to have been professionals; and it is therefore not

[1] British Museum, Add. 10338, f. 43.

surprising to find masques written entirely for amateurs after
political disturbances had put an end to the entertainments
at Whitehall. Shirley's masque *The Triumph of Beauty*, printed
in 1646, but probably acted in 1640,[1] was 'personated by
some young gentlemen, for whom it was intended, at a private
recreation'. In this, as in *Comus*, the strict form of the masque
is not maintained: there is an antimasque of rustics, very
closely imitated from the clowns of *A Midsummer Night's Dream*,
but instead of the set dance of masquers, with a little music
to lead up to it, the poet introduces a representation of the
judgment of Paris, which is treated at considerable length.
After the rustics have danced, a song is sung and Mercury
appears: he delivers the apple of discord to Paris and ascends.
The three goddesses are heard singing within, first singly,
then in chorus, after which they enter, dance, and deliver
a series of very lengthy speeches. Paris having given judgment, Cupid appears, with Hymen and Delight, the Graces
and the Hours, *i.e.* Eunomia, Diche and Irene, as introduced
in *The Triumph of Peace*. After some songs and dances, the
masque suddenly ends with a curious little piece of dialogue:

Venus: We want some of our nymphs, Eunomia,
Fair Diche and Irene; are they gone?
1 *Grace:* Although we did entreat them stay,
The pleasant Hours are stol'n away.
Venus: Which way?
2 *Grace:* That way,
To the elysian bowers.
Paris: We'll fly, and overtake the happy hours. (*Exeunt.*

This looks as if there was no curtain to fall, when we remember the methods of Corneille in *Andromède*; and the stage
directions show us that the scenery was of the simplest description. The scene is 'a grove' and remains unchanged throughout the play; the only 'machine' is the descent and ascent
of Mercury. Evidently the organizers of the masque had not
much money to spend on it. Our only guide to the planning

[1] J. Schipper, *James Shirley, sein Leben und seine Werke*, Vienna, 1911.

of the music (it is not known who composed it) is the typo-
graphy; but although we can be sure that everything printed
in italics was sung, we cannot be absolutely certain that
everything printed in roman was spoken, especially at this
period when 'recitative musick' was taking a very strong
hold on English audiences. It is possible that the concluding
words were set to music; in any case they form a kind of
epilogue, and it would be interesting if we could see whether
the composer had succeeded in making this part of a carefully organized scheme. There is, however, one strong argument against a musical setting, and that is that since the
three goddesses sing their songs behind the scenes before
their entry, they were probably represented by people who
could not sing.

Another play for 'young gentlemen of quality' was Shirley's
Contention of Ajax and Ulysses, remembered now only by the
famous song, 'The glories of our blood and state'. This was
the only piece of music in the little drama to which it forms
the conclusion, being sung as the body of Ajax was carried
in procession by the Greek princes. It is not known when it
was performed, but the words of the song show that it was
probably not written before 1649. As Shirley became a
schoolmaster during the Commonwealth, his occupation as
a dramatist being gone, it is very probable that these plays
were written for schools. Pepys (April 26, 1663) tells us how
his wife's maid Mary Ashwell entertained him by repeating
fragments of the masques in which she had acted at her
school in Chelsea; and in France the Jesuits regarded acting
as a very valuable educational influence.

Shirley's most important production during the Commonwealth was the masque of *Cupid and Death*. This masque was
also a private entertainment, organized by one Luke Channell
in honour of the Portuguese ambassador and acted on
March 26, 1653. As the preface ends with a compliment to
'the gentleman that performed the dances', I venture to
suggest that 'Mr. Luke Channen' was identical with Pepys'

'Luke Channell master of the school, where I saw good dancing', at a house in Broad Street,[1] and that the work was performed largely if not entirely by amateurs. There is no reason to suppose that it was beyond amateur abilities, when we remember that it was the pupils of a seminary for young ladies conducted by a dancing-master who first produced Purcell's *Dido and Aeneas*.

The declamatory style of Lawes and his school was in fact peculiarly suited to amateur performers. The original inventors of it in Italy were themselves largely amateurs; it was a literary rather than a musical movement that produced it. As Sir Hubert Parry has said,

the songs (of Lawes etc.) appear to be written for amateurs who have a cultivated appreciation of poetry, and no idea whatever of the beauty of well-produced vocal tone....The sole object of composers seems to have been to supply a kind of music which would enable people with no voice worth considering to recite poems in a melodious recitative, spaced out into periods in conformity with the length of the lines or the literary phrases.[2]

And it must be remembered that Lawes himself, like his contemporaries, was not sufficiently well-equipped in point of technique to solve his own problems with complete accuracy.[3]

Shirley's *Cupid and Death*, though described as a masque, is much more in the nature of an opera. Its literary form, as one might expect, has more affinity with the masques of

---

[1] Sept. 24, 1660. Mr Channell is mentioned by Downes in his *Roscius Anglicanus* as assisting 'Mr. Joseph Priest' in arranging the dances for D'Avenant's alteration of *Macbeth* in 1672 or 1673. The music to this production was by Locke. Mr H. B. Wheatley in his notes to Pepys' *Diary* suggests that Luke Channell was identical with one Luke Cheynell, mentioned as a hop-merchant. That a 'hop-merchant' was a facetious expression for a dancing-master we learn from Durfey's comedy *Love for Money, or the Boarding School* (1691), Act. III, sc. i, where Mr Coopee the dancing-master introduces the hero in disguise as 'a brother hop-merchant of mine that I brought here to teach a little, having a lame leg'.

[2] *Oxford History of Music*, III. 209.

[3] Cf. Dr Ernest Walker's criticism in *A History of Music in England*, Oxford, 1907. For a more detailed discussion of the relations of rhythm to declamation see Edward J. Dent, 'Italian Chamber Cantatas' in *The Musical Antiquary*, II. 142.

Ben Jonson than with those of D'Avenant, but the dramatic element is so much more developed that the allegorical element becomes almost naturalistic in its treatment. The subject is derived from a fable of Aesop, familiar to English readers of that date in the versified paraphrases of John Ogilby. Cupid and Death, overtaken by stress of weather, happen to spend the night at the same inn, and each, on his departure, carries the other's arrows away by mistake, with the result that Cupid causes young lovers to die, and Death awakens passion in the old and decrepit.

Shirley opens his play with a scene representing the exterior of the inn, situated in a forest. The Host, 'a jolly sprightly old man', comes out of the house and discusses with the Chamberlain the arrangements to be made for the 'immortal guests' whom they are expecting. Cupid enters, attended by Folly and Madness; the Host joins them in a dance (first antimasque), followed by a song, 'Though little be the god of love'. They all leave the stage; Death enters and dances the second entry, after which he calls for the Chamberlain, who shows him into the inn. A voice is heard calling on Death, and Despair enters. He agrees to make a will in favour of the Chamberlain if he will bring Death to him; the Chamberlain is delighted to arrange matters, and brings Despair a bottle of wine, for which he refuses to accept payment. Despair however changes his mind after drinking, and goes away refusing either to sign the will or to give the Chamberlain any payment for the wine beyond the halter which he has brought with him. At this point occurs the well-known song,

> Victorious men of earth, no more
> Proclaim how wide your empires are.

During this song we must suppose the night to have passed; the Host and Chamberlain re-enter, and the latter relates how Cupid went drunk to bed, followed by Death, who left the inn at dawn. The Chamberlain, to revenge himself on Death's friend Despair, has given Death Cupid's arrows to take away. While they are talking Cupid gets up, and musicians come to serenade him. Here follows the third song, 'Stay, Cupid, whither art thou flying?'

The scene changes to a garden, with ladies lamenting over their lovers slain by Cupid who is hovering in the air. A lover and his mistress dance. Nature enters and warns them against Cupid, but it is too late, and the lover is killed. Death enters, followed by two aged couples; he shoots, and they 'dance with antick postures, expressing rural courtship' (second antimasque). During this scene Nature comments in soliloquy.

After another song and chorus, six gentlemen enter armed, as if to fight three against three; Death strikes them, they embrace and dance. This may be regarded as a first appearance of the 'grand masquers'. Here the fifth song is sung. The Chamberlain enters, leading two apes. He has given up his post at the inn and intends to show his apes at fairs. Death strikes him; he falls violently in love with the apes, but his caresses are interrupted by a Satyr, who takes the apes from him and dances with them (third antimasque). Mercury then descends. He drives them all away, and discovers Nature sleeping in a bower. He then summons Cupid, unbinds his eyes, and shows him the corpses of the lovers; after which he calls in Death and makes the two exchange arrows again. The scene then changes to Elysium where the slain lovers appear as the 'grand masquers'. A sixth song is sung, the 'grand dance' is danced, and Mercury takes leave of the audience in a short epilogue.

The music to this masque was by Matthew Locke and Christopher Gibbons. Locke,[1] who was born about 1630, was at the very beginning of his career. He had spent some time on the Continent in 1648, and a collection of Italian songs which he copied abroad shows the direction of his

---

[1] For biographical details about Locke see W. H. Cummings, 'Matthew Locke, composer for the church and theatre', *Report of the Fourth Congress of the International Musical Society, London*, 1912.

musical tastes at that time. His *Little Consort*, published in 1656, was composed in 1651. Christopher Gibbons, son of Orlando, was about fifteen years older than his collaborator. His contribution to the work is comparatively small, though it fell to his lot to set 'Victorious men of earth'.

Whether the manuscript of the music now in the British Museum represents the masque as originally performed is doubtful. It is dated 1659, in which year the masque was performed publicly at 'the Military ground in Leicester Fields',[1] and it is quite conceivable that the music was elaborated for this occasion. Locke had sung the part of the Admiral in *The Siege of Rhodes* in 1656 and had composed the music of the fourth entry, and it is quite possible that the success of the opera led to a revival of the masque with considerable musical additions. In this case it is also possible to suppose that Christopher Gibbons' music was written for the earlier production. This is all a matter of pure conjecture; but as we shall shortly see, there is some ground for these suppositions in the fact that Locke set to music several speeches which from the printed libretto one would naturally suppose to have been spoken.

The music falls into three groups: the instrumental entries and dances, the 'songs' and the recitatives. Of these the 'songs' are dramatically the least important. Following the tradition of the masque, the poet and composers regarded them not as dramatic expression of human feeling, but more or less in the nature of choruses in a Greek tragedy. They are sung for the most part by single voices, partly perhaps from motives of economy, partly too from the tendency of the age towards solo singing; but the chorus generally takes part here and there, and the songs are never attributed to

---

[1] 'Behind *Leicester House* stood in 1658 the Military Yard founded by *Henry* prince of *Wales*, the spirited son of our peaceful *James*. M. *Foubert* afterwards kept here his academy for riding and other gentleman-like exercises in the reign of Charles II.' *Some account of London*, London, 1793. Leicester House stood at the north-east corner of Leicester Square, which at this time was not yet built upon.

any particular character. They are lyrical interludes totally independent of the dramatic action. The dances are often of great interest. Locke evidently had a strong sense of the stage, and a great determination to be expressive at all costs. The result is sometimes uncouth and awkward, but there is a great vivacity and energy about his music, just such as one would expect from the forcible and uncompromising style in which his literary prefaces are written. It is interesting to note that in the preface to his *Little Consort* he protests angrily against the practice of 'tearing [music] in pieces with division', that is, of extemporizing grace notes and rapid passages, instead of 'playing plain'; and the angularity of his rhythms and melodies would indeed make them as little suited for 'divisions' as was in a later century the music of Rameau for the vocal *fioriture* of Italian singers.

The recitative begins at the scene where the Lovers are slain by Cupid, with Nature looking on. This is all printed in roman type in both the original editions of 1653 and 1659, like the rest of the spoken dialogue—the musical portions being, as was the custom, printed in italic; but Locke has taken the opportunity of setting the whole scene.

As might be expected, Locke's style in recitative is very Italian, more so sometimes than that of Lawes. It was perhaps due to his being a singer himself that he has a frequent tendency to indulge in florid passages, not always very judicious, and often set to the most unimportant words; but they are evidently intended to be musically expressive, and not mere exhibitions of virtuosity. Locke's style is never conventional, like that of the Italians. It is derived from an Italian style which his Venetian and Roman contemporaries would have considered very old-fashioned; but it fits the English of the poet with great care, and even if it is at times ill-managed, it is always of interest as an early attempt in a style perfected later by Purcell. A more serious defect is the unsettled nature of Locke's tonality in recitative, which is very apparent in the extract here printed. It compares ill

in this respect with the example from William Lawes given
in Chapter II. But it is the inevitable result of an experi-
mental style. Locke is grappling with a very much more
difficult problem than Lawes; he attempts to cover a much
wider range of emotion, and he not only attempts but succeeds in giving the various emotional phases a much greater
intensity of expression. How strongly this is enhanced by
Locke's harmonic sense is seen in the passage beginning 'He
faints, 'tis now too late'. It may seem strange to a modern
reader that no attempt is ever made to describe instrumentally
the events happening on the stage. Such a conception is of
much later origin. If anything happened on the stage in
view of the audience, there was naturally no necessity to
indicate it in the music, although dances were often made
expressive, and out of them developments on modern lines
became more possible. But although no *leitmotiv* announces
the entrance of Death, the shock of his appearance is well
suggested by the change of harmony in the accompaniment,
from the chord of E major (as dominant of A minor) to the
chord of G minor. The same progression occurs in more
than one place expressive of great emotional stress both in
the *Euridice* of Peri and in Monteverdi's *Orfeo*.[1] The monologue of Nature which is here printed is preceded by three
short dances, headed 'fourth entry', and they are printed here
as in the manuscript. There is a note—'Play not the following suit of Ayres till after the song before the Hectors
Dance'—presumably added for the performance of 1659.

Each entry is as a rule prepared by a set of three or four
dances, and as the stage directions indicate a dance of the
lovers in this case, we may reasonably suppose that the three
dances printed were originally intended to accompany the
change of scene.[2] The first of these is extremely expressive,
and should be compared with the 'symphony' in A minor

[1] They are quoted in Morton Latham, *The Renaissance of Music*, London,
1890.
[2] A few short extracts from later scenes are quoted in the *Oxford History of
Music*, vol. III.

quoted from W. Lawes' masque in Chapter II, to see how Locke, though maintaining the same form and the same general style of bass and syncopated melody, yet produces poignant emotional effects such as we never find in the older writer.

The two following dances have less individuality, but are musically a great advance on earlier work. Even here we see that Locke under Italian influence is aiming at that directness, or even violence, of expression which made Italian opera so repugnant to the ears of French audiences trained in a gentler and more delicate school. The last dance is also very full of character; we must however beware of regarding this scene from a sentimental point of view. To the seventeenth century there was nothing poetical about elderly love-making: that age took too natural and frank a view of life to regard senile passion as anything but grotesque.

The first eight bars of the 'song' will be sufficient to give an idea of its style. It is written for a voice of wide compass extending from high F to low D. There are several changes of movement, both in the solo and in the chorus which concludes it, and the whole is rather baroque in the exaggerated vehemence of its sudden leaps and aggressive flourishes. But it has at least the advantage of presenting a strong contrast to the declamation of the preceding scene, and makes a very reasonable attempt to sum up the whole 'entry' in a vigorous piece of solid music built up to an effective climax of sound.

The remainder of the masque is almost entirely sung, and there is a very interesting monologue for the Chamberlain when he brings in his pair of apes, but it is too long for quotation here, and short extracts give very little idea of any theatrical scene.

The masque, if it can be said to have survived at all, survived now solely as an entertainment for school 'speech-days'. *Cupid and Death* seems to have been the model for another school masque written in 1676 by Thomas Duffett,

(The scene is changed into a pleasant garden, a fountain in the midst of it; walks and arbours delightfully expressed; in divers places, Ladies lamenting over their lovers slain by Cupid, who is discovered flying in the air.

Enter a Lover, playing upon a lute, courting his Mistress; they dance.)

‡6

[Repeat again from the 𝄋]

90

(Enter Nature, in a white robe, a chaplet of flowers, a green mantle fringed with gold, her hair loose. They start, and seem troubled at her entrance.)

Nature

Fly, fly, ... my child-ren! Love, that should pre-serve And warm your

hearts with kind and active blood, Is now become your e - ne - my, a

mur - - der- er. This gar - - den that was once your enter -

tainment With all the beauty of the spring, is now, By some strange

curse upon the shafts of Cu - pid, Design'd . . to be a

91

grave. Look ever -y - where The noble lovers on the ground lie

bleeding, By fran - - tic Cu - pid slain; into whose wounds Distracted

virgins pour their tears so fast, That having drain'd their fountains they pre-

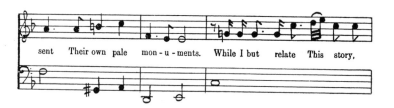

sent Their own pale mon - u -ments. While I but relate This story,

see, more added to the dead: Oh, fly, and save yourselves! I am your parent,

(Enter Cupid, who strikes the Lover, and exit)

Nature, that thus advise you to your safeties. He's come al - ready.

Lover (tenor)   *(Lover dies)*   *Nature.*

Ha! what winter creeps Into my heart? He faints, 'tis now too

late. Some kind-er god call back the wing-ed boy, And give him eyes to

look up - on his murders. Nature grows stiff with horror of this

spectacle. If it be death to love, what will it be, When Death itself must

93

(Enter Death)

act his cru - - el - ty? And here he comes: what tragedies are

(Enter Old Men and Women, with crutches)

next? Two aged pair: these will be fit for Death: They can ex-

pect but a few minutes more To wear the heavy bur - den of their

(Death strikes them with his arrow, and exit; they, admiring one another, let fall their crutches and embrace)

lives. Astonishment to Nature! they throw

off All their infirmities as young men do Their airy upper garments.

These were the Effects of Cu-pid's shafts; pro - di -gious change!

(They dance with antique postures,
(Exit) *expressing rural courtship)*

I have not patience to be - hold them longer.

4th Song

What will it, Death, ad - vance thy name, Up-

95

on cold rocks to waste a . . . . . flame, Or by mis-

take to throw Bright tor - ches in - to . . . . pits of snow? etc.

whom we shall meet in a later chapter as a writer of burlesques. *Beauties Triumph*, as it was called, was 'presented by
the scholars of Mr Jeffery Banister and Mr James Hart, at
their *New Boarding School* for Young ladies and Gentlewomen
kept in that House which was formerly *Sir Arthur Gorges*, at
Chelsey'. The masque deals with the story of Paris and the
three goddesses; it is evidently designed to bring in as much
music and as many characters as possible, both speaking
and singing. From the Epilogue we learn that the principal
occupations of young ladies at boarding-schools were
embroidery, music and modelling in coloured wax.

Nevertheless these school masques are of importance, for
they eventually led on to the production of Purcell's *Dido
and Aeneas*. We shall have to consider later on Blow's so-
called masque of *Venus and Adonis*; but that, as we shall see,
is a real opera, though on a very diminutive scale. Moreover,
Venus and Adonis was performed at court, not in a school. It
was only in a school that so novel a work of art as *Dido and
Aeneas* could have been attempted; and its performance in
school was only made possible by the fact that English

schools still kept up the Commonwealth tradition of performing masques which were musically, if indeed not
scenically, elaborate. During the first ten years of the reign of
Charles II 'recitative musick' seems to have declined rapidly
in public favour. It was kept up by the amateurs; Pepys
showed a consistent interest in it. His favourite subjects for
musical settings of his own or his master's seem to have been
taken from plays; the famous 'Beauty, retire' is from the
Siege of Rhodes, and so is 'This cursed jealousy',[1] though this
latter was purely lyrical. He mentions Lawes' recitative
songs with great enthusiasm, and the most curious testimony
to his passion for recitative is the setting of 'To be or not to
be' composed for him by Cesare Morelli,[2] which is a remarkably fine piece of musical declamation, the more so
when we reflect that it was the work of an Italian. As
Morelli did not come to England until 1675 this composition
is an interesting document for the length of time that the old
style of declamatory settings remained in favour.

But the genuine operatic movement, initiated by D'Avenant,
was short-lived. As soon as the theatres were placed on a
firm footing, there was no more need to disguise plays under
the title of 'moral representations'. The majority of the public
no doubt wanted plays, and not operas; moreover actors and
actresses were more easily obtained than dramatic singers.
D'Avenant himself evidently had a greater interest in plays
than in music, and the permanent influence of *The Siege of
Rhodes* was not musical but dramatic. Even Pepys, for all
his musical enthusiasm, clearly regarded *The Siege of Rhodes*
not so much as an opera as in the light of a great work
of literature, for though he delighted in hearing Edward
Coleman and his wife sing their old songs in later years, the
play is oftener mentioned as being his constant companion

---

[1] *Diary*, Feb. 26, 1661–2. 'Mr Berkenshaw with me all the morning composing
of musique to 'This cursed jealousy, what is it', a song of Sir W. Davenant's'.
[2] It has sometimes been stated that this music was composed by Pepys
himself; but the MS. in the Pepysian Library leaves no doubt that it was
composed by Morelli.

on land and on sea, a poem which he never tired of reading again and again.

It was more than ten years before another attempt at opera was made in London. During those ten years many new developments took place, dramatic and musical, both in England and in France. English audiences wanted plays, but they still liked to have their plays liberally interspersed with music, and D'Avenant had no scruples about adapting Shakespeare for this purpose. The music, however, was not really of a dramatic nature, except in rare cases. It did not intensify the drama; the drama was often twisted out of all sense merely in order to provide an excuse for introducing it. Moreover music had undergone its own changes. Under French and Italian influences melodies in triple time had become popular. These had been rare in earlier generations, although they no doubt existed in the music of the uneducated classes; the artistic music, except for a few dance-forms, was almost always in duple rhythms, and it even happens that melodies based in themselves on a rhythm of three beats are forced into one of four or two when accompanied contrapuntally. For the popularity of triple rhythms in the middle of the seventeenth century the *coranto* is largely responsible, and it is amusing to note that it was the favourite musical form of the amateur composer. Burney and Hawkins both quote Sir Bulstrode Whitelocke's *Corant* composed (with the assistance of Simon Ives) about 1633, which the composer tells us was much admired and constantly played in public for another thirty years. Shadwell alludes to the amateur composer of a later date in *The Sullen Lovers* (1670), where the 'foolish knight, that pretends to understand everything in the world' insists on letting his unwilling friends hear his production:

I have made this morning a glorious Corrant, an immortal Corrant, a Corrant with a soul in it.

One of the other characters, Ninny the conceited poet, observes later:

Yes, doubtless, Sir *Positive* has a great Soul of Musick in him; he has great power in Corrantos and Jiggs, and composes all the Musick to my plays.

Another play of Shadwell's, *The Humorists* (1671), introduces a coxcomb, Mr Briske, who thus describes his method of meeting one insult with another:

Why, faith when he kicked me, I told him very smartly, I scorn'd such ill-bred Sots from my heart, and that I thought him as much below me as the fellow that cries Tinder-Boxes and Mouse-Trapps; and then sang a Corant of *Berkenshawes* in D, sol, re, fa, la, la, ... At this he was amaz'd, and said I was a Stoick, but I sang on, fa la, la, la, which by the way is an excellent Corant, thou shalt hear 't, fa la, la.

He goes out singing his coranto and re-enters singing it again:

Fa, la, la, la, that's an excellent Corant; really I must confess *Grabu* is a very pretty hopeful man, but *Berkenshaw* is a rare fellow, give him his due, fa la, la, for he can teach men to compose, that are deaf, dumb, and blind.

It will be remembered that Berchinshaw gave lessons to Pepys.

The popularity of the coranto is of some importance, for it left its mark on the lyric verse of the day, and the plays of the next generation are full of songs written for tunes in triple time, such as Purcell's famous 'What shall I do to show how much I love her?' It was a great change from the days of Lawes, when the musician set almost all songs in common time, and did his best to disguise the fact that they had any symmetrical rhythm at all.

Chapter Six

'PSYCHE'

It is necessary at this point for us to take into consideration the development of dramatic music in Paris subsequent to the production of Caproli's *Le Nozze di Peleo e di Theti* in 1654. It was in the following year that Lulli first came before the public as a composer,[1] and for some time he continued to write Italian songs, dialogues and choruses for insertion in the *ballets de cour*. He generally acted in these himself, and as these diversions are always either in Italian or in some nonsense language, even after he had begun to assume the character of a French composer, it has been deduced that he never succeeded in speaking French without a foreign accent. Up to the death of Mazarin he was definitely and almost exclusively Italian in his style, but this did not prevent him from becoming a person of considerable importance in the musical world of Paris. He had written some French airs in *Alcidiane*, a ballet produced in 1658, and in the *Ballet de la Raillerie* (1659) he showed a remarkable mastery of both French and Italian idiom in an amusing dialogue between *La Musique Italienne* and *La Musique Française*.[2]

It was on the occasion of the marriage of Louis XIV that Mazarin made his final efforts in the interests of Italian opera at Paris. In November 1660 he produced Cavalli's *Xerse* with only moderate success; in March 1661 he died. But he had already initiated preparations for another opera of Cavalli, *Ercole Amante*, a work on an immense scale specially composed for the occasion to a libretto by Buti. After three years

[1] H. Prunières, *L'Opéra italien en France*, p. 193.
[2] The music is quoted in full in the appendix to H. Prunières, *L'Opéra italien en France*. It illustrates in a nutshell the essential differences of style between the music of France and Italy.

of ceaseless labour and vast expense, it was produced in February 1662. As on previous occasions, the main interest of the work for the spectators of the time lay in the dances, the dresses and the scenery. The records of contemporary chroniclers have plenty to say about the spectacle, but allow the music to pass almost unmentioned. One reason for this was, it is said, the defective acoustic properties of the gigantic new theatre which had been built for the occasion by Vigarani, the designer of the scenes. There were however more potent but less definitely accountable motives in the background. The anti-Italian party was still strong, and there seems to have been some personal rancour against Vigarani, for the workmen were bribed to put his machinery out of order. The last performance of the opera was given in May and Cavalli went back to Venice in a great rage, swearing that he would never write another opera as long as he lived.

Cavalli's departure was all to the advantage of Lulli, who was now bent upon making himself as much of a Frenchman as possible. He had naturalized himself in the country of his adoption directly after Mazarin's death, and now drew public attention to his new policy by marrying the daughter of a French musician, Michel Lambert. It was some time however before he succeeded in definitely establishing opera in the French language. Corneille's *Andromède*, as M. Prunières says, 'presents an eminently French solution of the operatic problem. The play calls in the assistance of music only at moments when the attention of the spectators is not occupied by the development of the plot; the music is a diversion to the ear, as the scenery is a delight to the eye, but poetry alone is allowed the right of appealing to the emotions'.[1] The tragedy had several successors, in which the music gradually assumed a more and more important place. Among other plays produced at the Théâtre du Marais was Quinault's *La Comédie sans Comédie* (1654) which may perhaps

[1] Prunières, *op. cit.* p. 327.

have suggested to D'Avenant the idea of *The Playhouse to be Let*, as it is simply an excuse for bringing in several short dramatic entertainments of different kinds.

The piece known as the *Pastorale d'Issy*, written by Pierre Perrin and composed by Robert Cambert (1659), has generally been accepted as the first real French opera, but it has recently been shown[1] that it was preceded by a pastoral, *Le Triomphe de L'Amour*, acted before the court in Mazarin's apartments at the Louvre in January 1655. This was sung from beginning to end, the music being by Michel de la Guerre. And even as early as 1650 Dassoucy, the composer of the *intermezzi* for *Andromède*, had produced a 'comédie en musique' entitled *Les Amours d'Apollon et de Dafne*. This however is more like an *opéra-comique* of the eighteenth century; the legend is treated in a spirit of burlesque, and the dialogue is spoken. The music consists of a number of songs, one of which is in Italian, and also includes a duet in dialogue. The other opera, if it has any right to be so called, was a pastoral of the simplest and most conventional kind, modelled on Tasso's *Aminta*; it consisted merely of short scenes given each to two characters in dialogue, not sung in recitative, but in a definite metrical form of fourteen lines, so that each 'scene' could be sung to the same music. As the play consists merely of love-making in the most conventionally Arcadian manner, it may be supposed that there would be no particular inappropriateness in singing the same tune to each conversation.

The first performance appears to have been given in concert form only; in 1657 the work was enlarged and acted, but nothing more is known about the performance. The *Pastorale d'Issy* of Perrin and Cambert (1659) did not carry the dramatic scheme much further. 'Les bergers et les bergères chantent ou se taisent, paraissent ou disparaissent, on ne sait trop pourquoi; ils ne prennent part à aucune espèce d'in-

[1] H. Quittard, 'Le Triomphe de l'Amour', in *Bulletin de la S.I.M.* April-May, 1908.

trigue, gaie ou triste, bonne ou mauvaise; c'est d'une insuffisance parfaite, d'une monotonie désespérante.'[1] Perrin had a very high opinion of his own powers, and has succeeded in obtaining more credit as an opera-librettist than he deserves. The type of opera at which he was aiming was merely an evasion of the whole problem, and could never be developed into anything of real dramatic power. The Italian experimenters of the opening century had aimed at drama alone, and had sacrificed almost all musical interest to the expression of the words which they set. Since they took care to provide themselves with a well-defined story and one which all the world knew already, and further clothed it in language which has the merit of real literary beauty, they evolved a new style merely by their sincerity and their devotion to what they supposed to be the ideals of antiquity. The English composers followed their example within a few years, as far as the setting of poetry to music was concerned; but they did not turn the new system to dramatic account on the stage. When opera became established in Italy as a popular diversion, it was inevitable that recitative should become quickened up and conventionalized, and the emotional moments be developed in the more strictly musical form of the aria. Perrin and his contemporaries, like many opera-goers of all generations including the present one, wanted to have an opera which was all aria and no recitative; but that is a form of opera which even all the resources of modern technique have as yet failed to accomplish. The reason of this is musical as much as dramatic: it might indeed be possible to construct a series of situations so conventional as to need no explanation; but it is impossible to make a satisfactory piece of continuous music merely by stringing together arias one after another. Even if there is no attempt at symphonic construction, as for instance in the operas of Alessandro Scarlatti, arias gain in effect if they are separated by recitatives. If spoken dialogue

[1] Nuitter et Thoinan, *Les Origines de l'opéra français*, Paris, 1886.

takes its place, the complete work is not worth consideration as an opera unless definite effort is made to build up the musical portion towards some sort of symphonic climax, as in Mozart's German operas or those of Weber.

The *Pastorale d'Issy* had to wait twelve years for a successor, and it was during the intervening period that were produced first the two operas of Cavalli already mentioned, and secondly a series of ballets for which the music was written by Lulli. It is interesting to compare the state of dramatic music at this moment in Paris and London. In England, as we have seen, the technique of both music and drama in the earlier years of the century had been more advanced than it was in France. But although England had been the first country to imitate successfully the new Italian recitative style, the very fact that the English drama was already so far in advance of that of the rest of Europe prevented the application of recitative to the regular stage. Only when the theatres were closed was there an opportunity for genuine opera to make its appearance. In France, on the other hand, there were no obstacles either to drama or to opera, and the new dramatic style of Corneille and Molière was evolved just at the moment when English drama was in a state of suspended animation. The Puritan dominion was advantageous to English opera at least in one respect: no time was wasted over pastoral opera, for the Puritans would undoubtedly have condemned the amours of Arcadia as contrary to good morals. The classical divinities beloved of the Romans would have fared no better, and the result of these prejudices was the evolution of the peculiarly English heroic opera. In this respect England was ahead of France; but the more stable economic conditions of court life in Paris made it possible for steady progress to be made there when England was only able to attempt opera by spasmodic fits and starts.

The first of these attempts since the collapse of D'Avenant's operas shortly after the Restoration was made in the autumn of 1673. It is the first English experiment on a French model.

Molière had invented the form of *comédie-ballet* in 1661. Being commanded to produce a comedy and a ballet as well, with a very small number of dancers at his disposal, it was suggested to him that the ballet should be distributed between the acts of the comedy, in order that the same dancers might appear several times in different costumes; Molière however hit upon the happy idea of making the ballets an integral part of the play. Beginning with dances only, Molière and his collaborator Lulli gradually increased the musical element, until it included songs and choral movements as well, and became so important as almost completely to overshadow the play itself, difficult as it is for a modern reader to realize this in such a case as that of *Le Bourgeois Gentilhomme* (1670). On January 17, 1671, they produced the *comédie-ballet* of *Psyché*, in which the parts of the play which were set to music were written by Quinault, Lulli's future collaborator in the operas of his maturity.

It was in imitation of this work that Shadwell and Locke brought out a so-called 'opera' with the same title. Both the motives and the circumstances of its production are difficult to ascertain. It is tempting to suppose that it was put forward at the Duke's Theatre in imitation and rivalry of the French operas that were being acted at the Theatre Royal about the same time. Downes in his *Roscius Anglicanus* tells us that *Psyche* was acted in February 1673.

In *February* 1673. The long expected opera of *Psyche*, came forth in all her Ornaments; new Scenes, new Machines, new Cloaths, new *French* Dances: This opera was Splendidly set out, especially in Scenes; the Charge of which amounted to above 800 *l*. It had a Continuance of Performance about 8 days together it prov'd very Beneficial to the Company; yet the *Tempest* got them more Money.

Mr Montague Summers[1] maintains that Downes is certainly wrong in his dating, and that *Psyche* was not produced until about October of 1673.

---

[1] Montague Summers, *Shakespeare Adaptations*, London, 1922.

Concerning the French opera season we have little information. Perrin and Cambert after many years' interval had followed up the *Pastorale d'Issy* with *Pomone*, produced in 1671, Perrin having obtained a privilege from Louis XIV ten years previously to establish 'des académies d'opéra, ou représentations en musique en langue française, sur le pied de celles d'Italie'. Lulli, who was anxious to get rid of all rivals, immediately bought up Perrin's right, and obtained the exclusive privilege of performing French operas in Paris. Cambert transferred himself to London, where he had a friend at court in the shape of his pupil Louis Grabu, who in spite of some hostility on the part of English musicians had got himself established as Master of the King's Musick.[1]

French writers have made various statements about Cambert's position at the court of Charles II, but no record of any appointment has been found in England. It is not even possible to state what was his connection with the French operas performed in 1674, though we know that he was directing the King's music at Windsor in July of that year.[2] But in 1673–4 there were printed in London French and English versions of Perrin's opera *Ariane et Bacchus*, the English title being 'Ariadne or the Marriage of Bacchus an opera, or, a Vocal Representation; First compos'd by Monsieur P. P. Now put into Musick by Monsieur Grabut, Master of his Majesties Musick. And Acted by the Royal Academy of Musick at the Theatre Royal in Covent Garden. In the Savoy, Printed by Tho. Newcombe, 1763⁄4'.

Ariane was intended to celebrate the marriage of James with Mary of Modena; he married her by proxy on September 30, 1673, and she landed at Dover on November 21. The prologue to the opera introduces three nymphs representing

---

[1] He was appointed 'composer in his Majesty's musique' on March 31, 1665, and 'master of the English chamber musick in ordinary to his Majesty, in place of Nicholas Lanier, deceased' on November 24, 1666. H. Cart de Lafontaine, *The King's Musick*, London (1909).

[2] H. Cart de Lafontaine, *op. cit.* pp. 273 and 280.

the Thames, the Seine and the Tiber; after they have sung there enters a nymph of the Po, singing

> Soufre que je vienne en ces Lieux
> Malgré les Destins & l'Envie,
> Joindre ma Divine Marie
> Au plus Grand de tes Demidieux.

The influence of the *ballet de cour* is apparent in the number of grotesque dances, such as that prescribed in Act v:

Enter Clowns, who being all drunk, fall a dancing after their manner. These Rusticles come to dance at *Bacchus's* Wedding, bringing with them Presents of such things as their Village affords; some bring in their Baskets Sawsages, others Eggs dy'd in several colours, and others Truffs. Old Silene, while they are dancing, changes their Baskets and gives them others, where instead of Sawsages they find live Eels; instead of Eggs, Frogs; and for Truff, live Rats.

The dedication to the King is followed by an address to the Reader which is an apology for the translation and for the original libretto too:

the *Original* itself being neither a Strain of Wit, nor yet the Stile of it Puft up; but onely a bare *Collection* of *Phrases*, and *Expressions* made fit for *Sound* and *Harmony*....But let it run what fortune it will, it can fare no worse than a Thousand far better things have done: and, were both the *Original* and the *Version* much worse than they are, the Pomp and Magnificence of its *Representation* will alone prove sufficient to plead their excuse.

It has been assumed by Professor Schelling[1] that this opera is the entertainment referred to by Evelyn in his *Diary*, January 5, 1673–4:

I saw an *Italian opera* in musiq, the first that had been in *England* of this kind.

On this assumption we may suppose that Shadwell and Locke's *Psyche* was produced as a counter-attraction. Mr Lawrence, however, argues that the French season lasted a fortnight only, at some date between March 27 and April 27,

---

[1] *The Cambridge History of English Literature*, vol. viii, chap. v.

the dates of entries in the Lord Chamberlain's accounts authorizing Grabu to borrow and to return after fourteen days time such scenery belonging to the private theatre at Whitehall as he might require for the French opera. He further points out that Shadwell's libretto must have been written about September 1673, since it was published before February 15, 1674–5, and the author says that it was written sixteen months previously. Lastly he suggests that Evelyn's 'Italian Opera' was not *Ariane*, but *Psyche* itself. Evelyn's entry can in fact be applied equally well to either opera, for he evidently means by an 'Italian opera' not an opera in the Italian language, or by an Italian composer, but simply a dramatic performance set to music, or, as the English expression of the day was, 'a vocal representation'.

The English theatres since the Restoration were always closely in touch with those of Paris. Various troupes of French actors had appeared in London, and among the pieces they presented was Chapoton's *Le Mariage d'Orphée et d'Eurydice*, revived in Paris in 1648, as we have already seen. Mr Lawrence identifies this with 'The Description of the Great Machines of the Descent of Orpheus into Hell. Presented by the French commedians at the Cockpit in Drury Lane in 1661', without apparently being aware that the original title of the French play as acted in 1640 was *La Descente d'Orphée aux Enfers*.[1] Of later French companies in London little is known, but there is no doubt that the plays of Molière were quickly made familiar to English audiences, for a version of his *Sganarelle ou le Cocu Imaginaire* (1660) formed part of D'Avenant's *The Playhouse to be Let* (1662) and various plays of his were adapted by Shadwell, Dryden and others.

Allusion has already been made to the incidental music which was so popular a feature of the plays produced during the first ten years of the Restoration. It will be convenient to postpone the more detailed consideration of this till a later chapter, as this system continued for many years after the

[1] Prunières, *op. cit.* pp. 322, 323.

performance of *Psyche*, which is a completely isolated pheno-
menon. But although the scheme of *Psyche* is not derived
from the English plays which preceded it, it must certainly
have owed its success largely to the fact that these plays had
gradually prepared audiences for drama in which music bore
a more important part.

Molière's play[1] begins with a prologue the opening of which
is set to music. Flora, Vertumnus and Palaemon, accompanied
by appropriate minor divinities, invite Venus to descend to
earth since Louis has established peace there. They dance
and sing dialogues on the subject of love until Venus appears
accompanied by Cupid and two Graces. She is in a state of
great indignation because she has heard it said that Psyche is
more beautiful than herself. She orders Cupid to avenge her
by causing Psyche to fall in love with the lowest of mankind.

In Act I the two sisters of Psyche, Aglaure and Cydippe,
meet the two rivals for her hand, Cléomène and Agénor.
Psyche refuses to decide between the two, saying that her
father must settle the matter and that her two sisters must
be married first. Lycas enters and after sending Psyche to
her father the King tells the sisters that an oracle has decreed
that Psyche is to be taken to the top of a mountain and left
there to become the bride of a monster. The sisters express
their satisfaction at the news, and the scene changes to a
rocky desert where Psyche is to be exposed. At this point
there is an *intermezzo* of *personnes affligées*, some of whom sing
laments in Italian, while the others express their despair in
a dance.

In Act II Psyche is conducted to the spot by the King and
left there alone. The two lovers enter and offer to rescue
her, but she declines, and is carried off before their eyes by
two Zephyrs. The second *intermezzo* represents the palace
which Vulcan by Cupid's orders is preparing for the reception of Psyche. He sings a song, and a ballet is danced
by six Cyclopes and four Furies.

[1] It was revived at the Odéon in Paris with Lulli's music in April 1914.

Act III consists of a love-scene between Psyche and Cupid in disguise, followed by an *intermezzo* of other Cupids and Zephyrs.

Act IV shows us another magnificent palace. The jealous sisters enter and persuade Psyche to ask her lover to reveal himself. She does so; Cupid flies away, the garden disappears, and Psyche is left alone by the bank of a river, with the river-god reclining before her on his urn. He forbids her to drown herself and warns her against Venus, who enters at this moment more angry than ever at hearing of Cupid's disobedience. The *intermezzo* brings a view of Hell, with a dance of Furies. Psyche crosses the Styx in Charon's boat, carrying a box which Venus has sent her to fetch from Proserpine.

In Act V she is visited by her old admirers Cléomène and Agénor. After they have left her she opens the mysterious box; fumes rise from it which cause her to lose consciousness. Cupid enters, followed by Venus, with whom he has a long wrangle, after which Jupiter descends and unites the lovers. Various divinities appear and celebrate the happy occasion with songs and dances.

Shadwell in his preface admits having borrowed some ideas from the French *Psyché*, but maintains that he has greatly improved upon it, although he confesses to having written the play in haste, and frankly states that he did not consider it worth while to revise or polish it, having a very poor opinion of rhyming plays for music, though not of his own literary skill. He evidently thought well of himself as a musician too, for he goes on to say:

In all the words which are sung, I did not so much take care of the Wit or Fancy of 'em, as the making of 'em proper for Musick; in which I cannot but have some little knowledge, having been bred, for many years of my youth, to some performance in it.

I chalk'd out the way to the Composer (in all but the Song of *Furies and Devils*, in the Fifth Act) having design'd which Line I wou'd have sung by One, which by Two, which by Three, which by Four Voices &c. and what manner of Humour I would have in all the Vocal Musick.

In this respect his self-praise is by no means unjustified: as we shall see, the opera is planned with a good deal of musical understanding, and the next paragraph of the preface shows that he had a proper appreciation of his collaborator's abilities, and a genuine desire to give him full scope for them, rather than merely to tickle the long ears:

And by his excellent Composition, that long known, able, and approved Master of Musick, *Mr. Lock* (*Composer* to His Majesty, and Organist to the Queen) has done me a great deal of right; though I believe, the unskilful in Musick, will not like the more solemn part of it, as the Musick in the Temple of *Apollo*, and the Song of the *Despairing Lovers*, in the Second Act; both which are proper and admirable in their kinds, and are recommended to the judgment of able Musicians; for those who are not so, there are light and airy things to please them.

The prologue, instead of being an allegorical scene all in praise of the King, after the French manner, is merely the customary English prologue in rhymed couplets, apologizing with rather unnecessary humility for the shortcomings of the piece, and showing that the author fully understood the difference of style proper to an opera libretto as compared with a play. The first act brings Psyche on the scene at once, instead of leading gradually up to her entrance as Molière does. Psyche is attended by two ladies, whose only purpose is to assist the heroine in explaining to the audience her gentle and retiring nature, and her preference for a rural existence. Music is heard, and Pan enters with his followers, to sing the praises of Psyche and crown her with flowers. This scene is developed at some length, with dances and choruses in echo. It is immediately followed by the entrance of four females representing Ambition, Power, Plenty and Peace, who invite Psyche to leave her solitudes. Envy and six Furies rise, and foretell her future woes. Psyche remains confident in her own innocence. The rival lovers then appear, Nicander and Polynices, who discourse at some length rather in the French style, after which Psyche induces them to embrace each other, and forbids them to invade her privacy.

She leaves the stage, and the jealous sisters enter. They invoke the aid of Venus, who descends from above and tells them in song that she has arranged with the oracle of Apollo to inflict injury on the offending Psyche. The act ends with the entrance of the King Theander, accompanied by Psyche; he bids them all follow him to the temple of Apollo.

Act II begins with a long and elaborate ceremony in the temple of Apollo. A solemn procession enters, headed by 'the Chief Priest crown'd with Laurel in a white Vestment, over that a Purple gown, over that a Cope embroidered with Gold, over all a Lamb-skin Hood with the Wool on', boys attending 'clad in surplices', carrying various objects, followed later by 'six Priests with books of Hymns, clad in Surplices and embroider'd Copes'.

The ceremony is all set to music, except for a short litany in which all the gods and goddesses are invoked, seventeen of them singly by name, the people responding 'Be propitious to our vows and prayers'. Theander inquires of the oracle who is to be Psyche's husband, and the image of Apollo delivers the following lines:

> You must conduct her to that fatal place,
> Where miserable lovers that despair,
> With howls and Lamentations fill the air;
> A Husband there your Daughter shall embrace.
>> On *Venus* rock upon the sea,
>> She must by you deserted be:
> A poysonous Serpent there She'll find,
> By Heav'n he *Psyche's* Husband is design'd.

A conversation of some length follows amongst the principal characters, which is interesting for the very rationalistic views on miracles brought forward by Psyche's two admirers. The Chief Priest, as might be expected, endeavours to stifle discussion with timely thunder, but although Psyche is meekly willing to submit, Polynices and Nicander get the last word before the scene changes to the rocky desert where the 'miserable lovers that despair' are presented to view. After

they have sung a quartet and committed suicide one by
one, Theander enters with Psyche, her sisters and attendants.
They leave her alone; Nicander and Polynices enter and
offer to rescue her, but infernal spirits drive them away, and
Psyche is taken up into the clouds by Zephyrs, Cupid ob-
serving from above.

Act III shows us the palace of Cupid, Vulcan and the
Cyclopes being at work on the decorations, though their work
consists mainly of singing, drinking and dancing. Cupid and
Psyche have a long love-scene, interrupted by a song from
invisible singers. Cupid at the request of Psyche sends Zephyrs
to invite her sisters to visit her. The scene then changes to
the principal street of Theander's city. The two princes have
slain the monstrous serpent, and are received with acclama-
tions by the Praesul and the Priests of Mars. This is all set
to music. While they are preparing to sacrifice to Mars, the
god himself appears in the air, Venus meeting him there at
the same moment. At her request he summons Furies, who
strike the altar and break it. After some mild consternation
Cidippe and Aglaura suggest that the princes should regard
Psyche as devoured and marry them instead; the princes,
however, with that scientific spirit which always charac-
terizes them, have already examined the monster's 'rav'nous
maw' and, finding no remains of Psyche inside it, conclude
that she is still alive. Aglaura and Cidippe therefore arrange
to have them dispatched by a trusty villain.

In Act IV the sisters visit Psyche, who entertains them with
music and dancing. They arouse Psyche's suspicions, and
even make an attempt to stab her while she is looking the
other way, but in this they are prevented by the Zephyrs,
who carry them off. As soon as the sisters are gone, Psyche
questions Cupid, and is abandoned by him. As in Molière,
the palace vanishes, and Psyche finds herself by the bank of
a river. The sisters enter and tell her that their father has
killed himself for grief. Psyche is going to throw herself into
the river, but is restrained by the river-god and his nymphs

who address her in song. Venus makes a short appearance, merely to assure Psyche of her undying hatred. The princes enter; Psyche is carried off by Furies; the soldiers of the jealous sisters attack the princes and are repulsed, after which the princes, arm in arm, fling themselves into the river in the hopes of meeting Psyche in the other world. Finally the sisters enter, in a great rage with the soldiers on account of their inefficiency, but are carried off to Hell by Furies at the bidding of Cupid.

Act v presents a view of Hell, described in some detail in the stage directions. A song is sung by Furies and Devils, followed by a dance. Aglaura and Cidippe express their satisfaction at the tortures of Psyche, who is consoled by Pluto and Proserpine. They give her the casket of beauty to present to Venus and bid her be gone; these speeches are set to music. The sisters sink to lower regions, and Pluto vanishes with all the Devils and Furies. Psyche, after an interview with the ghosts of Nicander and Polynices, is transported to the river-bank again. Here Shadwell follows Molière fairly closely: Psyche swoons from the fumes of the casket; Cupid appeals to Venus in vain, Jupiter revives Psyche and unites her to Cupid, after which Apollo and other divinities descend with songs and dances. Jupiter ends the drama with a few platitudes.

Shadwell was notorious for his hasty and careless writing, and *Psyche* shows his faults no less clearly than his plays. He begins well, with a style of his own, and treats the subject quite differently from Molière, but towards the end his invention breaks down, and he takes the plan of several scenes straight from the French: the first scene of Act iii and parts of Acts iv and v. But although the libretto may seem very French by comparison with such semi-operas as the contemporary adaptations of *Macbeth* and *The Tempest*, yet by comparison with Molière's play it is very characteristically English. Molière is throughout fettered by a very strict form of a play with a prologue, *intermezzi* and *finale*; he is further restricted by certain considerations of literary style. Shadwell, an Englishman and a romantic, is utterly indifferent to form, and presents the story as a play with plenty of incident, and as much music as he can find an excuse to bring in. Although he borrows freely from Molière in detached episodes, he uses the material for totally different effects. His employment of music is always picturesque; he visualizes a stage picture, such as that of Pan and his followers paying homage to Psyche, the scene in the temple, or the appearance of the river-god, and proceeds to elaborate it with a very strong sense of musical effect. Shadwell, in fact, whatever his short-comings as a dramatist, had the makings of a really good librettist; he could imagine an essentially musical situation, and make his play lead up to it as a dramatic climax. It was his misfortune to belong to a generation which produced no musician better than Locke, whose technical accomplishment was decidedly limited. Had he been able to work in actual collaboration with Purcell, he might have profited by Purcell's wonderful command of all musical resource, and English opera might have been set firmly on its feet; but Purcell's music to his plays was not written until they were revived some years after their first production.[1]

Molière's entertainment regards the play, the machines and the music as three separate things, connected with each other but not interdependent; Shadwell's is conceived as a whole, almost in Wagner's manner, all three arts uniting to produce an effect such as none could achieve by itself. The weakness of Shadwell's play is that the poet has made the plot so complicated, by his elaboration of various episodes which Molière passes over in a few words, that the last two acts become scrappy and disconnected for want of space to develop the ideas properly; and further, it is obvious that the poet was either lazy or pressed for time, and did not take very much trouble about the arrangement of his musical episodes.

[1] Shadwell's *Psyche* seems to have served to some extent as a model for Congreve's *Semele*.

The music has come down to us somewhat incomplete. It was the joint work of Locke and Giovanni Battista Draghi; Locke printed his own portion of it, but the dances and other instrumental music composed by Draghi have not survived. Some twenty years had elapsed since Locke had composed the music to *Cupid and Death*, and a distinct change had taken place in his style, not altogether for the better. Shadwell rightly praises the scene in the temple of Apollo, and the scene of the Despairing Lovers; the former is a dignified and effective pageant, the latter is expressive and full of feeling, though not really necessary to the drama. The first musical episode (Pan and his followers) is very attractive, the echo chorus being especially charming, and there are other fairly effective numbers—the symphony for the descent of Venus, the song of Vulcan, and some of the songs and dances at the end of Act v. One of the most effective moments is the appearance of the river-god. Molière shows us the river-god reclining on his urn throughout the scene,[1] and his remonstrance to Psyche is spoken. Shadwell causes him to rise from the river just at the moment when she is about to throw herself in, and heightens the effect enormously by making him sing, with the nymphs to echo his words. The music gives a much greater impressiveness to his entry, and adds a touch of mystery and solemnity to his prediction of her immortality.

Psyche. No longer these misfortunes I'll endure;
      Of all such wounds, death is the sovereign cure.
      In this deep stream that softly by does glide,
      All my misfortunes and my faults I'll hide.

She offers to throw herself into the river. The god of the River arises upon a seat of Bulrushes and Reeds, leaning upon an Urn. The *Naiades* round him sing.

---

[1] As represented at the Odéon it was a very effective stage picture.

MATTHEW LOCKE

River God (alto)

Stay, · stay, this Act will much defile my streams; With a short
pa - tience suffer these ex- treams. Heav'n has for thee a milder fate in
store, The time shall be when thou shalt weep no more. And yet fair Psy

1st Nymph · *Ritornello 1st Violin* · *1st Nymph*
She ne'er shall die, · And yet fair

2nd Nymph · *2nd Violin* · *2nd Nymph*
She ne'er shall die, · And yet fair

Viola · *River God*
- che ne'er shall die, · And yet fair

Psyche ne'er shall die, But shall be crown'd with im - - mor - ta - li -

Psyche ne'er shall die, But shall be crown'd with immor - ta - - li -

Psyche ne'er shall die, But shall be crown'd with immor - ta - - li -

- ty, but shall be crown'd but shall be crown'd with

- ty, but shall be crown'd with im - mor -

- ty, but shall be crown'd with im - mor -

Soft

im - mor - ta - li - ty, but shall be crown'd, but shall be

Soft

- ta - - li - ty, but shall be crown'd

Soft

- ta - li - ty, but shall be crown'd

Soft

It is not necessary to give more quotations here, since other specimens are to be found in *The Oxford History of Music*, vol. III.

Considered as a whole, Locke's music has serious weaknesses. In *Psyche* he seems to have lost much of that passionate striving for expression which marked *Cupid and Death*. Short extracts give a rather misleading idea of the work. There is a certain poetry in the utterance of the river-god, there is a vigorous lilt about the song of Vulcan; but these two styles represent all that Locke has to offer us. His characters either declaim in common time or sing definite tunes in a rhythm of three beats. Beyond this there is no differentiation of personality, and the songs in triple time are no more appropriate to any one character than to any other. They are moreover undistinguished from a purely musical point of view. In this Locke suffers perhaps from the limited technique of his period; even the best Italian music of his day is often marred by the practice of never giving the voice a moment's rest. This breathless concatenation of phrases is only tolerable when the phrases have a very sharply defined melodic character, and are arranged with a strong sense of

key-distribution and form, as in Stradella.[1] The best piece
of musical construction in the vocal portion is the echo
chorus of Pan's followers in Act I, where each phrase is repeated by a double and sometimes a triple echo, each echo
having a few notes less than its predecessor;[2] but this particular effect seems to have been largely the invention of
Shadwell, although the idea of musical echoes was by no
means new at that date. Of Locke's powers as an instrumental composer *Psyche* gives us little idea. There are
symphonies for the appearance of the deities; and when Mars
and Venus appear together the second half of the movement
makes a clear allusion to the symphony for Venus in Act I.
The symphony for the descent of Mars (the beginning is
quoted in *The Oxford History of Music*) is curious for its contrapuntal treatment; Locke seems to have been interested in
imitations and canons, which often involved him in extremely
awkward harmonic progressions. His writing for strings moreover suffers from a fault common in his Italian contemporaries, the frequent crossing of the two violin parts, which
obscures the melodic line. But there is a good deal of character about his crudities, for they show that he was bent on
expressing something serious and not content with facile
trivialities. Triviality indeed is totally absent from Locke's
music, and in his lightest moments he never can shake off
an inherent heaviness and clumsiness of style.

Psyche is an important landmark in our musical history,
because it is the first systematized attempt at a musical and
dramatic scheme which for a long period was characteristic
of English opera. The principal characters do not sing at all,
but there is a continual attempt to bring them into contact
with music, and to employ music as often as possible to
heighten dramatic effect. There is indeed one character in

---

[1] For a more detailed discussion of the point see Edward J. Dent, 'Italian
Chamber Cantatas', in *The Musical Antiquary*, II. 142, 185.

[2] Purcell adopts exactly the same device in the trio or chorus 'May the god
of Wit inspire' in *The Fairy Queen*.

Psyche who plays quite an important part, both in speech and in song, namely Venus. The whole drama is in fact enveloped in an atmosphere of music, and this idea is essentially English and romantic, a foreshadowing of the symphonic type of opera which was eventually to be perfected by Wagner.

Early in 1674 there was produced at the rival establishment, the Theatre Royal, an amusing parody of *Psyche* by Thomas Duffett, with the title of *Psyche Debauch'd*. Mr Montague Summers rightly says of it, 'It is a clever and amusing skit, at times astonishingly akin to more modern pantomime'. It was printed in 1678. It follows Shadwell's *Psyche* almost scene for scene, and often line for line. King Theander appears as King Andrew (acted by Mrs Corbett), Nicander and Polynices as Nicholas and Philip; the former of these was acted by Pepys' friend Mrs Knepp. Psyche is called None-so-fair, or more generally Nonsey, and was acted by the famous comedian Joe Haines; her sisters Wou'dhamore and Sweetlips (Aglaura and Cidippe) were allowed to be of the female sex. Mars is turned into Justice Crabb, and Venus into Mother Woossat, who was probably one of the two witches summoned by Hecate in the epilogue to *The Empress of Morocco*.[1] This is probably one of the earliest occasions on which women acted male parts on the English stage.

The prologue makes scornful allusions to the grossness of Shadwell's plays at the Dorset Garden Theatre, especially *Epsom Wells*, and alludes equally disparagingly to his literary style:

> Take off this *Psyches* borrow'd plumes awhile,
> *Hopkins* and *Sternhold* rise, and claim your style;
> Dread kings of *Brentford*! leave *Lardellas* Herse,
> *Psyches* despairing lovers steal your verse;
> And let *Apollos* priest restore again
> What from the nobler *Mamamouchy's* ta'en.

---

[1] In the original Hecate calls them by the names Puckle and Stradling; Duffett's printer gives in each case merely 'W—'.

As in *Psyche* the first scene shows us the heroine attended by two ladies enjoying the delights of country life. None-so-fair is here represented as a young lady who has run away from a boarding-school.[1] Costard, a countryman, and his wife Redstreak, who was also represented by a male actor, propose to entertain her. Their dialogue is worth quoting in full for its caricature of *Psyche* and of Shadwell's rather self-satisfied preface.

Redstreak. And we'l have a Masque, and Crouder[2] shall be *Pan*, and he must sing in resitantivy;

> Great *Psyche* go dress up the silly Rogues,
> And then *Piper* shall be *Chorus* and he shall sing:
> Now *Pan* with his fooling has made a fair hand.[3]

Then there must be Symphonie.

Costard. Shan't I be Symphonie, *Redstreak*?

Red. Hold thy tongue, Wilta? Lord to bless us; what rowly-powly, all Fellows at Foot-ball? Thee *Symphony*; No, *Symphony* must be a woundy cranck, short, tall, squat vellow with rusty Musick: and he must cry like a Bird;[4] and then we must have An Eccho—

Cost. Oh! there's an Eccho down at hollow Bank I'le call it Presently—

Red. No, no, we'l make an Eccho of our own.

Cost. How? prythee, *Redstreak* how;

Red. Why look thee: One must be Voice, and another must be Air, and another must be Rock; then Voice must talk soundly to Air, and beat her against Rock; and Rock must beat her back again; and then Air must cry out, and scold with Voice, and that's Eccho—Let me alone for Plot; if you will but work up the Sense and Passion as they say.

---

[1] Her description of school life throws a curious light on female education in England at this period. Compare also T. Durfey's play *Love for Money, or the Boarding School*, and the epilogue to Duffett's masque *Beauties Triumph*.

[2] *I.e.* the village performer on the crwth or crowd, a primitive kind of fiddle.

[3] *Pan.*   Great *Psyche*, goddess of each field and grove,
Whom every Prince and every god does love:

>   *   *   *   *   *

Chorus. And *Pan* who before all here did command,
Now resigns all his Empire to *Psyche's* fair hand.

[4] 'A short *Symphony* of Rustick Musick, representing the Cries and Notes of Birds....Then a short *Symphony* of Rustick Musick, representing an *Eccho*.'

A song and dance follows by the Crowder, Morris Dancers, Milkmaids and others. After the music Redstreak continues:

Red. It may be sweet Princes, You like not this solemn Musick, *Fiddle Fiddle, hey down Diddle.*—I value not myself upon the wit, but the fitness of the words; for Air and Melody.

> *Faddle fiddle hey down Diddle,*
> *Faith let's be merry.*

I have skill though I say't that shudn't, as they say for the *Jews* Trump-Citizen and Trump-Marine, I'le turn my back to none, though some have been bred up many year to't; I myself chalk'd out the way to the Tune-Maker; I know I have many Foes, that say I make not what I own, but Mum for that: This Rare *Opera* is all mine I'le swear; but for the Dress and Trim, give the Divel his due, I am beholding to the most serene and clear Monsieur *Stephen*, the King's Corn-cutter, and so are you all, for he put me upon't.[1]

Mention has also been made in this chapter of the litany sung in the temple of Apollo (Act II) with its invocations to various divinities. Here is Duffett's parody of it:

Two Priests: James Naylor, Pope Joan, Wat Tyler, Mall Cutpurs, Chocorelly—
All answer: Help our *Opera*, because 'tis very silly.
Two Priests: Massaniello, Mosely, Jack-straw, Jantredisco, Pimponelli—
All answer: Help our *Opera*, because 'tis very silly.
Two Priests: Hocus-Pocus, Don Quixot, Jack Adams, Mary Ambry, Friar Bungy, William Lilly—
All answer: Help our *Opera*, because 'tis very silly.
Two Priests: Carpentero, Paintero, Dancero, Musickero, Songstero, Punchanelly—
All answer: Help our *Opera*, because 'tis very silly.

In Act III, instead of Vulcan and the Cyclopes we have paviors with beaters; in Act V, when Psyche descends to Hell to fetch the casket of beauty for Venus, None-so-fair goes to 'a common prison' and is presented with a bottle of brandy for Mother Woossat. A monologue follows in which she sings a song about 'the delights of the bottle' and ends by falling

---

[1] Compare the extracts from Shadwell's preface quoted on pp. 110, 111.

down dead drunk. The play ends with the appearance of Justice Crabb in a wheelbarrow, after which there is a masque of gods and goddesses, which in print at any rate does not seem very different from Shadwell's.

Both the opera and the parody seem to have enjoyed considerable success; but Locke evidently thought that his work was not appreciated as it ought to have been, for when he published the music in 1675 he printed with it a rather peevish preface in which he defended his innovations. He observes that in his music

...you have from Ballad to single Air, Counterpoint, Recitative, Fuge, Canon, and Chromatick Musick; which variety (without vanity be it said) was never in Court or Theatre till now presented in this nation: though I must confess there has been something done (and more by me than any other), of this kind.

His replies to those who carped at his title 'opera', at the extreme compass of his voice parts, at his 'extravagance' of style and at the fact that the performers sang out of tune, need not be reproduced here. Any musician will sympathize with Locke in his resentment of ignorant criticism; but in these days we should consider it both undignified and useless to express it in print.

Chapter Seven

PLAYS WITH MUSIC

The joint effort of Shadwell and Locke has so far been considered rather from a French point of view, as an isolated experiment. We must now take into account the general movement of musical drama in England of which it forms a part. There are two powerful reasons for the very different course which opera took in England and in France, although the particular period was one in which French influences were exceptionally strong in the life and literature of this country. First, the English theatre, whether musical or not, depended mainly upon the support of the general public. If it pleased the King and his friends, so much the better; royal patronage doubtless encouraged the attendance of the ordinary playgoer. In Paris the theatre was much more directly dependent on the court. Molière and Lulli wrote primarily for Louis XIV and the society which had the *entrée* to the palace of Versailles. The classic tradition showed itself in music as much as in literature, and if we compare the operas of Lulli with those of Italian contemporaries, we shall notice not merely the difference of melodic idiom, but, what is much more important, the difference between French and Italian conceptions of an opera as a whole. An opera, especially a modern opera, presents us with so large and complicated a mass of material of all kinds, musical and otherwise, that it is very difficult for us to grasp the idea of regarding it as an organic whole in exactly the same sense as we regard a symphony or a sonata. It may be replied that this is a purely technical matter which appeals only to trained musicians. But our English attitude towards the drama is not very dissimilar; and though it is not necessary for the musician to acquiesce entirely in Voltaire's criticisms of Shakespeare, it must still be said that our national indifference to constructive principles in drama is a serious hindrance to the development of English opera. The first requirement of music is continuity, not merely continuity of sound, but continuity of idea. In French classical drama this continuity was attained by never allowing the stage to be empty; each character who enters is connected directly with some other character who is already on the stage, and each act moves consistently towards a definite end—a constructive system somewhat analogous to the principle of a fugue, in which the whole construction would tumble down completely if the music were allowed at any intermediate point to come to a definite close; a cadence may mark the division of a section, but a new theme must be proposed at once and the action carried on so that the movement shall never come to a standstill until the end is reached. The French, we may say, aimed at erecting a palace: the English at an agglomeration of irregular buildings which could never attain formal beauty, but only picturesqueness. Once admit picturesqueness as an ideal, and music is a most valuable resource towards heightening emotional effect and disguising irregularity of plan. English drama and, *à fortiori*, English opera presented its audience not with architecture, but with landscape gardening. If Versailles belonged to an Englishman, the façade would be smothered in crimson ramblers and Virginia creeper.

This brings us to the second point of difference, the difference which depends on the contrasting genius of the two languages.

The complex origin of the English tongue has enabled English writers to obtain those effects of diversity, of contrast, of imaginative strangeness, which have played such a dominating part in our literature. The genius of the French language, descended from its single Latin stock, has triumphed most in the contrary direction—in simplicity, in unity, in clarity and in restraint.[1]

[1] Lytton Strachey, *Landmarks in French Literature.*

It is this which accounts for the wide difference between the declamation of Lulli and that of English composers.[1] French recitative takes sentences as wholes, and seeks to reproduce their general contour even at the cost of perpetual changes of time-signature. An English composer never changes his time-signature: I cannot recall a single instance of an English recitative which fluctuates between common and triple time, nor indeed of any declamatory music in triple time at all. When Locke, for instance, breaks from common time to triple time, it means that he momentarily abandons the *parlando* style, and sets his words to a definite tune. English composers, especially of the earlier period, seem to have aimed not at expressing sentences, but at intensifying single words. A song of Lawes almost compels the singer to deliver the poem with a lingering enjoyment of the associations which each separate word suggests, and it is interesting to note how the English composers of the last generation, for example Parry and Stanford, achieved their effects in precisely the same way, due allowance being made for differences of technique. This tendency is rather less marked in Purcell, mainly because Purcell did not have such subtly imaginative words to set; moreover by Purcell's time the purely declamatory lyric was a thing of the past. But although Purcell's method is to express in his own music the fundamental idea which the poet expressed in words, rather than to take those actual words as a starting point and regard them not as symbols but as things of intrinsic value in themselves, yet he still shows a romantic intention in his habit of regarding not so much the character of the person singing as the meaning of the separate phrases which he sings. Just as the romantic play made character a mere peg on which to hang poetry, instead of making poetry the expression of character, so the romantic

---

[1] It must of course be realized that detailed criticism of this point is a matter of great complication and delicacy, because of the Italian origin common to all recitative, including that of Lulli, which, though accepted by most French critics as typically French, is yet very different from the attempts of his French predecessors.

composer and the romantic librettist, instead of employing music to express a dramatic idea, made drama merely an excuse for musical entertainment. It must not be supposed however that every musical play in the latter half of the seventeenth century merits this condemnation in an equal degree.

The romantic play with music was a gradual growth, and was the natural outcome of Elizabethan traditions. The importance assigned to music in the plays of Shakespeare's day has already been mentioned, and it appears that no scruple was shown even then about making musical additions to the works of Shakespeare himself, as the Folio of 1623 shows. The scenes for the witches in *Macbeth* not being sufficiently developed, additional matter was added from Middleton's play *The Witch*, which was set to music by Robert Johnson, composer of the songs in *The Tempest* and other dramatic music. When D'Avenant revived *Macbeth* after the Restoration, he not only retained the interpolations set by Johnson, very possibly with Johnson's music, but added some more of his own, for which music was provided by Locke. The play was extremely popular, and we gather from Pepys that the scenery, music, and dancing were among the features that contributed most largely to its success. It must be remembered that the music which Locke wrote for this early revival was quite distinct from the music to *Macbeth* popularly attributed to him.

The first revival of *Macbeth* under D'Avenant has been assigned to 1663. It was evidently given again early in 1673, and Duffett parodied it in 1674 in the epilogue to his skit on Settle's *Empress of Morocco*. The parody shows the importance which was attached to the scenic effects and to the flying of the witches.

The most renowned and melodious Song of *John Dory* being heard as it were in the Air, sung in parts by Spirits, to raise the expectation, and charm the audience with thoughts sublime and worthy of that Heroick Scene which follows. The scene opens:

Thunder and lightning is discover'd, not behind Painted Tiffany to blind and amuse the Senses, but openly, by the most excellent way of Mustard-bowl and Salt-Peter.

Three Witches fly over the Pit Riding upon Beesomes...*Heccate* descends over the Stage in a Glorious Charriott adorn'd with Pictures of Hell and Devils, and made of a large Wicker Basket.

Two spirits enter with burning brandy, which they drink; Hecate and the witches sing

A health, a health to Mother C[resswell]

to the well-known tune of *A boat, a boat.* Mr Montague Summers curiously supposes this tune to be identical with that of *Here's a health unto his Majesty.*

Of Locke's original *Macbeth* music only a few fragments have survived. Revivals of *Macbeth* took place in 1682 and 1689, and Mr W. J. Lawrence has suggested that it was for one of these that the music popularly ascribed to Locke was written. This music was published in 1750 under the editorship of Boyce. Various manuscripts of it exist, which differ from each other. Dr Cummings, who possessed one of them, maintained that it was a youthful composition of Purcell. This view has been accepted by Mr W. J. Lawrence and also by Dr Ernest Walker; Mr Barclay Squire refused to admit the possibility of Purcell's authorship, and suggested that it may have been written by Leveridge.

If the *Macbeth* music is by Purcell, it must have been written for the revival of 1682. For Purcell's style at this period we may look at the *Welcome Odes* of 1680–83 and the twelve sonatas of 1683. For 1689, the other date suggested by Mr Lawrence, we have *Dido and Aeneas* as an example of Purcell's dramatic method.

Compared with the opera, compared even with the earliest *Welcome Odes*, the *Macbeth* music is crude and awkward. If we are to choose between 1682 and 1689 as possible dates for it, the earlier year is certainly to be preferred. The rough and sometimes even ungainly style of the music might be assumed to be due to a recognized traditional treatment of the subject, as well as to the necessity of conforming to popular demands. There is nothing terrible about these witches; but the mere fact that the additions from Middleton were always considered inseparable from Shakespeare's tragedy shows us that these characters were not regarded as very different in their nature from Shadwell's grotesque Mother Demdike and her crew.[1] It is important to remember this, because in reading the *Macbeth* music nowadays we are naturally tempted to look for a romantic interpretation such as Weber might have given us. Also we must be careful not to judge the music as a concert-piece, and our inevitable difficulty in visualizing a stage performance will be much aggravated if we are out of sympathy with the theatrical methods and principles of the Restoration. If we can once bring ourselves to accept the grotesque view of the witches, we can see many merits in the music. It may be useful to analyse a short extract from the opening of Act III.

One's first impression of this is that it is childish and trivial, the melody barren and the harmony undistinguished. It has neither the thrill of romance nor the grotesque uncouthness which a later age expects. It suggests no picture to the mind. But let us make our own picture of the stage at the theatre in Dorset Gardens. A shrill voice calls 'Hecate!'; Hecate answers in the moment of rising from the nether regions. The rhythmical flow of 'My little, little, little spirit' carries on the sense of motion, while Hecate makes ready for flight. Before the song is well started, it is interrupted by the same shrill, insistent voice, calling quicker than before.[2] Again the time quickens; the rhythm of Hecate suddenly changes from the easy swing of triple time to a new and more energetic figure, the effect of which is heightened by responsive imitations in the accompaniment. The firm and decisive cadence in C major brings Hecate to a standstill to call the witches by name. They answer promptly in turn, the bass stamping on

---

[1] See *The Lancashire Witches*.
[2] The various signs for common time indicate a series of accelerations.

MACBETH

?LERIDGE   *From the Fitzwilliam MS.*

Symphony at the descending of the Machine in the Third Act

Strings

Slow   (*Hecate*)

Hackett,   Hackett,   Hackett,   Come a - way   Hark, Hark, I'm call'd,

Strings

My   little, little, little   spir - it,   see,   see,   see,   see,

Sits   in   a   fog - gy   cloud   and   waits   for   me,   My

little,   little,   little,   spi - rit,   see,   see,   see   see,

132

Sits in a fog - gy cloud and waits for me. Hackett,

Hackett, I come, I come, I come, I come, I come, I

come, I come, I come, I come, with all the speed I

And Hopper too and Hellway too, We

Here   Here

may. Where's Puckle? Where's Stradling?

In the Machine

want but you, we want but you!   Come a - way, Come a - way, Come,

Come, Come, Come, Come, Come, Come, Come, Come a - way, make

from subdominant to subdominant—C, F, B flat, E flat—as the last witches seem to tumble over one another in their eagerness to join in the fun.

'We want but you, we want but you!' The same high F is heard on which Hecate was first called, as the climax of the scene, before they mount their broomsticks for the *Walkürenritt* of 'Come away, come away'; even the repetitions of the word 'come', so characteristic of Purcell and his contemporaries, to the scorn of Burney, add to the hammering force of the phrase. This is only the beginning of a scene too long for quotation here. The vocal phrases are constantly interrupted by scraps of instrumental music of a violently energetic character; Hecate sings a sustained song of regular form, followed by a short chorus which develops to a quite Handelian climax, the orchestra repeating the last eight bars as the witches finally fly away.

It is not great music by itself, but it is effective stage music. It cannot thrill us as the music of the Wolfsschlucht can at the mere sight of the printed page; but if we have the stage action before us, it can excite our nerves and help to create an illusion of the supernatural by its energy and swiftness.

It is worth noting that the whole of the *Macbeth* music, including four separate scenes, is in the same key, F major. As we have already observed in the music of the masques, this gives the work a musical unity, and enables the composer to emphasize rhetorical points by momentary allusions to other keys, and to arrange his movements so as to work towards a final climax with a sense of definite purpose.

There exists yet another musical setting of *Macbeth* by John Eccles. This was probably written at a much later date, perhaps even after Purcell's death. It shows to a slight extent the influence of the music popularly ascribed to Locke, but it is more skilful in its musical technique. On the other hand, it has much less dramatic force. It has not even the merit of crudity; it is thoroughly conventional and uninspired. Eccles often showed considerable talent for a swinging English tune of popular character; but he possessed nothing of the rhythmical originality which makes Locke, in his genuine and much earlier work, an outstanding figure in the dramatic music of the seventeenth century.

More important than *Macbeth*, in the history of English stage music, are the various operatic versions of *The Tempest*. This play was revived in 1667. The version used was the joint production of D'Avenant and Dryden, and is chiefly notable for the additional characters introduced. Dryden in his preface alludes to plays on the same subject by Fletcher and Sir John Suckling,

'but Sir William D'Avenant', he continues, 'as he was a Man of quick and piercing imagination, soon found that somewhat might be added to the Design of *Shakespear*, of which neither *Fletcher* nor *Suckling* had ever thought: and therefore to put the last hand to it, he design'd the counterpart to *Shakespear's* Plot, namely that of a Man who had never seen a Woman; that by this means those two characters of Innocence and Love might the more illustrate and commend each other.'

To balance Miranda, who has never seen a man, Hippolito is introduced, a young man who has been secluded in a cave by Prospero from infancy. As it is necessary to provide Hippolito with a wife at the end of the play, Miranda is given a sister, Dorinda, and even Ariel is not allowed to remain a bachelor. The main purpose of these new characters is mainly to display their 'innocence and love' in remarks to which the audience could attach double meanings. The play is often mentioned by Pepys, who saw it several times. It has generally been supposed that the music for this performance was written by John Bannister and Pelham Humfrey; but Mr Barclay Squire has shown that the music of Bannister and Humfrey belongs to Shadwell's version of the play.

In 1671 the Duke's company opened a new theatre in Dorset Gardens, which was a building of some magnificence, especially adapted to spectacular plays. Sir William D'Avenant had died in 1668, but his theatrical privilege was carried on by his widow and her son, Dr Charles D'Avenant.

Macbeth was revived again

being drest in all its finery, as new Cloath's, new Scenes, Machines, as flyings for the Witches; with all the Singing and Dancing in it: The first composed by Mr. *Locke*, the other by Mr. *Channell* and Mr. *Joseph Preist*; it being all Excellently perform'd, being in the nature of an Opera, it Recompens'd double the Expence; it proves still a lasting Play.[1]

Of *King Lear*, Downes goes out of his way to tell us that it was acted 'exactly as Mr. *Shakespear* wrote it'. In 1673 or 1674 *The Tempest* suffered a further change, being 'made into an Opera' by Shadwell.[2]

---

[1] Downes, *Roscius Anglicanus*.

[2] For the complicated bibliographical history of Shadwell's version see W. J. Lawrence, *The Elizabethan Playhouse*, First Series, and W. Barclay Squire, 'Purcell's Dramatic Music,' *Sammelbände der Internationalen Musikgesellschaft*, v. 551. Mr Squire has thrown further light on the problem in 'The Music of Shadwell's 'Tempest'', *The Musical Quarterly* (New York), October, 1921.

Shadwell based his version on that of Dryden and D'Avenant, but added more songs, and a masque of Neptune and Amphitrite at the end. The music was the work of various hands. Uninteresting settings of the Ariel songs were made by Bannister and Pelham Humfrey; an Italian composer then resident in London, Pietro Reggio,[1] set the new song, 'Arise, ye subterranean winds', and a large amount of instrumental music was written by Locke and another Italian, Giovanni Battista Draghi.[2] Draghi's music has not survived; Locke's was printed along with the music to *Psyche* in 1675. It consists of dances and other pieces for instruments, some of which are of great interest.

There is some difficulty in fixing the exact date of Shadwell's version of *The Tempest*. Downes ascribes it to 1673, and suggests that it came out before *Psyche*,[3] in which case we might suppose that Betterton in suggesting the idea of *Psyche* to Shadwell had been directly encouraged by the success of *The Tempest*. Mr Lawrence, however, brings forward arguments to prove that *The Tempest* did not make its appearance until April 1674.

There seems to have been a great outburst of musical drama in 1674, for in addition to the French opera season already noted in the last chapter, there was a performance at court of a masque by John Crowne called *Calisto or the Chaste Nymph*, which contained a large amount of music. Crowne in his preface definitely states that the whole of the music was composed by Nicholas Staggins, a mediocre musician whom Charles II eventually foisted on the unwilling university of Cambridge as its first Professor of Music.

---

[1] Reggio is supposed to be the 'slovenly and ugly fellow, Signor Pedro, who sings Italian songs to the theorbo most neatly' mentioned by Pepys, July 22, 1664. A correct and rather old-fashioned composer, he appears to have had many admirers in Oxford.

[2] Draghi was a very popular composer in London, where he was generally known as 'Signor Baptist'. He is alluded to by this name in some of Shadwell's plays. Hardly any music of his has come down to us; his principal work is a set of suites for harpsichord published early in the eighteenth century.

[3] See his account of *Psyche* quoted in the preceding chapter.

It appears, however, that the direction of the performance was given to Cambert, and it is hardly likely that he would have consented to this if he had not contributed some of the music himself.[1] The question is, however, of little importance, since the masque is a very dull production as literature, and the music has not survived.

Other plays in which music had a considerable part were *Circe*, by Dr Charles D'Avenant (1676), and Shadwell's re-arrangement of *Timon of Athens* (1678). The music to the former was composed by Bannister, and for the latter play Grabu appears to have been responsible.

It is not necessary to consider all these plays in detail; but an analysis of *The Tempest* will give a general idea of the methods pursued at the Theatre in Dorset Gardens. Here is the first stage direction:

The Front of the Stage is open'd, and the Band of 24 Violins, with the Harpsicals and Theorbo's which accompany the Voices, are plac'd between the Pit and the Stage. While the Overture is playing, the Curtain rises, and discovers a new Frontispiece, joined to the great Pilasters, on each side of the stage. This Frontispiece is a noble Arch, supported by large wreathed Columns of the *Corinthian* Order; the wreathing of the Columns are beautifi'd with Roses wound round them, and several *Cupids* flying about them. On the Cornice, just over the Capitals, sits on either side a Figure, with a trumpet in one hand, and a Palm in the other, representing *Fame*. A little further on the same Cornice, on each side of a Compass-pediment, lie a Lion and a Unicorn, the Supporters of the Royal Arms of *England*. In the middle of the Arch are several Angels, holding the King's Arms, as if they were placing them in the midst of that Compass-pediment.

Behind this is the Scene, which represents a thick Cloudy Sky, a very Rocky Coast, and a Tempestuous Sea in perpetual Agitation. This Tempest (suppos'd to be rais'd by Magick) has many dreadful objects in it, as several Spirits in horrid shapes flying down amidst the Sailers, then rising and crossing in the Air. And when the Ship is sinking, the whole House is darken'd, and a shower of Fire falls upon 'em. This is accompanied by

---

[1] H. Cart de Lafontaine, *The King's Musick.*

Lightning, and several Claps of Thunder to the end of the Storm.

The first sentence shows the importance which was attached to the music. The orchestra was double the usual size[1] and was placed in the position now habitual, instead of being in the gallery over the stage, which was the usual practice of the time.[2]

The new arrangement was introduced from Italy and France. The advantages of it were many; it was no doubt possible to employ more instruments than could be accommodated above, and with a large body of singers on the stage, it must have been much easier to keep all the musicians in time together. The change of position had moreover a deeper significance. It meant that the presence of a band of instrumentalists was accepted as a recognized convention: that instead of the musicians being either invisible agents producing the mysterious sounds associated with angels above or devils below (in which latter position, as Pepys pointed out, 'there is no hearing of the basses at all, nor very well of the trebles'), or visible actors taking part in the play under such names as Simon Catling, Hugh Rebeck and James Soundpost,[3] the music which they made was to all present as normal a constituent of the mental atmosphere as the oxygen which entered the lungs of audience and actors alike, whether they were supposed to be in London or on an enchanted island, was of the physical.

The description of the stage shows how the Italian tradition of the early masques was still kept up. The 'frontispiece' was what we should describe as an inner proscenium, not permanent, but designed for one particular play only. The actual 'scene' does not appear to have been much of an advance upon the scenery of *The Siege of Rhodes*. The wings were probably conventional rocks, which could remain in

---

[1] The word violins must be taken as equivalent to the modern expression 'strings' so as to include instruments of all sizes.

[2] The music gallery is shown in the illustrations to Settle's *Empress of Morocco*.

[3] *Romeo and Juliet*, IV. v.

position all through the opera; it will be observed that the later scenes, like the 'tempestuous sea', could be represented simply by back flats. The great attraction to the public at this time was undoubtedly the 'flyings' which are constantly mentioned in the plays and their prologues, in Pepys and elsewhere. Thus Shadwell himself in his prologue to this very play says:

> Old sinners thus—
> When they feel Age and Impotence approach,
> Double the charge of Furniture and Coach;
> When you of witt and sence were weary growne,
> Romantick, riming, fustian Playes were showne,
> We then to flying Witches did advance,
> And for your pleasure traffic'd into ffrance.
> From thence new acts to please you we have sought ⎫
> We have machines to some perfection brought, ⎬
> And above 30 warbling voyces gott. ⎭
> Many a god and goddesse you will heare ⎫
> And we have Singing, Dancing, Devils here ⎬
> Such Devils and such gods, are very Deare. ⎭

The change to the second scene after the shipwreck was made in view of the audience.

In the midst of the Shower of Fire the Scene changes. The Cloudy Sky, Rocks, and Sea vanish; and when the Lights return, discover that Beautiful part of the Island, which was the Habitation of *Prospero*; 'Tis compos'd of three walks of Cypress-trees, each Side-walk leads to a Cave, in one of which *Prospero* keeps his daughters, in the other *Hippolito*: The Middle-Walk is of great depth and leads to an open part of the Island.

This scene may perhaps have been a 'releive' such as was designed for *The Siege of Rhodes*, employing more than one set of flats. Another scene, representing the wilder part of the Island 'compos'd of divers sorts of trees, and barren places, with a prospect of the Sea at a great distance', is employed in Act II. These two latter scenes are used alternately from this point to the end of the play. In Act II there is a scene corresponding more or less to part of Shakespeare's Act II, sc. i, in which Alonzo speaks of himself as the cause

141

of his son Ferdinand's death. Music is heard, growing gradually louder; the stage opens in several places and voices are heard singing. The characters on the stage are in great terror:

> *Antonio.* Ah! what amazing sounds are these we hear?
> *Gonzalo.* What horrid Masque will the dire Fiends present?

The Devils then rise singing a chorus, interrupted every now and then by spoken comments from Alonzo and the others. They are followed by four figures representing Pride, Fraud, Rapine and Murder,[1] who each sing a few lines, after which the Devils dance and all vanish. Alonzo and his friends propose to go and look for something to eat, but 'as they are going out, a Devil rises just before them, at which they start and are frightened'. Alonzo exclaims 'O Heavens! yet more apparitions!' on which the Devil sings the song 'Arise, ye subterranean winds'. At the end of this 'Two winds rise. Ten more enter and dance. At the end of the dance, Three winds sink, the rest drive *Alonzo, Antonio, Gonzalo* off'. This ends Act II.

Act III begins at once with Ariel singing 'Come unto these yellow sands'. This scene in Shakespeare belongs to Act I, sc. ii. It is perhaps worth while printing Ferdinand's few lines of reply in the words of Shakespeare, and in the versions of Dryden and Shadwell, so that the gradual process of ruin may be seen at one glance.

SHAKESPEARE.

> Where should this music be? i' th' air, or th' earth?
> It sounds no more;—and sure, it waits upon
> Some god o' th' island. Sitting on a bank,
> Weeping again the king my father's wrack,
> This music crept by me upon the waters,
> Allaying both their fury, and my passion,
> With its sweet air: thence I have follow'd it—
> Or it hath drawn me rather,—but 'tis gone.
> No, it begins again.

---

[1] Compare with this the appearance of the four allegorical figures in the first act of *Psyche*.

DRYDEN.

Where should this Musick be? i' th' Air, or th' Earth?
It sounds no more, and sure it waits upon some God
O' th' Island, sitting on a Bank, weeping against the Duke
My Father's Wrack. This Musick hover'd o'er me
On the waters, allaying both their Fury and my Passion
With charming Airs; thence have I follow'd it (or it
Hath drawn me rather) but 'tis gone;
No, it begins again.

SHADWELL.

Where should this Musick be? i' th' air, earth? it sounds no
more, and sure it waits upon some God i' th' island; sitting on
a Bank, weeping against the Duke; my Father's wrack'd; This
Musick hover'd on the waters, allaying both their fury and my
passion with charming Aires. Thence I have follow'd it, (or it
has drawn me rather) but 'tis gone: No, it begins again.

The song 'Full fathom five' is given to Milcha, Ariel's
companion spirit. After a few lines from Ferdinand the scene
changes. A scene follows for Prospero and the two girls,
after which the wild island reappears and Alonzo enters with
Antonio and Gonzalo. This scene corresponds to Shakespeare's Act III, sc. iii. Shakespeare here introduces 'solemn
and strange music'. Spirits bring in a banquet; just as Alonzo
is going to eat, Ariel appears as a harpy and the banquet
vanishes. Ariel makes a long speech, then vanishes in
thunder, after which the 'shapes' re-enter to soft music,
'dance with mocks and mows, and carry out the table'. In
Shadwell's version Ariel and Milcha, invisible, sing a song
'Dry those eyes which are overflowing';[1] then comes a 'dance
of fantastick spirits', after which the banquet is brought in.
After a short dialogue, two spirits descend and fly away with
the table. There is no appearance or speech of Ariel, and
the other characters merely leave the stage. A little later we
have Ferdinand and Ariel's echo song, somewhat extended,
with another song for Ariel, 'Kind fortune smiles'.

---

[1] These words are suggested by the song of Ceres in Shakespeare's Act IV,
sc. i.

Act IV is taken up mainly with the affairs of Hippolito and Dorinda; Hippolito being of a polygamous disposition excites the jealousy of Ferdinand, who fights with him. Miranda and Dorinda also quarrel. In Act v the characters are all reconciled, after which Prospero entertains them with a masque. 'Scene changes to the Rocks, with the Arch of Rocks and calm Sea. Musick playing on the Rocks'. Neptune, Amphitrite, Oceanus and Tethys appear in a chariot drawn by sea-horses; Aeolus is summoned with four winds, and a sort of masque is performed in which twelve tritons appear, more or less as if they were 'grand masquers', and dance with the singers. The play concludes with a change of scene to 'the Rising Sun, and a number of Aerial Spirits in the Air', after which Ariel and the rest sing 'Where the bee sucks'.

Successful as they were, Shadwell's 'operas' of this kind were not without their detractors. An amusing commentary on them is supplied by the travesties written by Thomas Duffett for performance at the rival theatre. It is not surprising that Duffett has been almost entirely ignored by literary historians; the entertainments which he parodied were from a purely literary point of view so contemptible that the caricatures would naturally seem to be nothing more than grossness and scurrility for their own sakes. They have none of the witty dialogue of *The Beggar's Opera*, and even that amusing work would have had little interest for modern readers if no record had survived of the music to which its songs were sung. But to anyone who will take the trouble to read Shadwell's 'operas' and try to visualize their effect in performance, setting aside all conventional prejudices in favour of Shakespeare, and endeavouring to look at the stage with the eyes of Pepys and his friends, Duffett's parodies are representative of the outlook of seventeenth-century audiences in the same way as the ephemeral burlesques of the modern pantomime and music-hall are representative of the theatre in our own day.

Dryden and D'Avenant's version of *The Tempest* had already been scoffed at in *The Rehearsal*.[1] This play is said to have been several years in preparation, and the principal character, Mr Bayes, sometimes represents D'Avenant (with the broken nose) and sometimes Dryden. First printed in 1672 and reprinted with alterations several times, it contains a good many allusions to music. The prologue for Thunder and Lightning is a parody of a song in dialogue between Jack-with-the-lantern and Evening in Sir Robert Stapylton's *The Slighted Maid* (1663), which may perhaps have been set to music by Locke;[2] the dance of soldiers to the tune which 'begins swift and ends slow' may perhaps refer to *The History of Sir Francis Drake*, especially as Locke was just the composer who would have puzzled his dancers by trying to make his music over-expressive. Bayes' first remark in the act which follows is, 'Now Sir, this I do, because my fancie in this Play is to end every Act with a Dance', and a few pages later he says, 'you must ever interlard your Plays with Songs, Ghosts and Dances'. In Act IV the banquet produced from Lardella's coffin, which is snatched away by Drawcansir, suggests the banquet offered by Ariel to Alonzo. The appearance of the two kings of Brentford in the clouds (Act V) singing a duet[3] is a close parody of the duet in Dryden's *Tyrannick Love*, Act IV, sc. i, when the two spirits Nakar and Damilcar descend in clouds and sing the duet 'Hark, my Damilcar, we are call'd below',[4] and the battle between the General and Lieutenant-General in the same act is derived from two or three separate scenes in *The Siege of Rhodes*. Mr Bayes sums up his whole battle 'in the representation of two persons

[1] Act II, sc. v: Udzookers, you dance worse than the Angels in *Harry* the Eight, or the fat spirits in *The Tempest*, I gad.

[2] Locke provided music for the same writer's *The Stepmother*.

[3] *Bayes*. Now, because the two Right Kings descend from above, I make 'em sing to the Tune and Stile of our modern Spirits.

[4] This was later set to music by Purcell (about 1695). Whether the parody was sung to the music of an anonymous setting dated June 9, 1681, which is preserved in the British Museum (Add. MS. 19759), cannot be definitely ascertained.

only, no more; and yet so lively, that, I vow to gad, you would swear ten thousand men were at it really engag'd'. The two combatants appear in armour with drawn swords and a scarlet ribbon at their wrists (apparently a recognized stage convention to represent fighting), each holding a lute in his hand.

I make 'em, Sir, play the battel in *Recitativo*. And here's the conceipt. Just at the very same instant that one sings, the other, Sir, recovers you his Sword, and puts himself in a warlike posture: so that you have at once your ear entertain'd with Musick, and good Language, and your eye satisfi'd with the garb, and accoutrements of war.

The long-standing popularity of *The Rehearsal*[1] and of Sheridan's *The Critic*, which is largely derived from the older play, is due to the fact that they satirize not merely the dramatic follies of the moment, but the perennial characteristics of authors, actors and managers. Duffett's parodies belong entirely to their own day, and are scarcely intelligible to those who do not know the originals. A parody of Settle's *The Empress of Morocco* was followed by an 'Epilogue in the manner of *Macbeth*', in which Hecate summons witches under the names of various well-known disreputable females. Duffett also wrote *The Mock-Tempest*, in which Ferdinand is transformed into a Quaker. This entertainment has very little to do with Shakespeare, and its satire is directed entirely at Shadwell's operatic version. Instead of the masque of Neptune and Amphitrite Duffett gives us a view of Bridewell 'with prisoners in several postures of labour and punishment'. Caliban and Sycorax sing a duet; the place of Aeolus and the winds is taken by a head-keeper and his assistants.[2] The play ends with the following version of Ariel's song:

> Where good Ale is there suck I,
> In a Cobblers Stall I lye,

[1] It was revived in 1914 by the Sheffield Repertory Theatre under the direction of Mr Orlando Barnett.

[2] Possibly Gay had some knowledge of Duffett's works when he wrote *The Beggar's Opera*.

While the Watch are passing by;
Then about the Streets I fly,
After Cullies merrily.
And I merrily, merrily take up my clo'se
Under the Watch and the Constable's nose.[1]

Mr Summers mentions another burlesque of *The Tempest* written by Robert Brough in 1848 as a skit on the Liverpool revival of 1847. Whether the Liverpool company followed Shakespeare's original version or that of the Restoration Mr Summers does not say; but the Restoration version was still current on the English stage. I am indebted to the kindness of Mr W. Bridges Adams for a copy of a playbill dated July 23, 1845, announcing a performance of *The Tempest* in the Theatre at Southwell, in which not only Hypolito (*sic*) and Dorinda appear in the list of characters, but also Rosebud and Bluebell, two spirits whose names suggest that they belonged to the same century as the performance.

Shadwell himself tried a strange experiment in *The Lancashire Witches* (1681), a play which encountered some hostility as it was alleged to be a satire on the Church of England. Shadwell protests against the accusation in his preface, and says that he could not imagine how any party could be offended by the play except the Papists. The play deals in the main with the usual subject-matter of Restoration comedy, but introduces also two ecclesiastical characters—Smerk, a Chaplain, 'foolish, knavish, popish, arrogant, insolent, yet for his interest, slavish', and Tegue O Divelly, an Irish priest, 'an equal mixture of fool and knave'. There is also Sir Jeffery Shacklehead, a justice and a great persecutor of witches. Sir Jeffery seems to have been introduced mainly as an excuse for bringing in the witches, and the witches, as Shadwell admits, were introduced for the sake of the machinery and music which accompanied them. The curious

---

[1] *The Mock-Tempest* is printed in full in Montague Summers' *Shakespeare Adaptations*, London, 1922.

thing about the play is that, whereas the superstitious perse-
cutors of witches are held up to ridicule, the witches themselves are treated as having genuinely supernatural powers.
Each act in the printed play is supplied with copious notes
giving all possible authority for everything that the witches
do or say, after the manner of Ben Jonson in his *Masque of
Queens*, though Shadwell professes himself, 'as it is said of
Surly in *The Alchemist*, somewhat costive of belief'. His
justification of the 'magical part', as he calls it, is interesting
as illustrating the view of the age both as regards the theatre
and as regards belief.

For the Actions, if I had not represented them as those of real
Witches, but had show'd the Ignorance, Fear, Melancholy,
Malice, Confederacy, and imposture that contribute to the belief
of witchcraft, the people had wanted diversion, and there had
been another clamor against it, it would have been call'd Atheis-
tical, by a prevailing party who take it ill that the power of the
Devil should be lessen'd, and attribute more miracles to a silly
old Woman, than ever they did to the greatest of Prophets, and
by this means the Play might have been Silenced.

The amount of actual music required in the play is not very
great, but it was no doubt a very essential feature of the
magical part, and the play is worth remembering as a tentative experiment in the direction of that mixed comic and
fantastic opera which we should naturally associate rather
with the German romantic movement of the nineteenth
century.

Chapter Eight

FRENCH INFLUENCES

During the period covered by the preceding chapter the main interest of English opera has been literary, dramatic and scenic rather than musical. With the advent of Purcell a new period begins in which the musical interest very soon throws all other features in the shade. There has been much controversy over the chronology of Purcell's musical career. The historians of an earlier generation (Hawkins, Rimbault etc.), assuming that his dramatic music was written invariably for the first production of the plays in which he collaborated, have assigned to a very early period of his life work which modern criticism tends to remove to a much later date.[1] But there seems no reason to doubt the statement of Downes as to Purcell's first appearance as a dramatic composer. Of *Theodosius, or the Force of Love*, a tragedy by Nathaniel Lee acted in 1680 at the Duke's Theatre, he says, 'All the Parts in't being perfectly perform'd, with several Entertainments of Singing; Compos'd by the famous Master Mr *Henry Purcell*, (being the first he e'er Compos'd for the Stage) made it a living and Gainful Play to the Company'.

Purcell was at this time twenty-one or twenty-two years of age. He had hitherto devoted himself almost exclusively to church music, studying under Pelham Humfrey and John Blow, whom he succeeded in this year as organist of Westminster Abbey. But he must have known something of the theatrical traditions: his father had acted and sung in the

[1] It is not possible here to discuss in detail the arguments on which these dates have been established: the reader must be referred to Mr Barclay Squire's article in *Purcell's Dramatic Music*, Sammelbände der Internationalen Musikgesellschaft, v. 489, and to Mr W. J. Lawrence's *The Elizabethan Playhouse*, First Series. These conclusions unfortunately appeared too late for inclusion in vol. III of *The Oxford History of Music* (1902).

first production of *The Siege of Rhodes,* and there is every probability that he himself was closely in touch with Matthew Locke. Locke had been a friend of his father's and the son composed an elegy on his death in 1677. Whatever his personal relations with Locke may have been it is at any rate abundantly clear that he was very much influenced by the study of his works in the formation of his own musical style. It must be remembered also that in the seventeenth century it was not so absurd as it might seem now for an organist to compose an opera. The English church music of the Restoration has met with much adverse criticism, both now and in its own day. Purcell and his contemporaries have often been censured for not writing in the severe style of the sixteenth century; but we might equally well censure the composers of the sixteenth century for not adopting the style of the fifteenth when they wrote for the church.

It was about 1663 that 'the king achieved the characteristic and subtle stroke of humour of sending Pelham Humfrey over to France to study the methods of the most celebrated composer of theatrical music of the time in order to learn how to compose English church music'.[1] It was in 1664 that Lulli composed that magnificent *Miserere* for double chorus and orchestra which caused Mme de Sevigné to exclaim 'Je ne crois pas qu'il y ait d'autre musique dans les cieux'. Its majestic dignity, its profound feeling and its technical skill place it on a level with any of Purcell's best work. Of frivolity it does not show the faintest trace.[2] Lulli's massive and imposing style of ecclesiastical music is well criticized by a more recent French writer:

Ce style harmonique que nous accusons aujourd'hui de mono-tonie, et auquel nous préférons l'agencement industrieux des combinaisons contrapontiques, était pourtant un progrès. Il

[1] C. H. H. Parry, 'The Music of the Seventeenth Century', *Oxford History of Music,* vol. III.

[2] Lulli's *Miserere* was performed under the direction of M. Félix Raugel at a recital of French church music organized for the congress of the International Musical Society in the chapel of the Invalides at Paris, June 9, 1914.

mettait fin à l'insupportable bavardage des compositeurs sujets
à la fugue chronique et à leur malencontreuse habitude de parler
sans cesse pour ne rien dire. Il permettait à la pensée musicale
de se libérer des formes traditionnelles, de s'exprimer plus naturellement. Il substituait au langage convenu de la rhétorique sonore,
un langage plus simple, plus touchant, plus humain.[1]

With English church music this book is not concerned.
But had Lulli never even written a note for the theatre, there
could have been no better influence on English dramatic
music than the tendencies summed up in the paragraph
quoted above. We can understand from this how the English
church of Purcell's day supplied no bad training for the
composer of English opera. The church composers had the
finest of all possible words to set. Our church composers
have the same words now, it may be replied. But Purcell
and his contemporaries had an enormous advantage which
it is most important not to forget; those sacred words were
the words of their own century, alive and direct, not yet
overlaid with the deadening tradition of two hundred years'
continual reverence. The literary movement of the earlier
generation had taught the composers to declaim words so as
to bring out their deepest poetical significance. Contact with
Italian and Franco-Italian music had added to their knowledge of purely musical resource. Their work in the theatre
must often have been hampered by the inevitable necessity
of considering popular taste and its effect on the receipts.
Church music in the grand manner (we must remember
that the age of bright and attractive $1\frac{1}{2}d$. anthems had not
yet arrived) gave the composer fuller scope for studying how
to combine forceful declamation with the technique of
structural development.

If the church demanded the music of the theatre, the
theatre was equally ready to utilize the music of the church.
The only musical scenes of any importance in *Theodosius* are
scenes of religious ceremony, the first being the reception of

---

[1] H. Prunières, *Lully*, in the series *Les Musiciens Célèbres*.

two ladies into a cloister and the second being the heroine's confirmation. Except for a few songs, mostly sung between the acts and having little or nothing to do with the drama, the music of the first act is all that has survived of Purcell's work. The play is in no sense to be regarded as an opera, and would have little claim to mention here if it were not for Purcell's connection with it. The description of the first scene is worth quoting, as it is very characteristic:

A stately Temple, which represents the Christian Religion, as in its first Magnificence—Being but lately established at *Rome* and *Constantinople*. The side scenes shew the horrid tortures, with which the *Roman* tyrants persecuted the Church; and the flat scene, which is the limit of the prospect, discovers an Altar richly adorn'd, before it *Constantine*, suppos'd kneels with Commanders about him, gazing at a bloody Cross in the Aire, which being incompass'd with many Angels, offers it self to view, with these words distinctly written, (*In hoc signo vinces!*)[1] Instruments are heard, and many Attendants: The Ministers at Divine Service, walk busily up and down. Till *Atticus* the chief of all the Priests, and successor of *St. Chrysostom*, in rich Robes, comes forward with the Philosopher *Leontine*. The Waiters in ranks bowing all the way before him.

A short chorus is heard at a distance, which was perhaps repeated later on, when after some explanatory dialogue Flavilla and Marina, two ladies of the Imperial house, are received into the monastic life by Atticus and the other priests. This scene is all set to music, and although Atticus is an important character in the play, the two ladies have no speaking parts at all and are not seen again. Purcell's music is of a very simple character, and the only employment of instruments is in a short symphony for two flutes.[2] There is nothing really dramatic though the music is in places decidedly expressive. Primitive as it may seem in comparison with Purcell's later scenes of religious ceremony, it is yet a considerable advance on Locke's temple scene in *Psyche*. Technically as well as emotionally its range is wider, and

[1] These characters are all represented in painting on the back flats.
[2] A flourish of recorders is indicated in the course of the preceding dialogue.

though it makes no use of curious effects, such as the echo, it shows a much greater command of the ordinary resources of melody, harmony and tonality.

In spite of the success of *Theodosius*,[1] Purcell's work for the stage was for the most part of a very slight order for some years. It is not necessary to consider here the few plays for which Purcell wrote nothing more than occasional songs, or perhaps an overture and a set of act-tunes. There is however one work of a more important character which must in all probability be assigned to this period, though there is much difficulty in fixing its date, and some uncertainty even in attributing it to Purcell.

The strongest musical influences on Purcell during his early period of activity must have been those of Locke, Pelham Humfrey, and Blow. Pelham Humfrey, as a pupil of Lulli, was naturally more familiar with the music of Paris; Locke and Blow leant rather to the Italian style, as represented mainly by Carissimi and Cesti. Purcell's *Welcome Odes* of this period may be described as on the whole English in character, showing Italian influence only in so far as all serious English music of the period did; but it is clear that Purcell, no doubt out of deference to the King's taste, has endeavoured conscientiously to assume a more definitely Parisian manner, especially in the instrumental sections. The French style is occasionally perceptible even in the recitatives. It seems however that in 1683 or slightly earlier, Purcell had made a very careful study of more modern Italian music, and had allowed himself to become very deeply impressed by it. The outcome of this was the set of twelve sonatas published in 1683, in which as he tells us himself, he had 'faithfully endeavour'd a just imitation of the most fam'd Italian Masters; principally, to bring the seriousness and gravity of that sort of Musick into vogue, and reputation

---

[1] The play was frequently acted in the eighteenth century, and Burney mentions the processional music (presumably the lost Act II) as still popular in his day.

among our Country-men, whose humor, 'tis time now, should
begin to loath the levity, and balladry of our neighbours'.
It was this strong modern Italian influence which made the
composition of *Dido and Aeneas* possible. Its first dramatic
fruits are to be seen in the music which Purcell wrote for
Circe, a play by Charles D'Avenant, son of Sir William. This
play had originally appeared in 1677 with music by Bannister,
and it is supposed that Purcell's music was written for a
revival in 1685. The play contains a large number of songs;
but Purcell appears to have set only the lengthy incantation
scene in Act I. The play is derived from the story of Iphigenia
in Tauris, but a love-interest is provided in the usual seventeenth-century manner. Circe appears as the second wife of
Thoas, King of the Scythians. Iphigenia is loved by Thoas,
and also by Ithacus, the son of Circe by Ulysses, but she
rejects their advances, and joins Circe in urging Ithacus to
marry Osmida, daughter to Thoas by a former Queen. At
the request of Ithacus, Circe summons Pluto by magical arts
in order to consult him on the difficulties of the situation.

The scene opens with an introduction for strings, the firmly
designed themes and solemn harmonies of which are clearly
ordered in a definite musical scheme which greatly strengthens
their emotional effect. A short solo for a priest leads to a
chorus, based on two themes, and constructed in a carefully
balanced binary form with an instrumental interlude in the
middle. There follows a recitative for tenor and bass priests,
the latter accompanied by strings. Hitherto all has been in
the key of C major. A third priest (alto) now sings an aria
of some length ('The air with music gently wound') in
C minor, and the same words are immediately repeated by
the chorus to a series of simpler phrases more or less derived
from the solo part. Here Circe speaks four lines and the
priests walk up to the altar. The first priest (tenor) now
invokes the demons in a song of two verses, of a decidedly
cheerful character; each verse is followed by a chorus of
about the same length, in a contrasting rhythm. Four spirits

enter, one of whom is sent off by Circe to fetch ingredients for further magical practices. Two women sing some lines describing the spirits' flight, whilst they are performing the Queen's commands, the chorus again having short alternating entries. At the bidding of Circe the magicians dance to a sort of grim minuet. This second section is all in the keys of G major and minor. Lastly Pluto is invoked directly by the second priest (bass) in an *arioso* recitative of some length, accompanied by strings throughout. This ends the scene in the original key of C major. There does not appear to be any music associated with the actual appearance of Pluto, or with the information which he proceeds to impart.

The music to *Circe* is far more interesting as music, but far less dramatic, than that to *Macbeth*. In *Macbeth* the composer seems to have witnessed a scene on the stage and to have written music to heighten its emotional effect only so far as was consistent with preserving a fairly exact synchronization. In *Circe* the poet has not planned a complete scheme of action but has roughly suggested an idea to the composer, supplying words of no dramatic value just as a peg on which the musician might hang his vocal and instrumental *scena*. There is no particular reason why anybody should sing anything, or why the scene should not have been enlarged to an indefinite extent. It is powerful and beautiful music; if a stage action can be fitted to it so much the better—if not, it does not make any very great difference. It is all held together by its symmetrical grouping of keys, and though it would have been improved by the addition of another dance and some sort of chorus at the end to make a more emphatic coda, we can still see that Purcell intended the general effect to rise to a climax in the last section. The first section, after the introductory assembly of the chorus, is intended to charm the spirits by the suavity of its melody; the second section (in G) asserts the enchantress's power over them; the third pronounces the final invocation, to which the first was only preliminary, in a tone of stately solemnity which contrasts strongly with the more vigorous rhythms of the middle section where even a slight touch of the grotesque may have been permitted. This final *arioso* is in fact one of the best declamatory solos to be found anywhere in Purcell's works. It begins on a long tonic pedal, and the bass even in the rest of the movement proceeds very slowly, though always with deliberate purpose; this gives the whole an air of immense dignity and serenity. The declamation of the voice is natural and free from exaggerations; the upper strings have parts of very independent character, and develop the salient themes of the voice part in effective imitations.

It must be frankly admitted that the whole interest of this scene is purely musical. It might be performed without action without losing any of its effectiveness; indeed a conscientious stage manager would find it a matter of some difficulty to arrange suitable movements and actions to accompany it. This fault is the inevitable outcome of Purcell's new technical developments. A comparison with contemporary opera in France or Italy only serves to show the remarkable nature of Purcell's genius. No Italian opera of that day ever turned the chorus to such effect, and few Italian composers took the trouble to write such elaborate string parts; Lulli had a stronger sense of his stage conventions, and a surer handling of his material, but within much more restricted limits of emotional expression.

Yet we must beware of basing our comparison on insufficient material. We must compare not isolated moments but operas as complete wholes. It is only rarely that Lulli rises to such scenes as Purcell has here given us, and they occur still more rarely in the Italian operas of which we may conveniently regard Alessandro Scarlatti as the typical composer. We have to make allowance for the long stretches of spoken dialogue which form the bulk of the English 'semi-opera' when we read a work of Lulli and complain of its tedious pomp and sterile melody, or when we weary of the endless alternation of *recitative secco* and formal aria that pursues its level course in an opera of Scarlatti. The operatic landscape must have its plains as well as its mountains, and a whole play set in the style of Purcell's most impressive scenes would be as monotonous and deadening to the nerves as those modern English operas which are modelled not on the Wagnerian drama but on the more popular 'grand Wagner concert'.

Nor must we speak of Lulli as if his style had been formed complete when he first began his career. Even between *Alceste* (1676) and *Bellérophon* (1679) there is as remarkable a development of resource as there is between *Macbeth* and *Circe*. In *Alceste* the style is notably primitive; the rhythm of the declamation is stiff and unchanging, the treatment of the orchestra and chorus rigidly homophonic, the sense of musical climax hardly perceptible. Hardly ever is a solo voice accompanied by the strings, and then it is invariably a bass which confines itself to singing the actual bass of the harmony without any attempt at individual expression. In three years Lulli had learnt to make much greater use of purely musical resource. He is always to some extent hampered by the custom of writing for the orchestra in five independent parts, and consequently treats them in a rather wooden style. To avoid overpowering the voice in accompanied solos he adopts the plan of making voice and instruments be heard alternately, breaking up an aria with frequent interludes, but never allowing the strings actually to accompany, except in the case of bass voices. But there are three big dramatic scenes in *Bellérophon* of the kind that Purcell would have loved to set: a magician invoking a monster, a scene in the temple of Apollo, with a prophecy by the Pythia and an oracle, and in Act IV a long descriptive chorus during which the monster is slain by Bellerophon. Lulli's music is however very dry as compared with Purcell's of a few years later. His weakness is that he never seems to have any ideas of suggesting character in his music. The Pythia (contralto) has a vigorous air with interludes for strings, but when Apollo himself appears and delivers his own oracle there is nothing whatever in the style to distinguish his utterances from those of ordinary mortals. Further progress is made in *Phaëton* (1683) which has several accompanied solos, among others a really fine scene for Proteus (baritone) whose part is quite independent of the instrumental bass. His prophecy of the fate of Phaëton makes a very effective end to the first act. Other interesting points are the air on a ground bass for Theone ('Il me fuit'), though this is not much developed; a lengthy *chaconne* on a very free ground bass; and in Act IV a ballet with airs for the Four Seasons and the Sun, some of which suggest that Purcell may have recollected this opera when writing *The Fairy Queen*. This act is well piled up to a climax with the fine chorus 'Allez respandre la lumière'.

It will be noted that Lulli, like Purcell himself, reserves his accompanied airs and striking musical effects for moments of abnormal exaltation: the prophecy of the Pythia, the appearance of Proteus; an analogous case will be seen in the madness of Roland, extracts from which are quoted in *The Oxford History of Music*, III. 242 ff. Lulli does not seem to have been closely in touch with more modern Italian music. He remains faithful to the traditions of Luigi Rossi, though in the twenty years that had passed since his day Italian composers had made swift progress towards that style which ultimately became the classical language of Europe. They had adopted more modern subjects for their plots, which necessitated a more rapid and unemotional type of recitative, since it had to explain facts instead of expressing polite sentiments in well-balanced phrases such as were put into the mouths of Lulli's mythological personages. This led them to concentrate their emotional effects on the arias, which stand to the general scheme of the play much as the similes and other literary tropes do to the heroic plays of Dryden and his contemporaries. The aria once accepted as a regular part of the musical scheme, the Italians proceeded to develop it in very subtle ways, so that for the history of classical forms in music the Italian operatic aria is a very important field for study. Purcell undoubtedly came under these Italian influences, but the English language did not lend itself to intricacies of musical construction on a delicate scale, and instead of stringing together forty or fifty little arias on a thread of plain recitative, the English chose rather to take their music in larger quantities at a time, and to let their composers draw upon all possible resources to the utmost for those supreme moments of passion or mystery.

English opinion was largely influenced by the doctrines of Saint-Evremond, who addressed his famous and often quoted 'Lettre sur les Opera' to the author of *The Rehearsal* in 1678. It should be carefully borne in mind that Saint-Evremond was then aged sixty-five, so that he naturally judged music by standards long forgotten, and was quite incapable of entering into the ideas of a younger generation. He was, above all things, that greatest enemy of new movements and staunchest ally of Philistinism, the 'man of taste'. Some extracts from the letter are worth quoting, if only to show that the type is no more near extinction now than in the days of Louis XIV.

La Langueur ordinaire où je tombe aux Opera, vient de ce que je n'en ai jamais vû qui ne m'ait paru méprisable dans la disposition du Sujet, & dans les Vers. Or, c'est vainement que l'Oreille est flattée, & que les Yeux sont charmés, si l'Esprit ne se trouve pas satisfait....Une Sottise chargée de Musique, de Danses, de Machines, de Décorations, est une Sottise magnifique, mais toûjours Sottise; c'est un vilain fond, sous de beaux dehors, où je pénètre avec beaucoup de desagrément.

Il y a une autre chose dans les Opera, tellement contre la nature, que mon imagination en est blessée; c'est de faire chanter toute la Pièce depuis le commencement jusqu'à la fin, comme si les personnes qu'on représente s'étoient ridiculement ajustées, pour traiter en Musique, & les plus communes & les plus importantes affaires de leur vie. Peut-on s'imaginer qu'un Maître appelle son Valet, ou qu'il lui donne une commission en chantant; qu'un Ami fasse en chantant une confidence à son ami? qu'on délibere en chantant dans un Conseil; qu'on exprime avec du chant les Ordres qu'on donne, & que mélodieusement on tuë les hommes à coup d'Épée & de Javelot dans un Combat?

Je ne pretends pas neantmoins donner l'exclusion à toute sorte de Chant sur le Théâtre; il y a des choses qui doivent être chantées, il y en a qui peuvent l'être sans choquer la Bien-séance ni la Raison. Les Vœux, les Prieres, les Sacrifices, & généralement tout ce qui regarde le service des Dieux, s'est chanté dans toutes les Nations & dans tous les Tems; les passions tendres & douloureuses s'expriment naturellement par une espece de chant; l'expression d'un Amour que l'on sent naître, l'irrésolution d'une Ame combattuë de divers mouvemens, sont des matieres propres pour les Stances, & les Stances le sont assez pour le chant.

Si vous voulez savoir ce que c'est qu'un OPERA, je vous dirai que c'est un *travail bizarre de Poësie & de Musique, où le Poëte & le Musicien également génés l'un par l'autre, se donnent bien de la peine à faire un méchant Ouvrage.*[1]

In spite of Saint-Evremond, Dryden does not seem altogether to have regarded opera as an absurdity, though it must be admitted that his one thorough-going experiment in this direction was not a success. There were however external reasons for this. The opera of *Albion and Albanius*, produced in 1685, was originally intended to have been nothing more than a prologue in one act to a play with music or semi-opera, the play in question being *King Arthur* which as a matter of fact did not make its public appearance until some years later. For some reason unknown to us, which Dryden does not explain, this project was abandoned, and Dryden turned the prologue into a complete entertainment by adding two more acts to it. Yet two more misfortunes contributed to its failure. After having been rehearsed in the presence of Charles II, its production was postponed by that monarch's death, and when it eventually saw the light in a revised form it so happened that the news of the landing of Monmouth arrived during the sixth performance and put a complete stop to the representations.

---

[1] *Oeuvres meslées de Mr de Saint-Evremond.* Londres, 1709.

Worst misfortune of all, the music had been composed by Louis Grabu.

English dramatic authors of the late seventeenth century seem to have had an almost Wagnerian passion for explaining their principles. Dryden is no exception, and the preface to *Albion and Albanius* is in fact a contribution of real importance to the theory of English opera. The author begins by pointing out that the libretto of an opera demands a style of its own just as much as any other sort of play.

An *Opera* is a Poetical Tale, or Fiction, represented by Vocal and Instrumental Musick, adorn'd with Scenes, Machines and Dancing. The suppos'd Persons of this Musical *Drama*, are generally Supernatural, as Gods, and Goddesses, and Heroes, which at least are descended from them, and are in due time to be adopted into their number.

From this it results that opera will admit of supernatural action and other impossibilities which the normal drama rejects; 'yet Propriety is to be observ'd even here: The gods are all to manage their peculiar Provinces'. Dryden accepts as a matter of course the distinction between recitative and aria, or what he 'for want of a proper English Word must call *the Songish Part*'. Just as other forms of poetry are derived from the fixed standard of antiquity, epic poetry from Homer, the ode from Pindar, so operatic poetry must conform to the tradition of its first inventors, the Italians. He cites *Il Pastor Fido* as a typical model, and incidentally points out that although the characters of an opera are properly supernatural, yet 'meaner Persons may sometimes gracefully be introduc'd', especially if they can be associated with the 'golden age'; 'and therefore Shepherds might reasonably be admitted, as of all Callings, the most innocent, the most happy, and also by reason of the spare Time they had, in their almost idle Employment, had most leisure to make Verses, and to be in Love, without somewhat of which Passion, no *Opera* can possibly subsist'.

Dryden then proceeds to discuss the relative values of

different languages for opera. It need hardly be said that his highest praise is for Italian; French, he says, has gained something in recent times 'by throwing off the unnecessary Consonants, which made their Spelling tedious, and their Pronunciation harsh', but he considers that the language must always suffer from its natural harshness and 'perpetual ill Accent'. The difficulties of our own tongue he finds to lie in the 'effeminacy' of English pronunciation, a fault shared by Danish, and in the scarcity of feminine rhymes. The scarcity of feminine rhymes is a difficulty which is only too well known to anyone who has attempted to translate other languages for musical purposes; but the English librettist of the future will probably not feel as much bound to them as Dryden did. It was, however, a difficulty which Dryden and the other poets of his day felt themselves in duty bound to overcome; their lyrics are indeed so rich in double rhymes that a foreigner might almost have supposed single rhymes to be as rare in English as in Italian.

'Tis no easie Matter in our Language to make Words so smooth, and Numbers so harmonious, that they shall almost set themselves, and yet there are Rules for this in Nature: and as great a certainty of Quantity in our Syllables, as either in the *Greek* or *Latin*: But let Poets and Judges understand those first, and then let them begin to study *English*....The chief Secret is in the choice of Words; and by this Choice I do not here mean Elegancy of Expression; but Propriety of Sound, to be varied according to the Nature of the Subject.

This advice still holds good for the modern English librettist.

It is a great misfortune that Dryden never carried into actual execution the plan which he outlines in this preface. As he himself hints, *Albion and Albanius* does not really conform to his ideal scheme at all; and the opera to which it was to have been a prologue was

a Tragedy mix'd with *Opera*; or a *Drama* written in blank verse, adorn'd with scenes, Machines, songs and dances: So that the Fable of it is all spoken and acted by the best of the Comedians; the other part of the Entertainment to be perform'd by the same

Singers and Dancers, who are introduced in this present opera. It cannot properly be called a Play, because the Action of it is supposed to be conducted sometimes by supernatural Means, or Magick; nor an *Opera* because the Story of it is not sung.

In its original form, therefore, *Albion and Albanius* would have corresponded exactly to the conventional prologue of a French opera, the first act being sufficiently complete in itself for this purpose. A prologue of this kind was not at all in accordance with English custom, but if we are to grant the adoption of a French tradition, Dryden's effort will serve the purpose no worse than any of Quinault's. But to expand such a prologue into a three act opera was an absurdity which not even the court of Louis XIV could have tolerated.

The number of characters—all of them either classical divinities or allegorical figures, except Albion and Albanius, who represent Charles II and his brother—is very large, and it is curious to note that Dryden in printing the play anticipated the modern custom of naming them in the order of their first appearance on the stage. The description of the scenery is elaborate, and amusingly characteristic of the most exaggerated symbolism of the period. We begin with a street of palaces leading to the Royal Exchange, adorned with equestrian statues of Charles I and Charles II. Augusta (London) and Thamesis are lying on couches at a distance from each other in dejected postures; to them Mercury descends in a chariot drawn by ravens, and opens the opera with an apostrophe to the 'glorious fabric' represented on the back scene. He reproves Augusta for her disloyalty and promises to restore Albion to her. Democracy and Zelota (Puritanism) enter with appropriate verses, but Archon (General Monk) takes Mercury's caduceus and sends them to sleep, and they sink below the stage supported on pedestals decorated with representations of Hypocrisy and Fanaticism. Thamesis calls for a dance of watermen in the king's and duke's liveries; Juno appears in a machine drawn by peacocks[1] to bless the nuptials of Albion and Augusta; Iris comes over from Holland 'on a very large Machine'[2] to announce that Albion has had a safe crossing. The scene changes to a series of triumphal arches; Albion and Albanius enter, preceded by Archon, with a procession, and the first act ends with universal rejoicings. This act, it will be seen, is complete in itself, as a mere prologue to lead up to the appearance of the two heroes, these being mere lay figures who neither act, sing nor speak.

In Acts II and III Dryden endeavours to be more dramatic. Hitherto his characters have been little more than living statuary; the few lines allowed to each are barely sufficient to show what they are intended to represent, and they have no chance whatever of expressing personality in action. The second act begins with 'a poetical Hell'; Democracy and Zelota, assisted by Alecto, concoct the Popish Plot in the presence of Pluto and the Furies. The scene then changes to the Thames, as seen looking up stream from the middle of the river, Lambeth on one side, Millbank on the other. Augusta enters, in a great state of jealousy, and listens to the advice of Democracy and Zelota. They apparently leave the stage, and a scene follows in which Mercury advises Albion to send Albanius away. Albion bids a reluctant farewell to his brother, Apollo makes a momentary appearance in a chariot to assure them of a satisfactory future, and Albanius is escorted to sea by Neptune, nymphs and tritons alternating chorus and dance in a *chaconne* of exceptional length.

Act III represents the port of Dover, viewed from the sea. Albion, who is in a state of melancholy, is consoled by Acacia (Innocence) and a chorus of nereids and tritons. This is followed by a lively scene for Tyranny and Democracy (men) with Asebia, or Atheism, and Zelota (women) who sing the

---

[1] The appearance of Juno in *The Fairy Queen* is evidently derived from this, as some verbal coincidences indicate.

[2] 'This was really seen the 18th. of March 1684 by Captain Christopher Gunman, on board his R.H. Yacht, then in Calais Pier: He drew it as it then appeared, and gave a draught of it to us. We have only added the Cloud where the person of Iris sits.'

praises of a commonwealth and witness a pantomimic dance of 'Property Boys' (adherents of the Duke of Monmouth) and Sectaries. Albion and Acacia return and invoke Proteus, whose cave of coral is carefully designed so as not to obscure the view of Dover pier. Proteus, after changing himself into a lion, a crocodile and a dragon, resumes his natural form and prophesies. The democratic party enter to attack Albion (this represents the Rye House Plot) but sink in flames. Venus rises from the sea with Albanius, attended by Graces, Loves and Heroes; Apollo descends from heaven attended by 'abundance of Angels and Cherubims' and takes Albion up again with him. Finally the scene changes to a view of Windsor Castle, with a procession of Knights of the Garter; Fame rises on a pedestal and sings the praises of Albion, the opera ending with a chorus and a dance.

This monument of stupidity is worth considering for a moment as an example of the way in which attempts have been made, and are still made occasionally, to achieve English opera at one blow. The court naturally supposed that whatever was done at Versailles must be right. Betterton had been sent over to France to obtain the latest scenic devices; Grabu was himself a Frenchman; and if anybody in England could write a libretto it should have been Dryden. Yet Dryden knew perfectly well that nothing had been so popular in England as *The Tempest*,[1] and he was himself planning another 'opera' on the same model. If anybody knew what the English playgoer appreciated, it should have been Betterton; if any English musician could have created English opera, it was Henry Purcell, but for some reason unknown, Purcell seems to have been looked upon with disfavour by Dryden at this moment. There can be little doubt that Purcell and Blow were among the group whom Dryden mentions as hostile to Grabu, and when we look at Grabu's music, we cannot be surprised at their opinion.

That the failure of the opera was due more to Grabu than to anyone else is fairly clear from the satirical poem quoted

---

[1] That is, of course, the operatic version of the play.

by Hawkins.[1] The rhythm of Dryden's verse, whatever other faults it may have, is always swift and lithe; Grabu's recitatives are a caricature of Lulli's *Paradeschritt*. The perpetual changes from bars of four beats to bars of three and *vice versa* are additionally destructive to the natural flow of the words, and this is made worse by 'perpetual ill accent' owing to Grabu's very inadequate knowledge of English. Even when he accents the syllables rightly he often makes nonsense of a sentence by an unsuitable melodic outline. Here is a specimen attempt to be English and popular in style:

ALBION AND ALBANIUS   GRABU

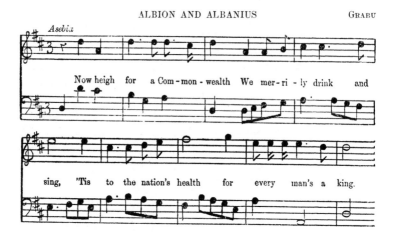

---

[1] A few verses may be given here:

  Betterton, Betterton, thy decorations,
   And the machines were well written, we knew;
  But all the words were such stuff we want patience,
   And little better is Monsieur Grabu.

  Damme, says Underhill, I'm out of two hundred,
   Hoping that rainbows and peacocks would do:
  Who thought infallible Tom could have blunder'd?
   A plague upon him and Monsieur Grabu.

  Lane, thou hast no applause for thy capers,
   Tho' all without thee would make a man spew;
  And a month hence will not pay for the tapers,
   Spite of Jack Laureat and Monsieur Grabu.

  Bayes, thou wouldst have thy skill thought universal,
   Tho' thy dull ear be to music untrue;
  Then whilst we strive to confute the *Rehearsal*,
   Prithee learn thrashing of Monsieur Grabu.

The instrumental and lyrical parts are indescribably dull. Grabu deserves praise for the idea of his great *chaconne* at the end of Act II, but the music itself is of the poorest quality. There can, however, be little doubt that Purcell studied the score with discriminating attention, for there are a few passages that can often and easily be paralleled in the English composer's operas. We may quote the dance and song of the nereids and tritons who rise from the sea to comfort Albion at the beginning of Act III. Professor Saintsbury cites these lines as 'excellent' and '(for the time) unusually cadenced'; but Grabu's tune effectually destroys all Dryden's delicate variation of the hackneyed rhythm.

The air for the Graces and Loves shows a certain charm
and variety of treatment; and lastly attention should be
shown to the air for Fame, or as Grabu prefers to call her
'The Renown', which is obviously the model for the air of
Fame in Purcell's *The Indian Queen*.

Strings in five parts.   *Ayre for the Graces and Loves*

The Renown (alto)

Re - nown, as - sume thy Trump - et from Pole . . .

. . . to Pole . . . . re - sounding, great Al - bion's

Name, great Al - bion's Name shall be the Theme of Fame.

Chapter Nine

CHAMBER OPERA

The entertainment produced by the joint labours of Dryden and Grabu had a weakness quite apart from its literary or musical qualities; it partook far too much of the nature of a masque. The influence of the masque had indeed been felt even in the 'semi-operas' to a certain extent, and it remained a characteristic feature of English operatic attempts for long after the period here under discussion. In *Albion and Albanius* we should never be suprised if at any moment the twin heroes walked down from the stage and selected partners from the audience; Democracy, Zelota and their friends correspond closely to the antimasque figures of Jonson and D'Avenant. But the really pernicious factor in the masque tradition is the perpetual introduction of allegorical figures which never get beyond the stage of explaining who they are and what they stand for. These Apollos and Proteuses are in fact of far less dramatic value than the parlour-maid who brings in a telegram on the modern Italian lyric stage. They are not even allowed to speak in their own characters, as they might have done in a Greek tragedy, or in an Italian Renaissance imitation of one: were they once allowed to behave as if they were real persons, even real divinities, they would cease to have any reason to appear on the stage at all in this type of spectacle. When almost all the characters in the play are gods from the machine, a mere mortal acquires an exceptional and peculiar distinction, and it may well be that this was precisely the effect which the courtier poet aimed at producing in the minds of those who were the originals of Albion and Albanius.

Contemporaneously with this petrifaction of the drama, an isolated attempt was made to give new life to the masque itself by a composer probably belonging to the hostile party, Dr John Blow. It is not possible to ascertain the exact date of his *Venus and Adonis*, described as 'a masque for the entertainment of the King', but it must certainly have been performed within a few years before or after Grabu's opera. The part of Venus was taken by Mrs Mary Davis, one of the mistresses of Charles II, and that of Cupid by her daughter, who is described as Lady Mary Tudor. Lady Mary, who was born in 1673, was not given the surname of Tudor until December 10, 1680, and was married to Lord Derwentwater in August 1687. It is perhaps reasonable to suppose that 'the King' for whose entertainment she and her mother sang was more likely to have been her father than James II; on the other hand, the part of Cupid is sufficiently exacting to suggest a later date as more probable, considering the young lady's age.

Although described as a masque and constructed on a very diminutive scale, *Venus and Adonis* is a real opera both in its libretto and in its music. It begins with an overture for strings in the form adopted by Lulli, although the handling of the instruments shows a decidedly English influence. It leads straight into the prologue, which begins with an address by Cupid to the audience in an *arioso* style, accompanied by the *continuo* only. A shepherdess sings a vocal minuet accompanied by a flute, repeated by the chorus and strings; a shepherd (tenor) sings a second stanza, the shepherdess and chorus taking up a quicker movement in praise of Cupid. Cupid and the shepherd sing a short dialogue, the chorus sing another minuet while a shepherd and shepherdess dance, and the prologue ends with a song and solo dance for Cupid.

After an act-tune for two flutes Venus and Adonis are discovered 'sitting together upon a couch embracing one another'. They sing an affectionate dialogue with two flutes, interrupted suddenly by music (violins) representing the arrival of the hunters. Venus starts from her love-dreams and bids Adonis hasten to the chase. This scene makes a very effective contrast, and the excitement is very cleverly worked up by instrumental interludes of a vigorous character to a spirited climax at the *ritornello*. Adonis refuses to go, and continues his dialogue with Venus. The characters are admirably brought out, Venus expressing her affection in graceful *coloratura* with a very independent accompaniment for a flute. A quicker movement follows in which they sing together, she encouraging him to go, he protesting resolutely that he will stay. The huntsmen enter and invite Adonis in chorus to join them; Adonis yields to their request and they leave the stage singing a chorus, the voices being still heard after they have passed from sight. A huntsman dances a solo dance to music evolved from the theme of the huntsmens' first entry; the dance is probably intended to be descriptive, but it is well constructed musically, and makes a very effective finish to the act, granted the Elizabethan stage convention of the solo dance at this point.[1]

After a very charming act-tune in rondo form, with a main theme built up of three bar phrases in triple time, the second act begins, discovering Venus, Cupid and a group of little Cupids. It is here that there occurs the so-called 'spelling lesson scene'[2] in which Cupid teaches the little ones not spelling but their duties of making the wrong people fall in love with each other. The word 'mercenary' is spelt out syllable by syllable because it happens to be rather a long one for divinities of tender years. Suddenly Venus becomes serious—'But, Cupid, how shall I make Adonis constant still'? 'Use him very ill', replies malicious Cupid, who has learnt his lesson; and Venus bursts into a wild hysterical laugh which is most startling. She recovers herself at once, and sends the Cupids to play, the Graces being invited to join them. This gives occasion for some very attractive choruses and dances. It is curious to observe that Blow makes the Graces treble, alto and bass! The act ends with a sara-

[1] Cf. *The Knight of the Burning Pestle.*
[2] Ernest Walker, *A History of Music in England*, p. 169.

band during which the Cupids dress Venus and adorn her with jewels.

Act III shows us Venus 'standing in a melancholy posture', sighing for Adonis who has not yet returned. A mourning Cupid crosses the stage and shakes an arrow at her; directly afterwards Adonis is led in wounded. A passionate dialogue ensues, at the end of which Adonis dies, and Venus gives vent to piercing inarticulate cries of grief. After a very expressive instrumental interlude, she rises and bids the Cupids bear Adonis to heaven, while the chorus call upon Echo and the wood-nymphs to mourn their departed huntsman.

Scant justice has been done by historians to this most remarkable and original work. Burney and Hawkins seem to have been entirely unacquainted with it; Dr Nagel and Sir Hubert Parry do not do more than mention it in passing; Dr Ernest Walker seems to have been the first to give it serious consideration, but he discusses it from a purely musical point of view, with no reference to its presentation on the stage.[1] He very justly criticizes its crudity, its unconvincing harmony, and its indefiniteness, both of melody and tonality. It is, however, most important to visualize this little opera in action. Blow seems to have had no regard for the regular operatic traditions either of France or Italy; he is not hampered by experience and routine, but takes whatever means happen to occur to his mind and concentrates on dramatic expression regardless of any conventional sense of style. He adopts a more or less French form for his dances; in his recitatives, or rather *arioso* passages, he is evidently much influenced not by Italian opera, but by Italian chamber cantatas; and we can have little doubt that he was well acquainted with Locke's music to *The Tempest* and to *Cupid and Death*.

It is not known who wrote the libretto, which has no particular literary merit. It has, however, the great merit of

[1] Musicians are indebted most of all to Mr G. E. P. Arkwright, who printed the work complete in *The Old English Edition.*

inconspicuousness and extreme simplicity. The story is as well known as that of Orpheus, so that there could never be the least difficulty in understanding what is going on on the stage, and the result of this is that attention is always concentrated on personality expressed in music. Venus stands out as a definite character, capricious and impulsive as Shakespeare's 'serpent of old Nile'; in the first act it is Adonis who loves, and she who plays with his devotion, in the second act she suddenly realizes her own passion for him, in the third she has lost him. It is the story of Rinaldo and Armida in its simplest form. Cupid and the shepherds provide the necessary contrast, and help to suggest the picturesque and voluptuous atmosphere of the whole.

There are many moments which for intensity of vocal expression almost recall Monteverdi's *L'Incoronazione di Poppea*, for instance, the opening scene:

VENUS AND ADONIS   BLOW

Note the whispered caresses of the first two bars, the languishing phrase of the flutes ending on a half-close; then the

movement of Adonis as the bass sounds the unexpected F
followed by the still more unexpected B flat that yet leads
so easily to the original dominant chord on E.

Still more striking is the outburst of Venus on the death
of her lover:

Short extracts can give very little idea of this work, the
interest of which depends so much on its presentation as a
complete whole: but space must be found for a few bars of
the hunters' music, if only to show how Blow anticipated
Weber's 'wild hunt' and the hounds of *Die Walküre*.

It is not at all surprising that Blow's masque was soon
forgotten. Its harshness of style would be more apparent to
its own generation than to ours; its indifference to accepted
models would be a certain bar to popularity. But it may
have been an encouragement to Purcell and those with whom
he collaborated towards the production of *Dido and Aeneas*,
which certainly shows traces of its influence.

The opera of *Dido and Aeneas*, for long supposed to be a
work of Purcell's extreme youth, has now been clearly proved
to date from 1689 or the early part of 1690,[1] the composer

¹ The evidence, which is too complicated to be summarized here, is set out

being then thirty years of age. It was not composed for the professional stage, and except for a performance in 1700, where it was inserted as a masque into Gildon's adaptation of *Measure for Measure*, it seems never to have been acted in public until some two hundred years later. This accounts for its peculiar form and style, and for the fact that it never had any successors of its own kind, although it may possibly have had something to do with Purcell's sudden popularity as a stage composer during the few remaining years of his life.

One can easily imagine that Purcell, when invited by the dancing-master Josias Priest to compose a musical entertainment for the young ladies at his school in Chelsea, may have felt that here was an opportunity of showing himself a better composer than Grabu. If Grabu had sneered at the want of good voices on the public stage, Purcell was hardly likely to find better ones among a body of youthful amateurs; but he must have known that he could count upon good will and hard work, with the additional advantage that some of

by Mr Barclay Squire, *Purcell's Dramatic Music*, Sammelbände der Internationalen Musikgesellschaft, v. 506 ff.

the girls were probably his personal pupils, and certainly free from the prejudices and vanities of the professional stage. He was not bound by the inevitable subservience of a manager to popular taste, and could try the experiment of writing, as all great composers have done, to please himself alone.

The libretto of *Dido and Aeneas* was by Nahum Tate, best known as the collaborator of Nicholas Brady in a metrical version of the Psalms, and is the most lamentable doggerel; but it is fortunately simple and unpretentious in its choice of words, so that its inaptitudes are to some extent masked by Purcell's music. In construction it is probably modelled on *Venus and Adonis*, with additional matter of such kind as had been observed to be successful at the public theatres.

Tate had been interested in the story for a great many years. In 1678 he had produced a tragedy called *Brutus of Alba*, the subject of which was the tale of Dido and Aeneas, although the hero is called Brutus and the heroine turned into a Queen of Syracuse. The play may also be regarded as a forerunner of *Albion and Albanius*, for Brutus deserts the Queen in order to found a kingdom in England.[1] In 1697 the tragedy was converted into an 'opera' by George Powell and John Verbruggen, with the alternative title of *Augusta's Triumph*; the play was cut down to the shortest possible limits in order to make room for excerpts from the music of Grabu's entertainment, and the description of the scenery suggests that the decorations of *The Fairy Queen* were utilized. *Brutus of Alba* has only very slight verbal suggestions of *Dido and Aeneas*, but a comparison of the two is interesting, as it shows us that the witches, who seem so inappropriate to a classical story, played an important part in Tate's original tragedy.

The music of *Dido and Aeneas* is accessible in various printed editions, but not all of them represent the composer's in-

[1] '[Geoffrey of Monmouth] reporteth that Brute, lineally descended from the demy god Eneas, the sonne of Venus, daughter of Jupiter, about the yeare of the world 2855 and 1108 before the nativitie of Christ, builded this citie [*sc.* London] neare unto the river now called Thames, and named it Troynovant or Trenovant.' Stow (1603).

tentions accurately. In the earlier part of the eighteenth century the work was sometimes performed at concerts, and for this purpose a version was made which omitted the dramatic dances, shortened much of the recitative and re-distributed the solo parts for different voices so as to avoid the necessity of engaging a separate singer for each character in the opera. There was also a considerable revision of the actual notes, in order to bring Purcell's melody and harmony more into conformity with the style of Handel and Galuppi. Purcell's autograph score seems to have been irretrievably lost, and the one really complete copy of it which still exists remained unknown until towards the end of the nineteenth century. This score, formerly the property of Sir Frederick Ouseley, is now in the library of St Michael's College, Tenbury. Macfarren, who edited *Dido and Aeneas* for the Musical Antiquarian Society in 1841, adopted the concert version, and his example was followed by Dr W. H. Cummings in the full score issued by the Purcell Society in 1889. Cummings possessed various early MS. scores and parts of the opera, which he also collated; he seems to have been already fairly well advanced with the work of preparing his edition when he made the acquaintance of the Tenbury score. He incorporated from the Tenbury score such move-ments as were missing from the others, but he does not seem to have regarded the Tenbury score as representing an altogether better authority.

The Tenbury score dates from the early years of the eighteenth century. It contains the entire opera, except for the prologue, which Purcell probably never set to music, and it has copious stage directions which agree with those of the printed libretto. Mr Arthur Cummings, son of Dr W. H. Cummings, kindly allowed me to see the collection of separate vocal and instrumental parts which had belonged to his father; these represent the concert version, and whatever their age may be, I cannot regard them as equal in authority to the Tenbury manuscript. A vocal score based on the

Tenbury manuscript has now been published by the Oxford University Press.

As printed, the opera begins with a prologue for Phoebus, Venus, Nereids, Shepherds, Spring, Nymphs etc., but Purcell does not appear to have set this to music and it is no great loss. After an overture in C minor Dido enters accompanied by Belinda (Virgil's Anna) and her train. Belinda calls upon the Queen to banish care, the chorus joining in; Dido expresses her agitation in a long air on a ground bass. Belinda guesses that she has fallen in love with Aeneas, and the chorus hails the idea of their marriage with great delight. A short dialogue between Dido and Belinda follows, which like Blow's masque shows the strong influence of the Italian chamber-cantata style. At this point the key changes to C major for the duet 'Fear no danger' in which Belinda and another lady assure the Queen of Aeneas' devotion. The duet is repeated in full chorus, and prepares for the entrance of Aeneas (tenor) with his train. He does not exchange more than a few formal words with Dido, but the chorus and Belinda comment openly on their passion. The act ends with a chorus of some length, 'To the hills and the vales', followed by 'the triumphing dance', which is a freely treated *chaconne*. Here, according to the libretto, ends the first act, which is all in C minor and C major. The score places the end of the first act after the following scene; but the difference is of no importance.

The scene changes to a cave of witches. A Sorceress (mezzo-soprano, not bass as in the concert version) after a gloomy prelude in F minor summons her sister witches in a recitative accompanied by strings. This accompaniment is noteworthy, as it maintains a striking rhythmical figure in almost every bar, quite independently of the voice. The witches enter with a short chorus in B flat major; the Sorceress continues in F minor with the same accompaniment. Her explanations are interrupted by a chorus of laughter in F major; she proceeds to tell them that Aeneas is 'bound by Fate to seek Italian ground' and at that moment the faint sounds of the Queen's hunting party are heard. This idea is no doubt suggested by Blow's masque, but the device employed is quite different. The Sorceress, out of pure unreasoning hatred towards Dido, arranges that a familiar spirit of hers shall assume the shape of Mercury and tell Aeneas to sail away. The witches then prepare to raise a storm; there is a duet for the witches in D minor and the well-known echo chorus in F major. This is followed by an 'echo dance' of furies in the same key, with rushing semiquavers after Lulli's manner, but much more contrapuntally treated, the phrases being alternately loud and soft.

This ends the first act according to the score, the first scene of the second act according to the libretto. Purcell here introduces more variety into his tonality, but is careful to make F the main key of the scene. The choice of F minor for the witches is interesting; Purcell evidently regarded it as a very extreme and mysterious key, only to be used on rare occasions.

After a ritornel or act-tune in D minor, we see Aeneas, Dido, Belinda and their train in a grove. Belinda and the chorus sing the charms of the forest. This air and chorus is clearly modelled on the air and chorus 'In these sweet groves' sung by Cupid and the shepherds in the prologue to *Venus and Adonis*. An attendant sings an air about Diana, followed by an instrumental movement which no doubt accompanied some pantomimic dance. At the end Aeneas presents a boar's head on his spear to Dido, after which the key changes to D major; a sudden storm begins, and the hunting party headed by Belinda proceed to 'haste, haste to town'. All leave the stage during this chorus except Aeneas, to whom the false Mercury suddenly descends with his message. This recitative is in A minor, and so is the long recitative in which Aeneas expresses his reluctant obedience and his embarrassment at having to explain his departure to Dido. According to the libretto, the witches should reappear at this point and end the act with a chorus. The inconclusive tonality of the recitative suggests that Purcell may have originally intended to set the chorus, but perhaps cut it out, feeling that the despair of Aeneas made a more dramatic end to the act. In this he was certainly right, but in view of Purcell's usual attention to tonal structure it is much to be regretted that he did not contrive his recitative so as to end the act in the key in which it began.

The third act shows us the harbour and the ships. The libretto had already indicated a dance of drunken sailors in the witches' scene, before the preparations for raising a storm; but there is no indication of this in Purcell's music, and it does not seem at all appropriate. The sailors make their first actual appearance in this third act, and are evidently drunk again. This chorus and dance of sailors was perhaps suggested by *Albion and Albanius*, or possibly by *The Tempest*. Purcell's vigorous and energetic music has however nothing in common with the conventionalities of Grabu. The witches enter, and rejoice over the prospect of shipwrecking Aeneas and setting Carthage on fire, from no motive but pure love of evil. They dance to some very curious music which must have been intended to represent definite and peculiar actions. The libretto here has a stage direction 'Jack of the Lanthorn leads the Spaniards (*sc.* Sailors) out of their way among the Inchanteresses'. To the modern reader these witches' scenes seem very inappropriate to the story and distracting to the development of the drama; but, as we have already observed, audiences of this period were never tired of seeing witches on the stage.

Dido, Belinda and a woman enter, followed shortly by Aeneas, who announces his departure, but on witnessing Dido's agitation offers to stay and brave the anger of Jupiter; Dido, however, is so indignant at his having so much as thought of leaving her that she sends him away in great wrath. He leaves the stage and Dido prepares to face death. The chorus sing a solemn setting of the words

> Great minds against themselves conspire,
> And shun the cure they most desire.

This may seem an awkward piece of dramatic construction: Dido's quarrel with Aeneas is so quickly over that we are tempted to find it a rather petty business, and the pompous platitude of the chorus merely emphasizes the undignified situation. But some sort of bridge was no doubt wanted to lead up to the recitative and air 'When I am laid in earth' with which Dido ends her life and the opera. Here again there may have been some recollection of Blow's masque; Blow certainly could never have written anything so poignant and so beautiful as this famous air, but he had attempted in his way a somewhat similar situation, and his successors may have remembered his closing chorus when they called on Cupids to come 'with drooping wings' and scatter roses on the tomb of Dido.

In this last act, as in previous acts, Purcell maintains his tonality on a definite scheme. The scene for the sailors and witches begins and ends in B flat; the scene for Dido and Aeneas is in G minor, and with slight deviations G minor is kept up until the end of the opera, Dido's last air and the final chorus being in that key. Blow does not seem to have grasped the importance of this, and though he uses very few keys in his masque, he pays no great attention to the grouping of them. It may be thought that this question of tonality is purely academic: but for the period under discussion, if not for the present day as well, it is of serious importance. An opera has no claim to be considered as a work of art unless it is a complete musical whole, organic from beginning to end. This sense of completeness may be achieved in various ways, the choice of which depends upon general conditions of musical technique at the particular time. It would have been intolerable if an Italian composer of Handel's day had written every air in each act of his opera in one and the same key, for practically every air is in one and the same conventional Da Capo form, and that in itself is a powerful means towards unification of style. But Mozart is as a rule extremely careful to make his operas or his single acts begin and end in the same key, although he allows himself and indeed rightly aims at a wide variety within these limits. The process of thematic development as seen in Beethoven's sonatas and symphonies was another source of unification for opera in the nineteenth century, and we see the results of this in the works of Wagner, whose use of *leitmotiv* has an enormous musical value quite apart from its dramatic interest. Yet the sense of tonality is still strong in his works, notably in *Die Meistersinger*, and even so late a work as Verdi's *Falstaff* depends equally largely upon unity of key. When we turn then to such composers as Blow and Purcell, whose range of tonality is extremely small, and whose knowledge of thematic development is practically non-existent, except in so far as it could be practised in the form of fugue, we must admit that a rather rigid system of tonality was the most satisfactory way of knitting together the constant succession of short separate movements, especially at a moment when variety rather than similarity of form in single movements was the habitual practice. The sense of tonality which dominates the whole period beginning with Bach and ending with Brahms was in fact only just beginning to be appreciated at this moment, and it was therefore all the more urgent that it should be emphasized to the utmost in complicated and elaborate works such as operas.

The construction of the opera is to some extent explained by that of *Brutus of Alba*. The situation which Tate and Purcell had to face was not unlike that which confronted D'Avenant when he produced *The Siege of Rhodes*. Purcell requires a libretto; Tate offers to make one out of *Brutus of Alba* or out of the original version of it in which the characters bore their right names. In *Brutus of Alba* we meet not only with the hero and heroine, the heroine's confidante, who corresponds to Belinda in the opera, and the sorceress Ragusa, but also with two other characters of some importance who do not appear in Purcell's opera. These are Asaracus, the confidant of the hero, who only succeeds in bringing Brutus to a sense of his patriotic duty by committing suicide himself, and Soziman, 'a designing lord, a Syracusan', who desires to obtain the crown of Syracuse for himself and calls in Ragusa the sorceress to assist him. Obviously Soziman, as villain, is a very valuable contributor to the dramatic scheme, and Soziman's villainy gives a plausible reason for the introduction of Ragusa. The reader will however have realized by this time that plausible reasons were quite unnecessary for the introduction of witches into an English opera; indeed one might imagine that Restoration audiences could not conceive of an opera without them. Purcell had to produce his work in a girls' school with only a limited number of girls who could take important parts; Asaracus has to be sacrificed and even Soziman as well. The witches must remain at all costs.

Some extracts from the third act of *Brutus of Alba* will make the construction of *Dido and Aeneas* more intelligible.

Scene a Desart. At some distance a Fountain with the statue of Diana.

(Soziman consults Ragusa)

Soz. Instruct this feeble Arm to shake a Throne,
And snatch a Crown.
Rag. Let it be steept in Bloud!
'Twas my initiating Ceremony
To my dire Art, I was install'd with Slaughter,
Nor could I raise me to my airy Rounds,
Till I had bath'd my Limbs in Infants Gore.

A Horn winded at distance.

Soz. Heark, the Game's rouz'd.
Rag. So merry!—well, 'tis odds I mar your sport.
By Contract, Son, I hate all humane kind,
But envy most the prosperous and great;
Thou art devoted to the Queen's destruction,
And so am I; this day begins her Ruine.
Take that.   [*Gives him a little Viol.*

Soz. Th' intent?

Rag. 'Tis the Queen's bane.
 Thou know'st the Custome when the sports are done
 The Court repairs to the *Diana* Fountain,
 To worship there the Goddess of the Woods,
 And drink of the cool Stream; the Queen drinks first,
 Into their Bowl see thou convey that Philtre,
 It fires the Chastest Breasts with loose Desires.

Soz. Speak on, for now thy voice grows full of Fate.

Rag. When they have drunk, an entertainment follows,
 That when the Philtre has for dalliance flush't 'em,
 I will by Magick pour a Tempest down,
 Hail, Rain and Fire, th' ingredients of the Storm;
 Scatt'ring the Company to th' Caves for Shelter.
 At the same Cell the Prince and Queen shall hide,
 Where she forgetfull shall resign her Honour.

The Restoration theatre teaches us a great deal about life in boarding-schools for young gentlewomen; but presumably even the dancing-masters who presided over them thought certain scenes unsuited for scholastic representation.

Later on Ragusa alludes to spells which will

> ...sink returning Sailers in the Bay

and after she has finished with Soziman she summons four women with whom she conjures up a storm. Again we have the stage direction

> *a Horn sounded at a distance.*

After this scene the witches vanish. Brutus enters with the Queen; they kneel before the fountain of Diana and Soziman gives them the philtre to drink. Thunder is heard; then comes a dance of masquers during which the storm gathers.

Asaracus. In all our Sea-disasters I ne'er knew
 So swift a change of weather.

Brutus. All shift for shelter.
 [*Exeunt All confusedly, Brutus and the Queen together.*
 Ragusa appears in the storm.

Witches also appear and shout 'Ho, ho, ho, ho!' The familiar crocodile appears in Act IV, but here it is Brutus who compares the Queen to the monster. When Brutus finally decides to sail there is a slight suggestion of the opera, or rather, the opera preserves a slight recollection of the play:

Brutus. Give notice to the Fleet we sail to Night.
   Said I to Night! forsake the Queen to Night!
   Forsake! oh Fate! the Queen! to Night forsake her!
   My word is past, 'tis giv'n, and those pale Lips
   With silent Oratory plead my Promise.

(The pale lips are those of Asaracus, who has just killed himself.) The farewell to the Queen follows immediately on this scene; her swoon ends the act. In the fifth act the witches appear again 'blowing black Powders from boxes'. The play ends with the suicides of the Queen and of Soziman, after which two Ambassadors (who seem to have stepped out of *The Rehearsal*) make the following final comment, which is not so very unlike the words of Purcell's final chorus:

2 *Amb.* Prodigious!
1 *Amb.* In Confusion I am lost.
   For their Enterments we will first provide,
   Then back to our expecting Court
   With mourning Trumpets in slow Marches move.
   Sad Cypress for Triumphant Lawrels wear,
   And Fun'ral Flags for Conquering Ensigns bear!

In judging *Dido and Aeneas* as an opera we have to make some allowances for the restricted conditions in which it had to be performed, but it is more important that we should put ourselves into the normal frame of mind of the 'select audience of parents' who witnessed that first performance by making some acquaintance with the general run of theatrical entertainments which they might have seen on other days. It is surprising how well the opera holds together in spite of all its shortcomings in construction; recent performances have often shown how convincingly effective it is even to a modern audience utterly unfamiliar with the traditions of its own period. That complete certainty of effect is due entirely to Purcell's individual genius; but to say that does not sum up the whole problem. German critics who have seen *Dido and Aeneas* on the stage characterize it as 'Shakespearean'; and in the mouth of a German this epithet carries perhaps more admiration than it would in England. A more detailed analysis of the opera will explain to a large extent the technical methods by which Purcell secured the intensity of his dramatic expression; and it is important that we should investigate these methods carefully, because Purcell's principles are in the main equally applicable to operatic composition in our own day.

Purcell's experiment, in spite of its obvious indebtedness to French and Italian sources, is a work such as no foreign composer could ever have written. It conforms to no tradition; it has no sense of style; but it is saved from falling into the merely picturesque by its robust directness. It is also quite original in its treatment of the chorus, though Purcell's real genius for dramatic choral writing was not fully developed until later. But although for the most part the chorus in *Dido and Aeneas* does no more than repeat exactly the airs sung by the ubiquitous Belinda, its presence is constantly felt as a factor in the drama, and in some places the mere suppression of Belinda's solos would give to the choruses an unexpected and striking individuality. We must regard Belinda in fact not as a definite person, but merely as a chorus leader, like the miscellaneous nymphs who start the choral movements of *The Fairy Queen*. In two choruses, 'Cupid only throws the dart' (Act I) and 'With drooping wings' (Act III), we find more individuality of choral treatment, more definite suggestion of gesture and movement, and we shall see this sense of the stage more conspicuously developed in the later operas.

It is naturally in the recitative that *Dido and Aeneas* is most remarkable, since, being the only real opera which Purcell ever wrote, it furnished his only occasion for writing musical dialogue of a genuinely human and dramatic character. Purcell's recitative is very obviously derived from the Italian chamber cantatas; this is shown by his expressive employment of florid passages, and his tendency to measured *arioso* rather than to free declamation on an almost stationary bass, as in Italian *recitativo secco* of the operatic type. Purcell never relaxes the sense of rhythm; his recitatives, like Mozart's, must be sung on a general basis of strict time. He does not even permit himself that common Italian formula, the dominant-tonic cadence independent of the general rhythm, which is scattered all over the works of Bach and Handel, to say nothing of the Italians, and which to the average reader is the most characteristic and the most annoying feature of recitatives. Nor does Purcell ever consider that recitative absolves him from the restrictions of key any more than from those of rhythm. The recitative in Act I 'Whence could so much virtue spring?' is a good example of his methods. The harmonies of Dido's first quatrain are as regularly disposed as the accent of the verse, simple in the extreme, yet always rhythmical; above them the declamation is forcible, the melody expressive, with a wide compass and rich variety of rhythm. To the modern reader perhaps the most striking features are the free alternation of major and minor modes in the same key of C, the bold *coloratura*, and the sudden burst of energy, heightened by its contrasting bass, in the concluding bar. Belinda answers in a gentler mood, moving through new keys—G minor, E flat and A flat, all untouched by Dido—and ending in suspense on the dominant; Dido leads the music back to the original tonality with a long ascending scale in broken rhythm that brings the whole movement to its emotional climax just before the end. The whole recitative is one continuous and logically constructed piece of music, beautiful and expressive even if no words were sung to it; yet the declamation is perfect, and every emotional point is seized with the most subtle delicacy and certainty.

The recitative of the Sorceress may appear at first less successful. The Sorceress has not the same human emotions to express. She is a type, not an individual. She is accompanied by the orchestra and Purcell requires the help of the orchestra to obtain the necessary 'atmosphere'. He seems to have had in this scene a prophetic vision of German romantic opera. The storm is suggested by the instrumental introduction and the Sorceress seems slowly and gradually to disengage herself from the storm, as if she became gradually visible out of the darkness which envelops the scene. Her invocation of the witches is almost a monotone; Purcell allows the words to dominate the music except just at those closing bars in which she suddenly bursts out with unconcealed exultation at the thought of the horrible things which she intends to do. Just as Dido throughout the first act stands out from the rest as the one person on the stage whose emotions are genuine and heart-felt, so the Sorceress stands out grimly self-controlled and intent on her fell purpose against the crowd of attendant witches who burst in upon her riotous and undisciplined.

The third scene brings yet a different type of recitative. Dido is on the stage the whole time, with never a word to say until the storm begins. She has two short lines to sing:

> The skies are clouded! Hark how thunder
> Rends the mountain oaks asunder!

Here again Purcell achieves a clear and definite musical form, at the same time giving us the contrast between her first half-whispered sentence and the outburst of terrified *coloratura* which follows. The recitative between the Spirit and Aeneas suffers musically from the loss of the concluding witches' chorus. The idea of ending the scene with Aeneas' agony is certainly very dramatic, but the fact of the recitative ending in A minor instead of leading back to the key of D minor in which the act began leads me to suspect that Purcell originally intended to write a chorus or dance of witches in D minor, and either discarded it or abandoned the idea, unfortunately without rewriting the close of the preceding recitative. The dialogue, simple as it is, contains many admirable points. The quick interruption of Aeneas 'To-night?' is Tate's invention; Purcell gives it additional effect by repeating the same notes, E, B, when the Spirit repeats the word. The severe dignity of the Spirit is balanced by the firm resolution of Aeneas as he answers him; then comes a pause—one of those pauses so frequent in Purcell's recitatives, pauses which thanks to the system of accompanying recitative on the harpsichord can be drawn out almost indefinitely in order to allow the actor to change his position and expression. The final soliloquy of Aeneas is another case where Purcell in a recitative covers a wide range of emotion. It is wider here than in Dido's dialogue with Belinda; but as in that case the whole movement is held together by rhythmical balance and careful distribution of key.

Purcell reaches his greatest heights in the long dialogue between Dido and the departing Aeneas in Act III. As on a previous occasion he begins with a tonic pedal, a favourite device of Italian chamber cantatas, though in opera it had hardly been used since the days of Peri and Monteverdi. Note how Purcell in setting the threefold repetition of the words 'earth and heaven' contrives to use the same notes in each case, but with different basses, planned so as to increase the emotional effect, an effect still further heightened by the harsh and scornful minor ninth on the last 'earth'. Aeneas speaks in subdued and broken tones; Dido bursts in upon him with fury, again making her emotional point by the repetition of and return to a single emphatic note. A moment later she does the same thing:

Aeneas. By all that's good—
Dido.   By all that's good! No more
      All that's good you have foreswore.

In each case the words 'all that's good' are set to the same notes; the third time, however, the bass moves, so as to make a very harsh 'false relation' of B natural against B flat. Yet again Dido employs the device, in the phrase 'Away, away' repeated for the last time quite by itself after the two have joined in a duet of protestations.

❚ Aeneas has nothing but recitative to sing, except for a few bars of measured duet with Dido in the last scene. The reason for this is doubtless the fact that Aeneas was the only character acted by a man at the first performance. His part is written in the tenor clef in the Tenbury MS., all the others being in the treble. No doubt the Spirit and the Sailor were both sung by girls in the school. I imagine that in the choruses the treble part was sung by schoolgirls and the alto, tenor and bass parts by men imported from outside, either from Westminster Abbey or from the theatre. The alto part in the choruses is obviously intended for a male alto. It has been said that Purcell himself took the part of Aeneas, but it seems much more probable that he directed the opera from the harpsichord. If, as is alleged, Purcell had an alto voice, the part of Aeneas would have been most unsuitable for him, for its compass is that of a high baritone rather than a tenor.

The songs are interesting in their form. Most of Belinda's are merely preliminary to a chorus; 'Shake the cloud' and 'Pursue thy conquest' are very neat little examples of the Italian *Da Capo aria* on a diminutive scale as practised by Stradella and by Alessandro Scarlatti in his earliest operas. In each act there is one long air on a ground bass: in Act I Dido's 'Ah, Belinda', in Act II the air for the Attendant 'Oft she visits' and in Act III Dido's death-song. This arrangement is part of the formal construction of the opera. Each song is entirely different in character in spite of the similarity of form; but as soon as the ground bass begins we know that we have here reached a point at which some vital emotion is to be seriously worked out. Tate probably had no such idea when he planned the Attendant's song, but Purcell saw that an air on a large scale was necessary to the form of his act, and utilized this one for the purpose. It serves its emotional purpose too because the words are suggestive of tragedy to come.

The dances are among the most interesting features of the opera. These also were introduced in view of the special conditions of the first performance, but they are a valuable ingredient of the opera even now, provided that they are rightly interpreted. Those of the first scene do not call for comment. The Echo dance at the end of the second scene is confusing if printed continuously as in the MS., but in the Oxford vocal score it is set out as for two orchestras. This explains its form at once, and it can be made very effective in performance if care is taken to secure a right balance and an exact synchronization of the two groups of players, one in front and the other behind the scenes. The amusing thing about the echoes is that they never reproduce the exact harmony of the original phrases; this ingenious device gives them a delightfully fantastic character, as if the human witches on the stage were answered by spirit dancers who strangely distort their movements. The sailors' dance, like the whole scene of the sailors, is irrelevant to the plot, but it is a welcome irrelevance and its boisterous gaiety prepares well for the tragic scene which follows. The sailors' dance ought certainly to be danced by men, and by men alone, as a definite exhibition of sailors dancing for the amusement of the crowd on the stage. The second dance (after the scene of the witches) is more difficult to understand. It is evidently an imitation of the capricious dances of Locke such as occur in *Cupid and Death* (Dance of the Satyr and Apes). The curious misprint of the original libretto adds to the confusion. The whole scene will become much clearer if we bear in mind the seventeenth-century view of witches. Witches in those days may or may not have possessed supernatural powers, but they were undoubtedly real human beings whom one might meet any day. The witches in *Dido and Aeneas* are therefore not to be represented as spirits; they are old women, and probably young ones too, such as might quite naturally be found among the crowd in the neighbourhood of the harbour. Duffett's parodies of the operas of

Shadwell show us plainly what sort of characters they were in normal life. The first section of this dance may well represent the gestures of the witches who are planning the ruin of the sailors; the second (3/4) will suit either 'Jack o' lanthorn'—a ragged child personating a will-o'-the-wisp—or the more dangerously attractive 'inchanteresses'; while the third section will serve to accompany a scene of general quarrelling, tumult and confusion.

Such descriptive dances as these may have led Purcell's mind on to those two extraordinary moments of musical scene-painting in the second and third scenes of the opera. The sorceress in imagination sees Dido and Aeneas on their hunting expedition. We have already noted the source of this idea in *Brutus of Alba*. Purcell having no horns at his disposal puts in a figure of repeated triplets for strings up and down the chord of D major. The result is far more thrilling than any horns could have been. Horns would have produced mere realism; the violins only suggest. When we hear them we feel that the horns are not really audible; it is an illusion in the minds of the witches on the stage created by the force of the sorceress's imagination. The other moment occurs when Dido first perceives the storm. Here again Purcell gives us repeated semiquavers on the chord of D major; it looks perfectly trivial on paper, but no one who has ever heard it in the theatre can forget its vividness. Purcell may have intended it as literal scene-painting, the musical equivalent of 'mustard-pot and saltpetre'; but it achieves its effect for us now because it gives us an emotional shock and does not call up any visual image.

What gives the whole opera its intense dramatic force is its swiftness of thought. Purcell expresses in ten bars emotions for which Bach or Handel would have required a hundred. For concentration of energy *Dido and Aeneas* stands alone among operas of all time. It is well that we should understand its technical methods. Purcell makes his effect by purely musical means. He has not merely the feeling for expressive harmony; he has a technical command of melody which enables him to balance unequal groups of bars, phrases of five bars where we should expect four, groups of three phrases where we might expect an even number. A good example is the chorus 'Harm's our delight'; it consists of a five-bar phrase ending with a definite cadence balanced by a group of ten bars, which divide not into five and five (in spite of the repetition of melody) but into six and four. A scheme such as this is only manageable by a composer who can conceive of his entire movement as a complete rhythmic whole; and we must feel this movement as a complete rhythmic whole if we are to sing it properly. In the recitatives the swiftness is obtained by the vigorous and accurate declamation of the words. Here the English language is an immense help; but the singer must contribute his share of the labour. A firm sense of rhythm must be established at once; when this is secured the singer will find that he can ultimately allow himself an amount of freedom in pace which would be impossible if he began the recitative with the oratorio-singer's reverent disregard of rhythm.

Dramatic as is Purcell's type of recitative, it must be admitted that the Italians were quite right in confining its model to the chamber. No composer could have kept it up, no audience could have borne the strain if it had been employed continuously throughout the dialogue of a full-sized Italian opera. Purcell could employ it here, and here only, because it forms only a small part—less than one-third—of the entire work, and the entire work is about one-third of the length of the average Italian opera.

In this matter Purcell and his fellow-workers were probably wiser than they knew. They had the choice between short opera of a highly concentrated quality, and long opera in which there must inevitably have been many tracts of comparatively little interest. The long operas of Lulli were held together more by the literary form of Quinault's drama than by any intrinsic musical method; the Italian operas were either shapeless masses of disconnected episodes, as at Venice, or formal dramas sung to more formal arias as at Naples. But Purcell, strong as was his sense of form, did not yet possess the musical technique to organize a whole opera on a large scale, and since the English poets of the period were utterly incapable of doing anything to help him in this direction, *Dido and Aeneas* never had a successor.

Chapter Ten

'DIOCLESIAN' and 'KING ARTHUR'

Among the spectators who witnessed *Dido and Aeneas* at the school in Chelsea we may probably imagine Betterton to have been present, remembering Priest's close connection with the theatre, and it is reasonable to conjecture that he was favourably impressed with the little opera, since in 1690 he engaged Purcell to compose music for a new play which he had adapted himself. This was *The Prophetess* of Beaumont and Fletcher. It appeared with the sub-title *The History of Dioclesian*, and it is under the name of *Dioclesian* that this new operatic version was generally known. The original play was itself almost a 'semi-opera', both in the predominance of supernatural influences in the action, and in the frequent opportunities for the introduction of music; Betterton did little more than elaborate the scenes where the original authors simply indicated 'music and a song'. The musical scenes are however very long, and a proportionate curtailment of the original dialogue was necessary.

The main character in the play is the prophetess Delphia, whose magic arts are employed chiefly in the matrimonial interests of her niece Drusilla. Drusilla is in love with Diocles, a private soldier, who has told her that he will marry her when he becomes emperor. Delphia gives him this prophecy—*Imperator eris Romae cum Aprum grandem interfeceris*—and Diocles sets out to kill as many boars as possible, but with no political result. Delphia is finally obliged to explain to him that the 'boar' in question is Volutius Aper, who has murdered the emperor Numerianus. The emperor's brother and heir Charinus has offered a reward for the murderer's head, promising to the avenger his sister Aurelia in marriage and half the empire.

In Act II Aper has the corpse of Numerianus guarded in a litter in order to make the soldiers believe that Numerianus is ill but still alive. Diocles discovers the deception and kills Aper, thus fulfilling Delphia's prophecy. Delphia on this occasion, as on many others, is watching the scene with Drusilla, both invisible in a chariot drawn by dragons. In the original play music is heard at this point, to indicate the approval of the gods; Diocles is made emperor and acclaimed by the soldiers with a song, the words of which are not given. Charinus and Aurelia enter; Charinus summons a flamen to marry Diocles to the princess on the spot, but Delphia sends thunder and lightning, whereupon Charinus suggests that the gods are angry because they have not yet buried the dead. The act ends in the original with the ascent of Delphia and Drusilla to perform more rites to Hecate.

Betterton here writes in a song for bass, 'Great Diocles the boar has kill'd', followed by a chorus, a second song sung by a woman and a second chorus. After a short dialogue taken from the original, another series of solos and choruses is sung while Diocles is being invested with the imperial robes. This is ingeniously made to lead into a musical entrance of Charinus and the bride Aurelia. Here the music stops, and the scene proceeds in dialogue. On the flamen's entrance a monster appears from the back of the stage, but as soon as Charinus has repented and ordered the funeral of Numerianus[1] the monster disintegrates into a number of furies who perform a dance. '''Tis wonderful', says Charinus, and the body is carried out to a dead march of trumpets and drums.

In Act III there is a long comic scene for Geta the buffoon of the play, who has been made ædile and proposes to arrest Delphia as 'a keeper of tame devils'. Delphia in the original summons a she-devil, Lucifera by name; Geta takes her on his knee, kisses her and dances with her. There was apparently some comic business with a chair at this

[1] In the original the corpse is that of Aper, not that of the emperor.

point[1], which was no doubt traditional, since Betterton enlarges on it.

In the operatic version Delphia makes the figures embroidered on the hangings step out and dance; 'when they have danced a while, they go to sit on the chairs, they slip from 'em and after join in the dance with 'em'.

This dance of chairs was evidently a great success, as is shown by the prologue of *The Fairy Queen* (1692):

> What have we left untry'd to please this Age,
> To bring it more in liking with the Stage?
> We sunk to Farce, and rose to Comedy;
> Gave you high Rants, and well-writ Tragedy.
> Yet Poetry, of the Success afraid,
> Call'd in her Sister Musick to her aid.
> And, lest the Gallery should Diversion want,
> We had Cane Chairs to Dance 'em a Courant.

In a later scene ambassadors from Persia vainly entreat Charinus to give up Cassana, the captive sister of the Persian king, who has been kept as servant to Aurelia. Maximinian, the nephew of Diocles, falls in love with Aurelia, and she by means of Delphia's spells returns his passion with great vehemence. On Maximinian's entrance the song 'What shall I do to show how much I love her?' is sung; it appears however that it is not sung by Maximinian himself, but probably by an invisible singer while Maximinian stands and gazes on the lady.

In the original play Act IV begins with a long dumb-show explained by a Chorus[2] and accompanied by 'Loud Musick', to indicate that the Persian ambassadors have carried off Cassana, taking with them Aurelia, Charinus and Maximinian as prisoners, in spite of the resistance of Diocles,

---

[1]   *Geta.*   Come hither, Lucifera, and kiss me.
    Delphia. Let her sit on your knee.
    Geta.   The Chair turns: hey-boys:
            Pleasant i' faith, and a fine facetious Devil.   [*Dance.*
                                        The Prophetess, Act III, sc. ii.

[2] This Chorus is of course a single speaker, as in some of Shakespeare's plays, not a chorus of singers.

which has been frustrated by the magic arts of the Prophetess. Betterton makes no use of this scene for musical purposes, as the whole idea was foreign to the operatic principles of his day. But in the course of this act he introduces a curious and very characteristic scene in which Delphia, after receiving Diocles' assurances of repentance, shows him a vision of Aurelia lying in state on a tomb. At a sign from Delphia the tomb vanishes, revealing another fantastic architectural scene behind; at a second sign this building falls to pieces and is 'turned into a dance of butterflies'. In the last scene of this act Diocles enters in triumph after having defeated the Persians; Betterton makes this the occasion of a spectacular entry, with a 'trumpet tune', song and chorus. In the course of this scene Diocles magnanimously restores the Persian king to his throne and hands over the imperial crown to Maximinian, himself marrying Drusilla and retiring to the country.

Act v shows us Diocles' rural retreat at which he and his wife are entertained by the songs and dances of the country people. Maximinian and Aurelia enter with soldiers, intending to put Diocles to death, since Maximinian considers that he has no real power as long as his uncle is alive. Delphia as usual saves the situation by thunder and lightning supplemented by other magical effects, and the original play ends with Diocles forgiving his assailants and preparing to entertain both them and his would-be rescuers, Charinus and his men, with universal feasting. Betterton in rearranging this act reduces the performance of the country folk to a single dance, but takes occasion at the end to introduce a lengthy masque, performed by a company of spirits under the direction of Delphia.

How far Betterton collaborated with Purcell in planning his rearrangement and additions we do not know. The music falls into four main groups: the overture and the 'first and second music' which precedes it, with which we may associate the act-tunes; the big choral scene in Act II; the lesser choral scene in Act IV; and the masque in Act V. In addition to this there are a few isolated dances, the song 'What shall I do' and two other songs which it is not possible to place, as they were not printed in the original score; they probably were composed for a later revival. It will at once strike us that, although the original play is more than usually full of supernatural effects, and although we have hitherto found music in the operatic plays of the Restoration almost invariably associated with effects of this kind, yet in *Dioclesian* the greater part of the music occurs in scenes of purely human character, and the supernatural element is confined to the three dances of furies, butterflies and cane chairs respectively. The masque at the end is so completely separate from the rest of the play that it can hardly be classed as 'supernatural', although it represents classical divinities and is supposed to be acted by Delphia's familiars. What then is the main purpose of all this music? How far is it operatic in intention, and on what principles is it planned?

The author-actor-manager, we may imagine, considered merely at what single points music might be introduced with good effect, and what excuses could be invented for bringing it in. The composer, on the other hand, being told to write a certain quantity of music for certain movements, probably considered how he might give his separate movements a general unity and make the audience feel that the whole play was set in a consistent musical framework. This is achieved in two ways, one dramatic, the other purely musical. The music is associated in the main not with apparitions and incantations, but with the crowd of men and women who form a sort of operatic chorus. It was evidently quite impossible at this moment to attempt a complete opera without any spoken dialogue; *Albion and Albanius* had been too conspicuous a failure, *Dido and Aeneas* not sufficiently conspicuous in its success. Moreover, while there was no lack of good actors, there was evidently a very inadequate supply of operatic singers. But a definite step towards opera could be made by treating the crowd as singers. It gave the play a musical background, it gave the music humanity; it heightened the spectacular effect and gave a new emotional weight to scenes which in spoken dialogue were wanting in due impressiveness. This is very noticeable in the first choral scene 'Great Diocles the boar has kill'd'. The other means by which unity was secured was the purely musical device of grouping the movements on a definite scheme of keys. In *Dioclesian* Purcell seems to be aiming at a wider sense of tonality than he had hitherto shown. The 'first and second music' are in C and C minor, but the Overture itself is in G minor. The first act-tune is in D minor; the choral scene of Act II begins in G major and minor, but in the third movement establishes the key of C which is then maintained to the end, the final air and chorus being in C minor and the Furies' dance in C major. The second act-tune is a repetition of one of the choruses. Act III begins with a *chaconne* in G minor, followed by the Chair dance in C major; the song and the next act-tune introduce the new key of D minor, the Butterfly dance returning to C major. The choral scene is in D major; then follows the country dance of Act v in G major, and lastly the masque, which begins and ends in C major but passes through A minor, D major and minor and also G major and minor. The main key of the opera is therefore C major, and Purcell, while obtaining variety by groups of movements in other keys, reasserts the key of C at intervals throughout; in the concluding masque, which forms one long continuous scene, he recalls all previous modulations in quick succession, ending with a long and elaborate movement which definitely re-establishes the original key.

Considered in detail, *Dioclesian* suffers to some extent from over-elaboration. The fact that Purcell printed his music in a similar *format* to that of *Albion and Albanius* may be taken as a fairly safe indication that he was bent on proving himself publicly the equal if not the superior of Grabu, perhaps indeed of Lulli himself, when we consider how extremely rare it was at that date for the music of operas to be printed at all. It is scored for a large orchestra—flutes, hautboys[1] and trumpets in addition to the strings—and there are very few airs which have not got an elaborately contrapuntal accompaniment for some kind of instrument. Another noticeable characteristic is the large number of movements on a ground bass, although none of them, not even the concluding chorus, is on so large a scale as that in the second act of Grabu's opera. The most interesting of these is the *chaconne* for two flutes, which is in canon all the way through.[2] It is clear that Purcell was determined to spare no pains in the matter of finished workmanship and careful attention to detail.

The choral scene in Act II falls into two well-defined sections. The first part, beginning in G and ending in C major, is concerned mainly with the vengeance of Diocles and the obligation of giving due funeral rites to the body of the murdered emperor. It may seem strange that this is almost entirely in major keys, whereas the second part, illustrating the entrance of Aurelia and the women to hail the new emperor Diocles, now to be called Dioclesian, is all in C minor. This is not at all in accordance with our modern ideas of the significance of the major and minor modes. It has often been remarked that Purcell in all his works shows a peculiar leaning to the minor mode, offering in this respect a great contrast to Lulli, whose employment of the minor mode is comparatively rare.[3] The reason of this is technical as well

[1] It is extremely probable that hautboys and flutes were generally played by the same musicians, both in this and in other works, as it is very rare to find them used simultaneously.

[2] The employment of strict canon in dance form is curious, but Locke's canonic dance (4 in 2) in *The Tempest* and the Dance for the Followers of Night in Purcell's *The Fairy Queen* (also canon 4 in 2) show that it was by no means considered as impracticable for stage purposes.

[3] Discussing Purcell with a French musician learned in all the music of the period, a great admirer of Purcell, but with a natural bias in favour of Lulli, I was interested to receive the criticism that Purcell was 'toujours anglais, toujours romantique et sentimental, toujours en mode mineur'.

as temperamental. At a period when chromatic harmony was just beginning to be common property[1] the minor mode naturally became associated with the more passionate emotions, since it provided a richer variety of harmonic colour.[2] Its comparative rarity in the work of Lulli does not point to the French temperament being more cheerful than the English, but merely to the dislike prevalent in French literary circles of that unrestrained and to them almost savage emotionalism of the Italians.

Purcell's devotion to Italian music has already been mentioned and he re-asserts it himself in the preface to the score of *Dioclesian*. If his music appears to us at first sight more melancholy even than that of his Italian contemporaries, it is because he makes much more use than they do of harmony for his emotional effects. Here then is the explanation of the scheme of this scene in *Dioclesian*, an explanation the principle of which can be applied to all Purcell's works. The first chorus is dignified rather than triumphant, based on a motive of righteous vengeance; the soprano solo 'Charon the peaceful shade invites' employs the minor mode for gentler feelings, until the trumpets break in in the key of C major. The choice of C major was here inevitable, owing to the fact that G major was an impossible key for trumpets. These instruments dominate the movement as long as it has a definitely military character. The change to C minor and the entrance of the flutes indicate not mourning but the predominance on the stage of the 'softer sex', and Purcell by developing the whole to a climax in this key wishes to transfer the attention of the audience from the political and military aspect of the scene to the purely personal interest centred in Dioclesian

---

[1] The chromatic tendencies of the previous century were confined only to small groups of advanced musicians, and, though of immense historical importance, were not at the time characteristic of popular music, even among the educated classes.

[2] This is especially noticeable in the effects derived from the melodic minor scale, which has a major sixth and seventh ascending, and the same intervals minor in descending. The works of J. S. Bach supply endless illustrations.

himself, whose love affairs are now to be the main motive of the drama.

The second choral scene calls for less comment. Here the situation is purely military, and no change of dramatic interest is involved, so that the three movements are all in the same key and of the same character. Here again the choice of key is dictated by the restrictions of the trumpets. To set the scene in C major would have made it only a feeble repetition of the previous one; D major, the only other available key for the trumpets, has the advantage of being more brilliant than C and so secures a heightened effect without undue expenditure of means.

The dances of furies and others, as well as the final masque, must be regarded purely as *ballet-divertissement*. They illustrate for the most part not dramatic situations or human emotions, but steps, movements and postures on the stage. The best form which criticism of these can possibly take is actual performance, and there can be no better way of entering into the intimate understanding of these and similar works of Purcell than by patiently planning out the details of stage grouping, gesture and attitude. Even if it is impossible to reconstruct accurately every detail of the original dances, it will be found not only that the resources of modern stage technique are well adapted to the interpretation of Purcell, but that the close study of his music reveals an infinity of delicate touches which even modern technique can take a pride and delight in making visible to the eye.

The success of *Dioclesian* obliged even Dryden to admit Purcell's genius. The preface to *Amphitryon* (October 1690) gives a warm commendation to 'the excellent composition of Mr. Purcell; in whose Person we have at length found an English Man, equal with the best abroad. At least my opinion of him has been such, since his happy and judicious performances in the late opera'. The music to *Amphitryon*, charming as it is, does not call for analysis here, as it is in no sense operatic; nor need we do more than mention

Distressed Innocence, a play by Settle, for which Purcell also wrote music in 1690. The music of these plays consists of act-tunes etc. and a few songs. Among the act-tunes of *Distressed Innocence* is an air in C minor of remarkable emotional power, but there is no indication in the play as to where it might have been inserted.

Dryden, being now convinced of Purcell's dramatic abilities, seized the opportunity to bring out his long-postponed opera *King Arthur*, to which *Albion and Albanius* had been intended as a prologue. We learn from the preface that the play required considerable alterations, and what is particularly interesting is Dryden's admission that he made various changes, not without reluctance, at the request of Purcell. He almost suggests that he had written his new words to Purcell's melodies, when he says that 'the Numbers of Poetry and Vocal Musick are sometimes so contrary, that in many places I have been obliged to cramp my verses, and make them rugged to the Reader, that they may be harmonious to the Hearer'. The opera was brought out at Dorset Gardens in 1691 and mounted with great magnificence; the expense of the singers and dancers was in fact so great as to excite some discontent on the part of those who were only actors.

Designed originally as a glorification of Charles II and rewritten seven years later with an eye to the favour of William III, *King Arthur* is aggressively patriotic in its plot. The scene is laid in Kent. Oswald the Saxon king of Kent, having been refused the hand of Emmeline the blind daughter of Conon duke of Cornwall, has made war on his rival in love Arthur, and has invaded the west of England. Arthur at the opening of Act 1 has succeeded in driving the Saxons back to Kent, and is on the point of fighting the last battle which will finally decide the struggle. The first act serves merely to introduce the characters: Arthur and his allies; then Emmeline and her companion Matilda; and finally, after a change of scene, Oswald, who under the direction of a heathen wizard Osmond prepares to propitiate his gods Woden, Thor and Freya by the sacrifice of six Saxons on their altars. Osmond is assisted by two spirits, Grimbald 'a fierce earthy spirit' and Philidel 'an airy spirit', for whose cowardice Grimbald expresses severe contempt. No sooner has the sacrificial ceremony been performed than a battle is supposed to take place behind the scenes, and the act ends with the Britons rejoicing over their victory in the well-known chorus 'Come if you dare'.

In Act II Philidel is encountered by the enchanter Merlin (who supports Arthur) and surrenders to him. Arthur and his soldiers enter preceded by Grimbald who in the disguise of a shepherd is leading them astray into bogs and marshes; Philidel warns them in a song, other good and evil spirits answering him in opposing choral groups. Grimbald himself sings a song in opposition, but on Philidel repeating his music, Arthur and his friends finally choose the right course and Grimbald, enraged, disappears in flames. Philidel and the good spirits lead the Britons off to safety with another song. The scene changes to a pavilion, and a short dialogue between Emmeline and Matilda follows, the object of which is to emphasize the heroine's blindness and inability to conceive of anything visual. Shepherds and shepherdesses entertain her with music, after which Oswald and his friend Guillamar enter and carry off the ladies. The Britons appear and there is a certain amount of trumpeting and clashing of swords, after which Arthur and Oswald have a long but ineffectual wrangle in the usual heroic manner.

In Act III Osmond has embarrassed the Britons by laying enchantments on a wood. Merlin sends Philidel to investigate; he is seized by Grimbald, but outwits him and leaves him bound by a spell. Merlin and Philidel restore sight to Emmeline (two songs for Philidel are here lost) who now sees Matilda and Arthur for the first time. Philidel also shows her a vision of spirits in the shapes of men and women (the music to this chorus is also lost). Osmond approaching, Merlin and Arthur depart, but are unable at present to

What does the cold scene symbolise?

release Emmeline from his spells. Osmond, having drugged his master Oswald, makes violent love to Emmeline, and by way of encouragement transforms the landscape to a scene of ice and snow, in order to show how Cupid can warm the inhabitants 'in spite of cold weather'. Osmond then offers violence to Emmeline, but is called away by Grimbald who is in need of assistance.

In Act iv Grimbald warns Osmond of Merlin's manœuvres. Arthur enters and is tempted by the songs of sirens in a river; he resists and is tempted again by a chorus and dance of Nymphs and Sylvans. Again he resists, and by way of forcing a passage to Emmeline strikes at a tree with his sword. Emmeline appears in the tree-trunk, but Philidel saves him from yielding to her charms and exposes the false Emmeline as Grimbald in disguise. Arthur hacks his way through the wood and Philidel drags Grimbald off in chains.

In Act v Arthur and Oswald fight a single combat, each assisted by his attendant wizard; Arthur disarms Oswald and the play ends with the surrender of the Saxons, the imprisonment of Osmond and the embraces of Arthur and Emmeline. Merlin waves his wand, and a masque follows concluding with a song by Honour in praise of St George and the Order of the Garter.

Apart from some absurdities of detail due mainly to the taste of the age, Dryden's libretto is a very skilful piece of work. The human and supernatural interests are closely interwoven, the spoken dialogue and the musical numbers are in general well balanced. The main interest of the play is inevitably centred on the music, but the dialogue is clear and not too prolix, and although the principal characters do not sing at all, the music is cleverly led up to so as to be an integral part of the drama. The influence of *The Tempest*, that is, of Dryden's own version of it, is everywhere apparent. Merlin is derived from Prospero, Philidel from Ariel; Emmeline's somewhat indiscreetly naïve conversation perpetually recalls Miranda.

To the modern reader there are various situations which seem to foreshadow Wagner—the hero accosted by sirens in the river, the duel in which each actor is but a puppet in the hands of visible supernatural powers, the slow appearance of the Frost Genius, not unlike the evocation of Erda; indeed the whole opera with its atmosphere of barbaric legend seems in some ways a prototype of *Der Ring des Nibelungen*. The cause of this is probably to be found in the influence of Tasso which was making itself felt in all literature at this time, and was by no means exhausted even as late as the early nineteenth century, although its effect on Wagner was probably quite indirect.

Although, as we have seen, the supernatural element was introduced expressly in order to provide opportunities for music, Purcell and Dryden do not confine their music entirely to this part of the play. Grimbald makes his first appearance without any music, and the music of the first act is devoted to a big choral scene similar to those in *Dioclesian*. This is effectively planned so as to form a climax at the end of the act. It begins with a sacrificial scene such as Purcell often wrote; after a short introduction for the orchestra a dialogue ensues between solo priests and the chorus, the repetitions of the choral phrases giving the movement musical form. This is entirely accompanied by strings, and Purcell has been very skilful in making the strings carry the music vigorously forward by insistence on strong rhythmical figures imitating and answering the voices. This is followed by a duet for two priests and a chorus in quicker rhythm 'To Woden thanks we render'. The priests and people then address the victims who are to be sacrificed; the chorus 'Brave souls, to be renowned in story' is treated fugally, with a strongly contrasting coda in the minor key at the words 'Die and reap the fruit of glory'. The whole of this fine chorus is very Handelian in character. It might almost justly be said that it is too severe and noble for the character of the savage Saxons who are supposed to be singing it; but 'local colour' was not much understood in any branch of art at this date, and Purcell was more concerned in setting the words themselves than in depicting the characters of those who sang them. In any case the mistake is redeemed by the song and chorus 'I call you all', the energetic bounding rhythm of which provides a violent contrast to the dismal harmonies of the sacrifice. On this chorus follows immediately the battle music, thirty-five bars in C major (the previous scene was in F) made up of answering trumpet calls, after which the victorious Britons enter to sing 'Come if you dare'. This well-developed chorus with its severely simple harmonies contrasts vividly with the chorus of Saxons, and makes a brilliant finish to the act.

At the beginning of Act II are two instrumental numbers, one of which may perhaps have been used at the descent of Merlin; neither of them has any very strongly marked character. Philidel's song 'Hither this way', lightly accompanied by two violins, has an airy grace that well suggests the character of the gentle spirit, and the chorus, by dividing antiphonally into groups of male and female voices respectively, fits the dramatic situation very well. Grimbald is a bass, and sings in the character of a shepherd, so that his song is of a plainer cast and more energetic in character. After a repetition of the previous chorus there follows a delightful movement for five solo voices and chorus, 'Come follow me', with which Philidel leads the Britons into safety.

Between each of these musical numbers there are a few lines of dialogue, not set to recitative but spoken; this helps by contrast to emphasize the supernatural character of the spirit choruses, without breaking up the musical unity of the scene. Here again a good effect is secured by making the characters leave the stage in the course of the last chorus, after which the scene changes. The music in the next scene is a good example of useful irrelevancy. There is no reason why a chorus of shepherds and shepherdesses should appear, but their songs and dances make a delightful point of repose in the action of the play, and are of great value in heightening the dramatic effect of the sudden abduction of the heroine by Oswald and Guillamar which immediately follows this episode. Considered simply as music this group of three movements is one of the most charming scenes that Purcell ever penned, and we must not fail to note the skill with which he has combined unity of style with the happiest variety of rhythm and melody, the concluding hornpipe chorus bearing a sufficient melodic resemblance to the first chorus to give a general suggestion of a *da capo* form. The remainder of the act is without music; Dryden here gives us a quick succession of exciting entrances, and to illustrate a dramatic effect of this kind the musical technique of the period was not sufficiently flexible.

The music to the first part of Act III is unfortunately lost; we can perhaps best judge by the model of Ariel's songs in *The Tempest* how Purcell would have treated the restoration of sight to Emmeline by Philidel. The next musical episode —also lost—is the chorus of spirits who sing to Emmeline of 'Sight, the Mother of Desires'. This again is a point of repose, corresponding in value rather to the contemplative *ensembles* of later Italian opera.[1] In an opera of Mozart's day we should no doubt have had at this point a quartet for Arthur, Emmeline, Matilda and Philidel, but as on this particular occasion Philidel was the only character able to sing, the necessary musical commentary had to be provided by other means. The advances of Osmond to Emmeline which follow on this repeat the idea of the abduction scene in the previous act; but the repetition is here effective, because every factor in it is greatly intensified. The chorus of spirits (we may at least imagine that Purcell's lost music did not fall below the general level of the rest of the opera) is on a higher emotional plane than the chorus of shepherds; the protracted violence of Osmond is more harrowing than

---

[1] We may compare it with the trio in Act II and the quartet in Act III of Mozart's *Idomeneo* or the quartet 'Mir ist so wunderbar' in *Fidelio*.

the hasty abduction, especially with the added interest of Emmeline's restored sight, a benefit of which she as yet hardly knows how to make use; lastly, there occurs here the long and elaborate musical scene of Cupid and the frozen people. It must be confessed that the actual conclusion of the act after the music has come to an end is not well managed, at any rate from a modern point of view.

The frost scene is one of Purcell's most famous achievements. It derives much of its celebrity from the curious notation which Purcell has employed in the voice parts to indicate an effect of shivering. It is probable that if Purcell had lived in a society in which opera was a matter of daily routine as in Italy, he would have noted his air not as we have it—

KING ARTHUR   PURCELL

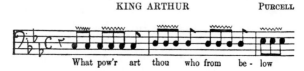

but thus—

adding perhaps some direction such as *tremolando*, or, it may be, trusting to the natural dramatic instinct of the singers to give the phrase a suitable emotional colour.[1] Nor is there anything remarkable about the accompaniment of repeated quavers: the device is quite common in the operas of Alessandro Scarlatti and other Italians, who sometimes even direct the strings to play '*orrido*'. To mention this is not to

---

[1] The curious and often apparently unsingable vocal phrases to be found in the works of Caccini and Monteverdi are in general nothing more than awkward attempts to render in normal note-values such *nuances* of interpretation as a modern composer would either leave to the singer's intelligence or indicate by grace notes and marks of expression. It must be remembered that in Purcell's day marks of expression were almost unknown; yet we cannot for a moment suppose that performers executed everything at a uniform *mezzo forte*.

detract from the value of Purcell's work. The greatness of the scene lies not in the quaint notation or even in the particular device of instrumentation, but in the musical idea itself. The whole scene is nothing more than a masque, and has no real connection with the drama, though its ostensible function is to excite the passions of Emmeline by the presentation of Cupid's effects in a visible form. It is extremely difficult for the modern reader to enter into the seventeenth-century point of view in a case of this kind. The whole idea is essentially baroque, and belongs to an age which on every conceivable occasion was ready to represent abstractions in the form of allegorical sculpture in attitudes of frantic gesticulation. Yet we can at least admire the picturesqueness of Purcell's imagination, the bold contrasts of style, and the masterly piling up of the music to a climax at the end of the chorus 'Tis Love that has warm'd us'. Here, or perhaps after a dance, the scene should have ended; the duet 'Sound a parley', interesting though it is as showing how completely Purcell was dominated by Italian influences, is much too long, and completely holds up the mimetic development of the scene, which although largely sung is in essential principle *ballet-divertissement*.

In Act IV the poet has employed music very skilfully to set the atmosphere of temptation and enchantment, in order to lead up to the episode of the false Emmeline imprisoned in the tree. It is only to be regretted that so little music is allotted in the opera to Grimbald, who might have been made a much more vivid personality. Probably some of the music to this scene is lost: we have no trace of the 'soft Musick' which is directed at the lines

> Hark, Musick and the warbling Notes of Birds;
> Hell entertains me, like some welcome guest,[1]

nor of any setting of the first song of the sirens. Their second song 'Two daughters of this aged stream' is a movement of

---

[1] We may perhaps imagine something like the nightingale music on a ground bass in Act II of *The Fairy Queen*.

exquisite beauty. Here again we note the employment of a minor key, indicating not melancholy but rather voluptuous-ness.[1] The same key of G minor is maintained in the next number, in which various combinations of solo voices and chorus are interwoven into a long *chaconne* in a most masterly way. This movement is directed by the poet to be danced all through, and corresponds in effect to the ballet of shepherds and shepherdesses in the fourth act of Gluck's *Armida*.[2] From a dramatic point of view the movement is much too long as a chorus, but if we regard it as a ballet with vocal accompaniment, its introduction here is most justifiable. There is no more music in this act, the climax being obtained by the scenic effect of the destruction of the forest, with a comic exit for Philidel and Grimbald, which corresponds on a small scale to the comic duet for *soubrette* and *basso buffo* which often comes at the end of a serious act in Scarlatti's operas.

The music in the fifth act is entirely confined to the masque at the end. Here, as in *Dioclesian*, Purcell displays his infinite variety of invention; but the individual episodes have no great connection with each other, and there is nothing in the entertainment that has the slightest dramatic character. For this reason the masque will not be analysed here; it will be more convenient to criticize Purcell's treatment of such forms in the next chapter.

Like *Dido and Aeneas*, *King Arthur* is a solitary specimen of its kind. Purcell wrote a very large quantity of stage music during the four years of life that still remained to him; but never again did he collaborate directly with a poet on a work conceived from the beginning as an opera, in which music and poetry were at least on equal terms, even if music was

---

[1] Cf. 'Shepherd, shepherd, leave decoying' (G minor) in Act II (in Mr Fuller Maitland's edition, 'Shepherd, shepherd, May invites you'), 'If Love's a sweet passion' (G minor) in Act II of *The Fairy Queen*, and 'Ah! how sweet it is to love' (A minor) in the masque in *Dioclesian* as specimens of Purcell's erotic style.

[2] The close resemblance to this scene shows Dryden's indebtedness to Tasso.

not always allowed to have the upper hand. In all the remaining cases the play if a new one was designed primarily as a play; if intended to be regarded as a sort of opera, it was never more than a rearrangement of an old play, sometimes even one to which music had already been written in a previous generation.

In spite of its essentially late-seventeenth-century character, *King Arthur* retained its popularity as recently as 1842, having had frequent revivals in the preceding century, though various alterations were made and additional music provided by Arne and others. It is in fact the classical example of typical English opera, and the influence of its form (though not of its music) may be traced even in Weber's *Oberon*, which was composed for London to a libretto by an English author and constructed on characteristically English lines.

Chapter Eleven

'THE FAIRY QUEEN'

It might at first sight be thought impossible that Purcell in the four years which remained to him after the production of *King Arthur* should have written music for all the plays which recent research assigns to this final period; but it must be remembered that though these amount to nearly forty names, there are only four which have enough music to be considered as operas, even putting the widest interpretation on that word. These four works are *The Fairy Queen, Bonduca, The Tempest,* and *The Indian Queen.* The first of these stands in a class by itself. We have already spoken of the independent masques which follow *Dioclesian* and *King Arthur. The Fairy Queen* (1692) is nothing more than a series of four masques, which are placed at the end of each act of the play (a barbarously mutilated version of *A Midsummer Night's Dream*) except the first, and for this there was written a curious and hardly less irrelevant comic scene when the opera was revived in 1693. *Bonduca* repeats the methods of *Dioclesian,* though with a more advanced musical technique.

The dramatic plan of *The Tempest* has already been discussed in Chapter VII, and the substitution of Purcell's music, probably in 1695, for that of Locke and others did not materially affect the general scheme of Shadwell's libretto. Much the same may be said of *The Indian Queen* (1695) which Purcell apparently was not able to finish before his death, as a few numbers were adapted from earlier works, and the final masque was composed by his brother Daniel. The interest of these 'operas' lies not in their form, which is in all cases a retrogression from the scheme of *King Arthur,* but in the musical and interpretative value of their single numbers.

For this reason I propose to make no attempt to analyse them singly in chronological order, but to pick out certain recurring types of musical or dramatic method and discuss them under separate heads.

The main types to be considered are (1) single songs of various kinds, from the simplest tune to the elaborated *scena*, and duets—all these roughly divisible into the two categories of tragedy and comedy; (2) scenes of magic, including religious ceremonies, most of which include choral numbers; (3) choral movements of a purely human character, sometimes associated with dances; (4) masques, under which heading most of Purcell's dance music will be considered. The dramatic value of these single specimens is often negligible, but Purcell continued to make progress in his powers of musical interpretation in spite of having no opportunity to show what he could do in continuous musical drama, and we must therefore criticize the body of this later work more as a series of studies towards that immortal masterpiece of English opera which he did not live long enough even to attempt.

Purcell's songs, enchanting as they are from a purely musical point of view, are of comparatively little importance as factors in the dramas for which they were written. They are never sung by any but subsidiary characters; in most cases they are given to persons whose only reason for being on the stage at all is to sing the song. The nearest approach to a song as an expression of personality by the character who sings it is in such cases as 'What shall I do to show how much I love her' in *Dioclesian*,[1] or 'O lead me to some peaceful gloom' sung by Bonvica, the daughter of Bonduca, in the play of that name. In this latter case, however, the song is introduced not as a spontaneous outburst of feeling, but as a piece of music, so that it has much the same dramatic value as when a character in a modern play sits down to the pianoforte. This device has its function, as we see both in

[1] See preceding chapter.

Shakespeare and in modern opera, but its value is well illustrated by such a case as that of Desdemona's 'willow song' in
Verdi's *Otello*, where the actual song itself would have no
importance dramatically if it were not for the constant inter-
ruptions, and the contrast supplied by the orchestral indications of those feelings which find no vocal expression.
A device of this kind was beyond the musical technique of
Purcell's day.

The songs which Purcell puts into positions of this kind
are always of a very simple nature. There are, however, a
certain number of songs which we should describe now by
the word *scena*. Several of these are introduced in the three
Don Quixote plays. Two of them, 'Let the dreadful engines'
and 'From rosy bowers', are well known to modern audiences.
But songs of this class are always introduced frankly as
musical performances, that is, they are intended to be so
regarded by the characters in the play. Thus in *Don Quixote,
Part III*,[1] Altisidora sets out to make Don Quixote unfaithful
to Dulcinea, and expresses her intention of 'teasing him with
a whimsical variety'; when he begins to make love to her,
she says 'Come now, you shall see me sing and dance, and
how far I excel dull Dulcinea'—the song 'From rosy bowers'
(to part of which she very probably danced) following immediately. It is what was commonly described as 'a Mad Song',
and the type is clearly derived from the Italian chamber
cantatas, such as Stradella often wrote, the object of them
being simply to exhibit in one long chain of movements what
Altisidora calls 'a whimsical variety, as if I were possess'd
with several degrees of passion'. It is easy to imagine how
successful they must have been, when we see how grateful
they were to the singer, how wide their range of emotion,
how vivid the presentation of each phrase. If there were
singers who could do them justice, why, it may be asked,

---

[1] The play of *Don Quixote* by Thomas D'Urfey (1694) was so popular that
it was followed at once by a sequel (*Part II*) and this by another in 1695; this
last, however, was not successful.

were they not set in a continuous frame of music, and allotted to the principal characters as the most intense expression of the sincerest feelings? Yet we can well understand that what the public wanted was, not to be faced with new and unwonted expression of complex emotions, but to see an old-established favourite, such as Betterton, in a part which gave scope for such effects as they had already learned to admire. It did not matter that the favourite was no singer. A singer could be introduced anywhere, and the audience came, not to be moved by the presentations of real emotion, but to admire and applaud the skill of the presenter, in which case it could not matter whether the emotion was presented as real or as deliberately feigned.

Most interesting, from the point of view of operatic technique, are Purcell's broadly comic scenes, and also certain songs of a light comedy character, such as Mozart might have given to Susanna or Cherubino. One of the best of this latter class is 'Dear pretty youth' sung by Dorinda in *The Tempest*. The dramatists of Purcell's day, following the example of Dryden, were sometimes able in their lyrics to exchange the high-flown poetic manner for a language that was surprisingly direct and conversational. Purcell seizes on this in the happiest style, and develops it in a most natural and amusing way by repetitions of words, which may appear ridiculous on the printed page or when sung with such seemly restraint and reverence as is of course due to classical music, but when backed up by appropriate gestures and movements are full of life and humanity. Somewhat similar in style, though not so accomplished, are the songs 'Celia has a thousand charms' (*The Rival Sisters*, 1695) and 'Pious Celinda goes to prayers' (words by Congreve), and there are also some duets of much the same type (*e.g.* 'Leave these useless arts' (*Epsom Wells*, 1693), and 'As Amoret and Thyrsis lay' (*The Old Bachelor*, ?1693). Another characteristic style of Purcell's is the blustering bass song, of which the best-known examples are 'I'll sail upon the dog-star'

(*A Fool's Preferment*, 1688) and 'Let the dreadful engines' (*Don Quixote, Part I*, 1694). This type is also to be found in duets, such as the dialogue 'Behold the man' in *The Richmond Heiress* (1693), where the fighting man so common in all seventeenth-century drama is contrasted with the sprightly lady; in this case both the characters are supposed to be mad. It is not far from duets of this kind to those scenes of broad low comedy which are among the most masterly and most intensely national things that Purcell wrote. An amusing example is the dialogue in *Oroonoko* (1695), 'Celemene, pray tell me'; a more easily accessible specimen is the dialogue between Coridon and Mopsa in *The Fairy Queen*, 'Now the maids and the men'. In songs and dialogues such as these Purcell exhibits not merely an inexhaustible vein of vigorous popular melody, but a great sense of humour in the setting of words which sometimes startles us by its life-like and even modern effect. One of the best specimens is the scene of the Drunken Poet in *The Fairy Queen*, in which the poet staggers on to the stage singing 'Fi-fi-fi-fill up the bowl' and is teased by Titania's fairies.

The scenes of magic and religious ceremony were very important features of the tragedies and spectacular plays of the Restoration. Those in *Theodosius*, *Circe*, and *Dioclesian* have already been discussed. Dryden's *Oedipus* (probably 1692) contains a scene in which Tiresias invokes the ghost of Laius. We find here the usual combination of recitative and chorus, with a definite air in the middle in which one of the characters calls for music, in accordance with obvious operatic device, to charm the infernal powers. This particular scene is curious as being set for three male voices only, alto, tenor and bass. It is, however, far surpassed by the scene in *Bonduca* 'Hear us, great Rugwith' in which the Britons address their deities. There is the usual introduction for strings, on the theme of the first chorus, showing a very modern understanding of the resources of chromatic harmony; the chorus, built up of short and striking entries in close imitation, is interrupted at frequent intervals by four soloists. This is followed at once by a noble recitative and air 'Hear, ye gods of Britain', accompanied by strings which enter in responsive phrases, as in *Dioclesian*. All this is in C minor. These prayers meet with no result. Caratach (Caractacus) then invokes the goddess in a speech of some length, and a flame arises on the altar. He next calls upon the Druids to sing. Here follows the usual invocation of the art of music, 'Sing, sing, ye Druids', given in this case to two priestesses; it is preceded by a very long introduction for two flutes, to which no doubt some sort of dance was performed. The movement (in G minor) is constructed on a freely treated ground bass, and as invariably happens in such cases it is extremely long; but Purcell has strengthened it by making the full chorus repeat the last eleven bars with the strings, so as to form a dignified coda and bring the duet to a climax. It is succeeded at once by an *arioso* in the same key for a tenor priest, asking the oracle (with an extended *coloratura* phrase) if the Britons will 'dye with Roman blood the field'. The judicious oracle replies with the words 'Much will be spill'd', which were presumably spoken. On this there follows at once a brilliant trumpet symphony in C major, the sudden entry of which is very striking. Two Druids take up the same melody to the words 'To arms, your ensigns straight display', and this leads straight on to the well-known 'Britons, strike home', played first by trumpet and strings, then sung as a solo, and finally repeated by the chorus. The similarity of this scene to that in the first act of *King Arthur* will be at once apparent. The scene in *King Arthur* is more interesting as drama, because a strong contrast lies between the two hostile choruses which are thus brought into close contact. In *Bonduca* the same chorus is on the stage the whole time, so that the interest of the scene is more purely musical; yet it is easy to see that a very imposing and exciting stage picture could be arranged to this chain of movements. It is hardly safe to attempt any conjecture as to what were the general principles of stage management practised in Purcell's day with regard to operatic scenes of this kind; but a modern 'producer' would certainly hail with delight the opportunities indicated by the imitative entries of the chorus in the first movement for the rhythmical carrying on of a striking gesture from one part of the stage to another, an effective contrast being obtained by the more rigid grouping and simultaneous action suggested by the clear-cut simple rhythm of 'Britons, strike home'.

Another fine scene of this kind occurs in *The Indian Queen.* The fifth act opens with a scene in the temple of the sun, with priests 'in habits of white and red feathers, attending by a bloody altar' ready to sacrifice the hero and heroine, with the latter's father, at the orders of Zempoalla, the usurping queen of Mexico, and her paramour Traxalla. Here we have only two choruses, separated by a ceremonial recitative with responses from the people, but Purcell has secured a fine effect by beginning in a dignified style with an introduction and chorus in F major, reserving the harsh and grim effect of F minor, with fugal entries and poignant discords, for the second chorus, which works up to the energetic declamation of the phrase 'there's nothing to be trusted here below'. The dramatic value of this is considerable, as the music is immediately followed by several violent deaths on the stage, with the news of a revolution and the final triumph of Montezuma the hero.

Attention may be drawn here to one or two other items of stage music which are better classed among scenes of magic than among songs. It is as a rule difficult for us now to see anything very terrible or marvellous in most of Purcell's supernatural scenes. Generally speaking, the mere fact of their being set to music instead of being spoken was considered enough to give them a supernatural character. But there are certain cases where Purcell has shown a fantastic imaginativeness which still appeals to modern readers. We can trace it in the freakish duet 'Hark my Damilcar' sung by the two spirits in Dryden's *Tyrannic Love* (probably written for a revival in 1695), the curious words of which were absurdly parodied, on its first appearance, in *The Rehearsal*. Another striking scene is that in the last act of Shadwell's Don Juan play *The Libertine* (? 1692), when Don John is entertained by the Statue in the church, and devils rise from below to give a performance of infernal music. This scene is remarkable for the employment of trombones, and it is curious that Purcell should have utilized the same material again (also for trombones) as part of the funeral music for Queen Mary.[1] Two more scenes of supernatural character are to be found in *The Indian Queen*, which is the most interesting of all Purcell's operas from this point of view. Zempoalla, the usurping queen, consults the magician Ismeron, who invokes the god of sleep in the hope that he will be able to forecast the future for her. The opening of Ismeron's solo 'Ye twice ten hundred deities' was described by Burney as 'the best piece of recitative in our language'. The whole solo is well planned for dramatic effect; opening with this magnificent piece of declamation it proceeds to a fantastic air in which the violins are well employed to enhance the interpretative power of the voice part; then after the remarkable dramatic passage to the words

> From thy sleeping mansion rise
> And open thy unwilling eyes,

which leads to a climax on the dominant of the key, the whole character of the song changes to a gentle lulling melody, which prepares well for the appearance of the god himself. He rises to the accompaniment of two hautboys, the entrance of which makes an effective contrast of tone-colour, and the effect is kept up by the solo hautboy which accompanies his air. Here again, as in so many of Purcell's airs, it must be admitted that the composer has allowed himself an undue length. There is some uncertainty about the arrangement of the music in connection with the rest of

---

[1] This scene is discussed at some length in my *Mozart's Operas*, London, 1913, in connection with Mozart's *Don Giovanni*.

the scene; the most important number is a duet for 'aerial spirits' on a ground bass, 'Ah! how happy are we', the sighing and (to us) melancholy phrases of which, together with the heaving rise and fall of the ground bass, suggest emotions of a very different kind; but Purcell very probably employed the minor mode to suggest the mysterious and voluptuous character of a scene of enchantment.

Still more curious is the musical scene in Act II. Zempoalla 'appears seated on a throne frowning upon her attendants'. Without any explanation of whether we are to regard the figures as real or fictitious, there appear suddenly Fame and Envy, each accompanied by a chorus of followers. Fame sings the praises of Zempoalla, joined by the chorus; then Envy asks

> What flattering noise is this
> At which my snakes all hiss?

At the end of each line—both, needless to say, are repeated several times—the followers of Envy (alto and tenor) pronounce the single word 'hiss' coinciding exactly with Envy's words 'hiss' and 'this', so as to form a complete chord; at the end of the main divisions of the air they repeat the first line in chorus. This experiment in musical imitation may strike us as crude and perhaps even childish; but it was an ingenious idea for the time and shows that Purcell was ready to make use of unconventional methods of expression. The movement as a whole is disappointing and somewhat deficient in real musical interest. The whole scene is in fact a masque, and it is difficult to understand why it should have been introduced at this point, especially as the lady whose envious detractors are silenced so emphatically by Fame is the female villain of the play. The probable explanation is that it was an attempt to reproduce the effect of a somewhat similar scene in Grabu's *Albion and Albanius*.

Choruses in other than religious scenes are not very common. The most important have been already criticized as they are in close connection with scenes of sacrifice or incantation. An example of quite different character occurs in *The Libertine*, in the fourth act of which there is a scene of rustic merry-making, to which belong the song 'Nymphs and shepherds' and the chorus 'In these delightful pleasant groves'. The greater part of Purcell's choruses are to be found in the masques, which are best considered as a separate category.

The masques have as a rule no real connection with the plays, except in so far as the appearance of Hymen or Juno might always be regarded as appropriate to the pairing off with which practically every drama was expected to end. Nor have they except in isolated cases any internal organization. They conform roughly to a general scheme in which we are fairly sure to find Hymen, Juno, Cupid, Bacchus and their followers, and also some sort of rustic and humorous characters. These vocal numbers are interspersed with dances, and in some cases the masque ends with a vocal or instrumental *chaconne* on an extended scale. It is quite useless to expect the masque to have any dramatic justification. It does not even attempt to tell a definite story, or to present any definite idea, except in so far as most of the masques are concerned with the passion of love in some form or other. We must therefore regard the masques simply as *ballets-divertissements*. To the idea of opera they are absurd and useless excrescences; but they contain many single numbers both vocal and instrumental which show that Purcell had a clear sense of the value of stage movement.

Examples of masques are to be found in *Dioclesian*, *King Arthur*, *Timon of Athens*, *The Tempest* and *The Indian Queen*. But the one opera in which the masque is developed to such an extent as to absorb practically the whole of the music is *The Fairy Queen* (1692). This is an adaptation of *A Midsummer Night's Dream*, which some critics have described as being itself almost more a masque than a play. The author of the operatic arrangement is not known. There are many verbal resemblances to *Albion and Albanius*, but whether they are to be taken as indications of Dryden's own hand or only of some indolent plagiarist is a question which must be left to professed historians of literature. The general idea adopted was to preserve most of the clowns' scenes, reducing their three entries to two by transferring some of the play-rehearsal to the first meeting, and most of the play itself to the rehearsal in the wood, and to cut down the scenes for the lovers as far as possible. By re-arranging the order of the scenes, the author contrives to bring Titania on at the end of each act, and on each occasion she is entertained with a sort of masque. The play was revived in 1693, when further additions were made to the music. The admirable scene of the drunken poet was inserted into the first act, the preliminary dialogue of Theseus, Egeus and the lovers being removed to make room for it, and two songs were introduced later, one of them—'The plaint'—being so singularly inappropriate to its surroundings that we can have no doubt that it was already known as a favourite song and was inserted simply for the benefit of a favourite singer. Either for the sake of variety, or because the inventors of the entertainment realized that an ordinary London opera-chorus was not likely to present a very convincing appearance in the character of fairies, each masque is given a different set of costumes. Thus in Act II the singers appear as attendants on Night and Sleep, in Act III they are Fauns, Dryads and Naiads, in Act IV attendants on the Four Seasons, while in Act V the whole scene is transformed to a Chinese garden with a chorus of 'Chineses'.

This arrangement gives each masque some slight consistency. That in Act II begins with an invocation to the birds, with a delightful little symphony representing two nightingales. An echo chorus follows, with a dance of fairies. Titania then prepares to go to sleep, and instead of the familiar 'Ye spotted snakes' we have a long and effective allegorical scene in which Night, Mystery, Secrecy and Sleep enter in turn, each singing a characteristic song. The song of Night, in a very Italian style, accompanied by muted violins and violas without violoncellos or basses, is singularly beautiful. From a stage point of view the most remarkable number is the air of Sleep and the chorus which repeats the same music in an extended form. 'Hush, no more', they sing, with long and measured silences separating each subdued exclamation; then at

> Softly, softly steal from hence,
> No noise disturb her sleeping sense!

the music becomes more continuous, breaking off suddenly at the words 'no noise', with more rests of several beats. One can almost see the sudden halt of the retreating figures, and their discreet gesture; then, repeating the phrase in a whisper, they glide away into the darkness and leave the stage clear for the mysterious evolutions of the dancers.

In Act III Titania, having made the acquaintance of Bottom, bids her fairies prepare a masque for his entertainment. There is an elaborate change of scene, with a river and trees in the distance which alter their positions as the music goes on. A troop of Fauns, Dryads, etc. sing a languishing chorus ('If love's a sweet passion'); two swans swim to the bank of the river, turn into fairies and dance; four savages enter, frighten the fairies away, and dance by themselves. These dances are very cleverly characterized; the energetic dance of savages contrasts sharply with the grace of the swans, and the successive entries of a well-defined subject with a rushing scale in each part in turn rather suggest the pursuit of the fairies by the savages first from one corner of the stage and then from another. A comic duet follows for Coridon and Mopsa, Mopsa being as usual the ugly shepherdess,[1] represented by a man. This dialogue is extremely spirited, and would have been acted in every bar. A nymph sings one of Purcell's characteristically gay and lilting tunes, and the act ends with a chorus that to some extent recalls the mood of the first one, thus giving a sort

[1] Cf. *A Winter's Tale.*

of poetical unity to the scene. After the music is over Titania and Bottom have a few lines of dialogue.

The fourth act brings the reconciliation of Titania and Oberon, which they celebrate by a masque of the Four Seasons, heralded by Phoebus and a complicated transformation-scene representing the sun rising in a garden of fountains. The description of the scene in the libretto is very elaborate, and shows us a picture of the most characteristically seventeenth-century design—fountains, cascades, marble staircases and columns, cypresses and statues, most of these objects being probably just painted on the back flats. During the sunrise a long and brilliant symphony is played, after which the chorus, headed by a soprano soloist, hail the birthday of Oberon. This solo and chorus, on a free ground bass, is one of the most imposing musical movements in the opera. Phoebus descends in a machine to a short trumpeting symphony, sings an air and is saluted by the chorus; then each of the Four Seasons comes forward in turn with an air and probably a dance of attendants, the second chorus being repeated as a conclusion to the masque.

The longest of the masques is that in the fifth act. Theseus and the lovers have returned from the temple, and the Duke has just delivered what is left him of the well-known speech on poets, lovers and madmen. Music is heard and Oberon enters with the rest of the fairies, 'to cure his incredulity'. Juno appears in a machine drawn by peacocks, and after a short presentation to Theseus by Oberon sings a recitative and air expressing her good wishes.

In the second version of the play the song known as 'The plaint' was introduced here by request of Oberon. As this represents the despair of a lady who has lost her lover for ever, it was a singularly inappropriate moment for its insertion. The scene then changes to an elaborate Chinese garden, 'the Architecture, the Trees, the Plants, the Fruit, the Birds, the Beasts quite different from what we have in this part of the World'. Chinese men and women enter and sing, with choruses and dances of various kinds; six monkeys come from between the trees and dance to one of Purcell's most amusing ballet-tunes. Two women, assisted by the chorus, invoke Hymen, who appears with some reluctance. At this point 'Six pedestals of *China*-work rise from under the Stage; they support six large Vases of Porcelain, in which are six *China*-Orange-trees'. The women sing to Hymen,

> Turn then thine Eyes upon those Glories there,
> And catching flames will on thy torch appear,

but it is probable that the 'Glories' which are to have so encouraging an effect on the 'dull god of marriage' are not the 'pedestals of *China*-work' but the four lovers, to whom Hymen, the two women and the chorus, offer their felicitations. Finally there is a *chaconne* for all the dancers.

A curious thing to be noted about *The Fairy Queen* is that in no case does the act end with the end of the music. On every occasion there is a certain amount of spoken dialogue after the music is over. This is no doubt due to the habit then prevailing of keeping the curtain up during the whole of the play, instead of lowering it between the acts as is done now. There was then no attempt to make a 'situation' or 'tableau' at the end of an act, since an effect of this kind depends essentially on the sudden obliteration of the picture by the closing curtain.[1] In *The Fairy Queen* the concluding dialogue for Oberon and Titania is nothing more than an epilogue, such as was invariably spoken at the close of a play: here it is incorporated into the play itself, just as in *The Indian Queen* the usual prologue is made part of the opera, and even set to music as a dialogue, although the words leave no doubt that it was meant to be addressed to the audience as an appeal for their favour.

The influence of the masque is also very noticeable in *The Tempest*. The masque of Neptune and Amphitrite belonged to Shadwell's original version, and Purcell's setting is of interest mainly for purely musical reasons. The songs are

[1] See *ante*, Chapter III.

particularly beautiful, and the Italian influence is very marked, more so perhaps than in any other opera of Purcell, since we find here several examples of the fully developed *da capo* aria, a form hitherto unknown in English music.

So much has been written about Purcell elsewhere in his capacity as a musician that the purely musical side of his work has been more or less neglected in the foregoing chapters, attention being concentrated as far as possible on his contribution to operatic developments. No great composer was ever so unfortunate in his surroundings. In spite of his popularity, to which the mere number of the plays for which he composed music is sufficient testimony, he was never trusted sufficiently to be given a free hand, and between the inevitable jealousy of poets or actors and the disastrous prudence of managers his wonderful genius for the theatre was condemned to a humiliating slavery. When we consider his marvellous power of setting English words to music, the massive nobility or the racy humour of his declamation, his unerring perception of a stage picture, his unrivalled fertility of invention and his unsurpassed handling of all technical resources, it is difficult not to believe that he only wanted an equally skilful librettist and the reasonable support of an intelligent public to have become the greatest operatic composer of his time in Europe.

What Purcell failed to achieve was not to be accomplished by the mediocre talents which survived him. There was just a moment's hope that Handel might have built up an English opera on Purcell's foundations, for it is by reason of his indebtedness to Purcell rather than by mere fact of his residence in this country that we are entitled to claim Handel as in the line of our own composers. The masque of *Esther* was originally intended for the stage, and was, on one occasion at least, actually so represented; but the prejudices of the Bishop of London would not permit of its public performance, and to this unfortunate circumstance we owe the fact that Handel's greatest works to English words, in spite of the

strong dramatic ability of his librettist Morell, were confined
to the narrow limitations of oratorio. During the last few years
there has been a great revival of Handel in Germany, and
by far the most successful results have been obtained from
the production of his oratorios in dramatic form with scenery,
costume and action. The oratorios have in fact proved to
be much more effective on the stage than the operas, and
this method of representing them has brought out very
strikingly Handel's indebtedness to Purcell and to the English
opera of Purcell's day in his treatment of the chorus.[1]

Taking a general survey of English music and drama
during the seventeenth century, we may observe two main
streams of progress, which we may roughly distinguish as
the tendencies of the amateurs and those of the professionals.
To the professional group belong the plays of Shakespeare
and his followers, the later school of D'Avenant and Dryden,
with the incidental music to them which has already been
discussed. To the amateurs we may assign the Elizabethan
chorister-dramas, the Jacobean masques, such works as *Cupid
and Death*, and those rare specimens of genuine English opera,
Venus and Adonis and *Dido and Aeneas*. The classification is
necessarily a very rough one; it is difficult to decide in which
category to place *Psyche* or *Albion and Albanius*. *Albion and
Albanius*, set to music by the worst type of hack composer,
was written by a poet who on that particular occasion, at
any rate, must be classed among the amateurs. On the other
hand, some of the Carolan masques are decidedly professional
in their routine, although by the circumstances of their
performance the form belongs to the amateurs.

The fundamental distinction lies between the work of
routine and the work of adventure; and it is only the adventurous who achieved anything significant in the field of
musical drama. It may seem blasphemous to class Shakespeare on the side of routine; but we are dealing here

---

[1] *Semele*, which is even more closely related to the opera of Purcell's type,
was staged with great success at Cambridge in 1925.

exclusively with operatic principles, and in the application of music to drama Shakespeare, however practised and effective in his stage-craft, is not adventurous. To us who have been brought up on Wagner and Verdi, it is extraordinarily difficult to realize the adventurousness of those early composers who interpreted a complete drama in terms of music. For their achievement, little though they themselves may have been aware of it, signified an attempt, at least, towards a complete inversion of the expressive values of music and poetry. To the average man poetry is sense and music sound; poetry supplies the element of reason, music that of imagination. This general attitude we have seen exemplified in the writings of Corneille and Saint-Evremond. They at least have this justification for their view, that they were Frenchmen, and therefore incapable of conceiving poetry and drama apart from the logic of formal design. But what the English temperament has always craved is a drama of romance: a drama doubly romantic indeed because romantic not only in its disregard of formal construction, but romantic too in the associational values of every word of its language. The result is that in an English opera the words, instead of supplying the reasonable, logical and constructional element, as the uneducated listener is apt to suppose, tend to become a violently disruptive force of exceptional power.

The fact is that in any language the words of an opera, even the words of a simple song, are bound to be disruptive, anti-logical, anarchistic in regard to the ordered intelligence of the music. Even in Italian opera, where the sense of music is inherent in the language, not because the open vowels and simple consonants facilitate the mere act of singing, but because its rhythmical values and its methods of grouping words and phrases are often essentially musical in character, it has needed the skill of a Metastasio to restrain this disruptive tendency.

Music is, in its most primitive essentials, form. Form is the quality which unites the two elements of melody and rhythm to make what we recognize as 'a tune'. Anyone who can grasp what is meant by 'a tune' has a sense of musical form. The 'form' of a symphony is simply an elaboration of the primitive principle; and when untrained listeners say that a modern work is unintelligible to them, they mean that they have been unable to grasp its form. It is not necessarily the listeners who are exclusively at fault.

Now if clarity of form is an essential to symphonic music it is all the more vital to the construction of an opera. No principle could be more misleading than to make the music subservient to the drama. The music is itself the drama: that is the fundamental principle of opera. A composer of opera must choose a dramatic idea which will lend itself to musical principles of development; the poet must cast his thoughts in forms which definitely require music for their complete expression. Yet as long as words are words and not music, the disruptive tendency will be inevitable, and since it is inevitable, the artist must realize that it is part of his materials, and must make up his mind to turn it to account as a technical device. It is an idiosyncrasy of the marble which is a blemish to machine-made work, but a stimulus to inspiration and originality in the true sculptor. English thought and English words are so full of 'flaws' of this kind, that to achieve homogeneity of texture becomes a practical impossibility, even if it were worth achieving. The difficulty of setting English to music is plainly shown by the extraordinarily small number of English songs, old or new, that can be considered as belonging to the rank of masterpieces.

It is not surprising then that English opera presents a more difficult problem than opera in French or Italian. The tendency of the 'professional' theatre, exemplified by D'Avenant and Dryden in the seventeenth century, still persists; our modern productions of Shakespeare—even our ultra-modern ones—are merely variations on the same theme. They have little or no value as contributory to the development of genuine opera; they are ingenious evasions of the problem, not attempts to solve it. If it is ever possible to learn anything from the past history of an art that can be of value in the present and future it is to the other group that we must turn. The modern composer may very reasonably say that Locke and Purcell fail to stir his emotions, that they belong to the limbo of forgotten things, that it is impossible to create a new art by the deliberate and self-conscious revival of an old one. Some of the works described in this book have recently been put on the stage at Cambridge, Glastonbury and elsewhere; their revival was in all cases due to the adventurous enthusiasm of amateurs. They have in no case been adopted into the professional repertory, and it is not likely that they will ever appeal to the professional mind—at any rate in their own country. They must in all probability remain what some of them were in their own day—instruments of education; yet performances of them may serve to educate grown-up composers as well as boys and girls. We must admit that they are dead; but there is at least one place where the dead are of definite use to us—the school of anatomy.

Index

INDEX

1) English View of Opera
2) Purcell's setting of the play. (conclusion accuracy not necessary)
3) The theme of enchantment
   i) how shakespeare creates
   3) how Purcell creates.

4) Comedy in shakespeare + Comedy in Faerie
   i) Bottem + the play
   ii) The drunk poets Act 1